Footprints of Feist in European Database Directive

Indranath Gupta

Footprints of Feist in European Database Directive

A Legal Analysis of IP Law-making in Europe

Springer

Indranath Gupta
Centre for Intellectual Property and Technology Law, Jindal Global Law School
O.P. Jindal Global University
Sonipat, Haryana
India

ISBN 978-981-10-3980-5 ISBN 978-981-10-3981-2 (eBook)
DOI 10.1007/978-981-10-3981-2

Library of Congress Control Number: 2017933061

Printed on acid-free paper

This Springer imprint is published by Springer Nature
The registered company is Springer Nature Singapore Pte Ltd.
The registered company address is: 152 Beach Road, #21-01/04 Gateway East, Singapore 189721, Singapore

Foreword

Intellectual property is not a monopoly on facts, information and data. Until recent years, this principle seemed to be safely entrenched in both national laws and jurisprudence across the world. Copyright laws instruct that authors have certain exclusive rights on their own original expressions, but cannot exclude others from accessing, using and benefiting from the information that such expressions convey. Similarly, patents give to inventors a temporary monopoly on certain uses of their own inventions, but on condition that the information on how to work the invention is fully disclosed and made accessible to anyone interested in the patent. Collections of data, or databases, made no exception. However many facts, information or data you collect, you do not acquire a right to exclude others from using the collection and pick up the information therein contained. As the US Supreme Court stated in the landmark *Feist* decision: "Common sense tells us that 100 uncopyrightable facts do not magically change their status when gathered together in one place".

With the Database Directive of 1996, the European legislator has challenged this commonsensical statement. A new, somehow "magical" right has been introduced, in the hope of creating an incentive to database makers. The latter now enjoy a right to exclude others from using facts, information and data, on the very ground that they have gathered them in one place—a database. Does the "database right" represent a departure from that revered principle of intellectual property recalled above? To what extent is this right a monopoly on facts, information and data? And what is its practical effect and significance?

The book of Indranath Gupta addresses these questions with rigour and in a variety of ways. It tells a fascinating story of unrealistic policy objectives, unwise lawmaking and unwanted consequences. It unveils the roots of the European lawmaking process in the background of the American experience and the persistent influence of the *Feist* decision. It tells how the European Court of Justice has in part succeeded in mitigating the harmful effect of the database right, by developing a subtle albeit occasionally convoluted interpretation of the requirement of subsistence of this right. Perhaps the most important lesson to be drawn from the story told in this book is that the use of intellectual property as "incentive" must be made with extreme care and caution, and not without sound supporting evidence. This is the challenge that databases present today to intellectual property scholars and legislators alike.

Maurizio Borghi
Professor of Intellectual Property Law
Bournemouth University

Acknowledgements

I would like to express my heartfelt gratitude to the unstinted support of Mr. Dipesh Ashok Jain as a research assistant.

A special thanks to Prof. Maurizio Borghi of Bournemouth University for kindly contributing the foreword and to all my peers and fellow practitioners with whom I have discussed the issues considered in this book.

I would like to thank the faculty and administrative staff of O.P. Jindal Global University. I would also like to register my appreciation for the constant support of Prof. (Dr.) C. Raj Kumar, Founding Vice Chancellor, Prof. (Dr.) Y.S.R. Murthy, Registrar and Prof. (Dr.) Sanjeev P. Sahni, Principal Director, Jindal Institute of Behavioural Sciences of O.P. Jindal Global University. Many thanks to all my friends for their support and suggestions.

Finally, I owe a debt of gratitude to the loving and constant support and encouragement of my family, my in-laws and especially my son Emon who has been wise beyond his years about my hectic work schedule. It is to them that I dedicate this work as without them I would not have been able to come this far and present this book as you see it today.

Contents

About the Author

Indranath Gupta is Associate Professor and Assistant Director of the Centre for Post Graduate Legal Studies and Assistant Director at the Centre for Intellectual Property and Technology Law. He is also co-director of the Jindal Initiative on Research in IP and Competition (JIRICO). Dr. Gupta received his LL.B. degree from the University of Calcutta, India, and holds an LL.M. with distinction from the University of Aberdeen, UK and a postgraduate research LL.M. in Computer Law from the University of East Anglia, UK. He obtained his Ph.D. from Brunel University, London, UK.

Dr. Gupta has been involved in qualitative and quantitative research. He was appointed as the research collaborator by the Universitȧ Bocconi, Milan, Italy, for a project funded by the European Commission under the 7th Framework Programme. He has also been appointed as a research assistant for a project relating to data protection compliance level at Brunel University, London. Dr. Gupta has also worked as an advocate in a solicitor firm at the Calcutta High Court. He has published in European and Indian Law journals and has spoken at international conferences and seminars. His research areas include database right, copyright, data protection, cyber law and interface of IP and Competition Law.

Abbreviations

AOIC	Author's Own Intellectual Creation
Ariz. St. L J	Arizona State Law Journal
ASCII	American Standard Code for Information Interchange
BCL Rev	Boston College Law Review
Berkeley Tech L J	Berkeley Technology Law Journal
BGH-IZR	German Federal Court of Justice
BHB	British Horseracing Board
Can Bus L J	Canadian Business Law Journal
Chicago-Kent L Rev	Chicago-Kent Law Review
CIS	Congressional Information Service
CJEU	The Court of Justice of the European Union
CLR Int'l	Computer Law Review International
CLSR	Computer Law and Security Report
CMLR	Common Market Law Review
Colum J L & Soc Probs	Columbia Journal of Law and Social Problems
Colum L Rev	Columbia Law Review
COM	Commission
Comm & Law	Communication and Law
Computer L Rev & Tech	Computer Law Review and Technology
CDPA	Copyright, Designs and Patent Act
CRDR	Copyright and Rights in Databases Regulations
CW	Copyright World
DePaul-LCA J. Art & Ent L	DePaul-LCA Journal of Art and Entertainment Law
DMCA	Digital Millennium Copyright Act
E L Rev	European Law Review
EADP	European Association of Directory and Database Publishers
EBBA	European Border Breakers Awards

ECC	European Commercial Cases
ECDR	European Copyright and Design Report
ECJ	The European Court of Justice
ECR	European Court Reports
ECU	European Currency Unit
EDNY	Eastern District of New York
EEC	European Economic Community
EEPROM	Electronically Erasable Programmable Read-Only Memory
EIPR	European Intellectual Property Review
Ent L Rev	Entertainment Law Review
EWCA	England and Wales Code of Appeal
EWHC	High Court of England and Wales
Fordham Int'l L J	Fordham International Law Journal
Fordham Intell Prop Media & Ent L J	Fordham Intellectual Property, Media & Entertainment Law Journal
FSR	Fleet Street Reports
GDD	Gale Directory of Databases
Harv L Rev	Harvard Law Review
Hellenic Rev of Int'l L	Hellenic Review of International Law
High Tech L J	High Tech Law Journal
ICC Reports	Investors Capital Corporation Reports
IDEA Intell Prop L Rev	IDEA Intellectual Property Law Review
IIC	International Review of Intellectual Property and Competition Law
IJLIT	International Journal of Law and Information Technology
Iowa L Rev	Iowa Law Review
IPQ	Intellectual Property Quarterly
IVIR	Institute for Information Law
J Econ Persp	Journal of Economic Perspectives
J Intell Prop L	Journal of Intellectual Property Law
J Legal Stud	The Journal of Legal Studies
J of Tech L & P	Journal of Technology Law and Policy
Minn L Rev	Minnesota Law Review
Neb L Review	Nebraska Law Review
Notre Dame L Rev	Notre Dame Law Review
NRP	National Register Publishing
Ohio St L J	Ohio State Law Journal
OJ C	Official Journal of the European Union Information and Notices
OJ L	Official Journal of the European Union Legislation
Pat Trademark & Copyright J	Patent Trademark and Copyright Journal
RDF	Raw Data Feed

RIDA	The Revue Internationale Du Droit D'Auteur
Roger Williams UL Review	Roger Williams University Law Review
RPC	Restrictive Practices Court
RRP	Reed Reference Publishing
RTDcom	Revue trimestrielle de droit commercial et de droit économique
Santa Clara L Rev	Santa Clara Law Review
SDNY	Southern District of New York
Tex L Rev	Texas Law Review
The Geor Wash L R	The George Washington Law Review
TPM	Technological Protection Measures
TRIPS	Trade-Related Aspects of Intellectual Property Rights
U Cin L Rev	University of Cincinnati Law Review
U Dayton L Rev	University of Dayton Law Review
U Pitt L R	University of Pittsburgh Law Review
UCLA L Rev	University of California Law Review
UKHL	United Kingdom House of Lords
Univ of Ottawa L T J	University of Ottawa Law and Technology Journal
USPQ	United States Patents Quarterly
VA J L & Tech	Virginia Journal of Law and Technology
Vand L Rev	Vanderbilt Law Review
Wash U J L & Pol'y	Washington University Journal of Law and Policy
WIPO	World Intellectual Property Organization
WLR	Weekly Law Reports
Yale J of L & Tech	Yale Journal of Law & Technology

Chapter 1
Introduction

The importance of databases is paramount because technology enables us to access vast amount of information in a systematic manner. In a typical database, a publisher collects and makes the information available at a single place and in a simple way.[1] A special incentive in the form of a Database Directive was created in Europe for publishers to increase investments towards production of databases. It was believed that in a digital age, owing to the risk of free-riding, database producers may not be interested in investing in database production without any special incentives safeguarding their investment.[2] Further, there were legal reasons as a result of diverse structure of available protection measures for databases in Europe.[3] Other than the above reasons, the decision of US Supreme Court in *Feist Publications v Rural Telephone Service* was considered a benchmark for reasoning protection for databases.[4]

This book attempts to trace the footprints of the *Feist* case in the Database Directive in Europe. In the process it questions the interpretation of the *Feist* decision as it happened in the European Union and also explores the overall structure of the Directive through the interpretation of Article 3 and 7.

The Database Directive offers a two-tier protection to both original and non-original databases. Article 3 harmonizes copyright protection for databases and

---

[1]The Database Directive under Article 1 defines database and it is "a collection of independent works, data or other materials arranged in a systematic or methodical way and individually accessible by electronic or other means", Council Directive of 1996/9/EC of 27 March 1996 on the legal protection of databases [1996] OJ L 77/20 (Council Directive 96/9/EC).
[2]'DG Internal market and services working paper: First Evaluation of Directive 96/9/EC on the legal protection of databases' (*Commission of the European Communities*, 12 December 2005) available at <http://ec.europa.eu/internal_market/copyright/docs/databases/evaluation_report_en.pdf> (accessed 31 October 2016) (First Evaluation of Directive 96/9/EC), para [2.2].
[3]ibid.
[4]499 US 340 (1991).

I. Gupta, *Footprints of Feist in European Database Directive*,
DOI 10.1007/978-981-10-3981-2_1

protects original databases "by reason of selection or arrangement of their contents, constitut[ing] the author's own intellectual creation."[5] This copyright protection does not extend to contents, but to the way such contents are selected or arranged. Where a database producer has invested substantially in obtaining, verifying or presenting the contents of a database, he may prevent extraction or re-utilization of such contents by virtue of database right under Article 7.[6] The protection afforded under Article 7 is for databases where no author's own intellectual creation is present. These are commonly referred to as 'non-original' databases.[7]

1.1 Background to Granting Additional Protection for Databases

Although there were concerns regarding level of protection available for database producers, no concrete evidence of market failure was present to guide the formation of Database Directive.[8] The first draft proposal portrayed enough scope and potential for European database market to grow, and compete internationally in the ensuing electronic information market.[9] There was concern with existing fragmentation in the European market due to technical, legal and linguistic barriers.[10] Further, development of the internet and electronic business happened in US long before it started in Europe. Even the number of European databases produced in English language were less than 60% at the time of the first draft proposal.[11] Under these circumstances, the Commission warranted rectification of legal barrier in member states. Producers who were involved in database industry could rely on a combination of existing measures to prevent unfair extraction of contents. These measures broadly included use of copyright law, unfair competition law, breach of confidence and general use of contractual provisions.[12] However, existing structure of incentives was not considered adequate in an electronic age where there were

[5]Council Directive 96/9/EC, Chapter II; According to the Commission, in the member states there was a difference in the standard of originality for copyright protection of databases, Commission, 'Proposal for a Council Directive on the legal protection of databases' COM (92) 24 final (COM (92) 24 final), para [2.2.5].

[6]Council Directive 96/9/EC, Chapter III.

[7]The Database Directive offers protection to both original (Article 3) and non-original (Article 7) databases, First Evaluation of Directive 96/9/EC, para [1.1].

[8]The first draft proposal talked about the challenges and the possibilities without concrete evidence of any problems; COM (92) 24 final.

[9]COM (92) 24 final, para [2.0].

[10]ibid, para [2.1.3].

[11]ibid, para [2.1.5].

[12]Stopping parasitic behaviour constituting the act of misappropriating the contents of databases by using unfair competition law is present in some member states, which would have done similar sort of function as the database right, ibid, para [3.2.8].

ample opportunities for European industry to grow and compete with United States.[13] The biggest worry was with the available copyright protection, and it was feared that a single database might be treated differently in different member states owing to varied threshold of originality.[14] There existed the presence of 'sweat of the brow' standard involving skill and labour in Common Law member states, whereas in *Droit d' Auteur* member states there was standard based on 'intellectual creativity'.[15] It was believed that it would be difficult to protect the contents of an electronic database, since there were no reliable technical measures to stop the act of illegal downloading.[16] Under these conditions, a competitor database producer may not face any hindrance in copying contents, and re-selling it as part of his own product.[17] To the detriment of a database producer, there was a possibility that a competitor may be able to copy and reproduce electronic databases at low cost.[18]

Further, there was additional concern with the level of protection afforded to electronic databases. It was understood that electronic databases would be mostly comprehensive in nature, thereby excluding creativity in selection or arrangement of the contents.[19] As a result, it would be unlikely for electronic databases to be a subject matter under copyright. With this growing uncertainty, producers would have less incentive towards production of electronic databases. Thus, this Database Directive wanted to create a platform for European producers to invest more towards database production by ensuring an atmosphere of stability.

A cumulative effect of the above situations led to believe that electronic databases deserved a different type of incentive if Europe was to compete in the international market. While electronic databases were identified, there was no evidence mentioned in the proposal to suggest the type and amount of incentive required for database producers.[20] At this crucial juncture, the US Supreme Court decided *Feist*. The *Feist* decision involved copyrightability of a telephone directory. The Supreme Court held that a factual compilation must be original to merit copyright protection. This originality must be an outcome of creativity towards the selection or arrangement of contents.[21] The jurisprudence surrounding the *Feist* decision was believed to be detrimental for electronic databases where there would be less selection or arrangement.[22] On the contrary the perception in proposal was

[13]"The situation as regards to the legal protection of databases in the member states", Explanatory memorandum, COM (92) 24 final, para [2.2]; Pointing to the fact that US dominated the database market at the point of the first draft proposal, COM (92) 24 final, para [2.15.1].

[14]COM (92) 24 final, para [2.2.5].

[15]First Evaluation of Directive 96/9/EC; 'sweat of the brow' argument in the context of copyright protection of a compilation points to the labour expended towards its creation.

[16]COM (92) 24 final, 28-31.

[17]ibid 30.

[18]ibid, para [3.1.11].

[19]ibid 30.

[20]COM (92) 24 final.

[21]*Infra* chapter 3.

[22]COM (92) 24 final, para [2.3.3].

that databases in order to be useful, must be comprehensive in nature. *Feist* was believed to develop a new-line of jurisprudence replacing 'sweat of the brow' argument as a basis for copyright protection.[23] Further, the decision showed that copyright was not the correct type of protection measure for electronic databases. It was believed that *Feist* would have a negative impact on future production of databases.[24]

Other than referring to *Feist* decision in the explanatory memorandum to the first draft proposal, the evaluation report of the Database Directive questioned the implications of *Feist*.[25] Although the report was meant to evaluate the Directive, it only focused on whether the growth rate of European database industry increased after the introduction of database right. In other words, with protection in place, whether beneficiaries of the new right were producing databases at a comparatively higher rate than the period when the right did not exist. In the process the report primarily pointed out that the economic impact of database right was unproven.[26] There was no evidence of any substantial positive impact with database right in place other than the claims of publishers that such right ensured stability for future database production.[27] In fact, number of databases remained almost same in comparison to pre-Directive period.[28] US continued to be the market leader in database production, despite having no specific law for database protection.[29] There was no initiative to enact a special legislation for protecting databases, even after the landmark US Supreme Court decision in *Feist*.[30]

---

[23]ibid.

[24]ibid.

[25]First evaluation of Directive 96/9/EC, para [2.4].

[26]ibid, para [1.4].

[27]ibid, para [4.2.3].

[28]The report stated that the number of European databases were similar to the pre-Directive days. In 2001, there were 4085 EU-based "entries" while in 2004 there were only 3095, First evaluation of Directive 96/9/EC, para [4.2]; Although the European Association of Directory and Database Publishers claimed that there has been an increase in supply of information through databases, there was no empirical evidence or a procedure provided in this regard to quantify or measure information provided through these databases. The report, however, said that care should be taken to conclude on the basis of GDD. It was the best available data at the time of the evaluation, which acts as a guideline, and gives a rough estimate, First evaluation of Directive 96/9/EC, para [4.2.3].

[29]First evaluation of Directive 96/9/EC, para [4.4].

[30]*Feist Publications* (n 4); The term 'database' includes compilations under the broad definition of database and Article 1 (2) of Council Directive 96/9/EC, states that "'database' shall mean a collection of independent works, data or other materials arranged in a systematic or methodical way and individually accessible by electronic or other means". According to the Recital 13 "this Directive protects collections, sometimes called 'compilations', of works, data or other materials which are arranged, stored and accessed by means which include electronic, electromagnetic or electro-optical processes or analogous processes" Council Directive 96/9/EC. The European Court of Justice (ECJ), now known as Court of Justice of the European Union (CJEU), in the case of Case C-444/02 *Fixtures Marketing Ltd v Organismos Prognostikon Agnon Podosfairou (OPAP)* [2005] ECDR 3 para [37] said that the definition of a database is meant to be broad so as to cover any future electronic and non-electronic form (Organismos).

In the context of harmonization of copyright protection for databases under Article 3, the report said that many databases may still receive protection under the new threshold requirement.[31] The report, however, did not elaborate on extent of such protection. There were no specific details as to how many databases will meet that threshold. In conclusion, need of continuing with the database right was questioned.[32] The report contemplated severing the database right from the Database Directive.[33]

The dependence on the *Feist* case started from the first draft proposal. Although this case was referred in the evaluation report, the justification behind giving importance to this case in the first draft proposal was not discussed any further. Therefore, there is an opportunity in the book to study the impact of the *Feist* decision as it happened in the United States. In the course of this effort, it has been observed that the impact of *Feist* jurisprudence in US, and the belief that *Feist* had raised threshold of originality to a level that would have left many databases unprotected are largely incorrect.[34] From a doctrinal perspective, *Feist* mainly clarified the position of copyright in relation to compilations.[35] The decision was not as path-breaking as it is commonly believed, and did not introduce a legal reasoning that was unprecedented or unique in the US.[36] As a result, while registering compilations under copyright, there were no appreciable changes in the procedural steps followed at the US Copyright Office.[37] Cases decided subsequent to *Feist* have also followed similar threshold requirement. There were no substantial inconsistencies to deter producers from investing towards databases.[38]

So far as the economic effect is concerned, the impact of *Feist* was negligible, and there was no considerable distress among publishers.[39] It was contemplated in the proposal to the Directive that publishers looked to invest towards databases because of the incentive of 'sweat of the brow' argument.[40] This argument was removed by US Supreme Court in *Feist*. The idea that 'sweat of the brow' was a major incentive for database producers is faulty as producers were certain about protecting their investments.[41] Furthermore, the fact that the first database bill was tabled by US Congress after a long gap of five years confirms that there was no urgency towards enacting a special legislation protecting databases after the *Feist* decision. As a matter of fact, investments continued in US without a special legal

[31]First Evaluation of Directive 96/9/EC, para [1.5].

[32]ibid, para [6.2].

[33]ibid.

[34]*Infra* chapter 3 and chapter 4.

[35]*Infra* chapter 3.

[36]ibid.

[37]ibid.

[38]*Infra* chapter 3.

[39]*Infra* chapter 4.

[40]COM (92) 24 final, 17.

[41]*Infra* chapter 4.

incentive for databases.[42] Moreover, the prolonged American debate that followed immediately after the passage of database right in Europe, did not have *Feist* at the centre stage. Impact of the *Feist* decision in US has been negligible.[43] Therefore, the assumptions involving *Feist* decision and its influence on electronic databases at the preparatory stage of the Directive are questionable.

Further it has been observed that database producers will not face substantial difficulty to meet the threshold requirement under author's own intellectual creation (AOIC). A creative output, which does not result in an obvious selection or arrangement of contents in a database, is sufficiently original for the purpose of Article 3.[44] The national courts in three member states of UK, France and Germany have all converged to a similar threshold standard for copyright protection of databases.[45] This non-stringent standard is also reflected in the recent decision of *Football Dataco Ltd v Yahoo UK Ltd* (*Football Dataco*) in England, alongside the opinion of Court of Justice of the European Union (CJEU).[46] The recent opinion of CJEU in *Football Dataco* has qualified the type of creativity that can merit protection under Article 3.[47] According to the CJEU, any amount of creativity that goes towards creation of any data is not covered within the scope.[48] This opinion is different from the decision of Court of First Instance in England, since it accepted incorporation of creativity at any stage of creating the database.[49] For a single-sourced database, the opinion of CJEU meant that a producer is required to show separate creativity while selecting or arranging contents, which is separate from creativity at the stage of data creation. The threshold standard suggests that majority of databases would be able to meet the requirement.[50] Moreover, comprehensive commercial databases will meet the threshold requirement of AOIC. This is true for both electronic and paper-format databases, and they reflect enough creativity to merit protection.[51] Compilers do not necessarily produce comprehensive databases that are merely compilation of information. Instead, they expend creativity towards selection or arrangement of contents and this activity in most

[42]ibid.

[43]ibid.

[44]*Infra* chapter 5.

[45]ibid.

[46]Case C-604/10 *Football Dataco Ltd v Yahoo! UK Ltd* [2012] ECDR 10, 194 (*Football Dataco*); *Football Dataco Ltd v Brittens Pools Ltd* [2010] EWHC 841 (Ch) Sections 83-90 (*Football Dataco 2*); *Football Dataco Ltd v Yahoo! UK Ltd* [2010] EWCA Civ 1380, [2011] ECDR 9; CJEU was previously known as the European Court of Justice (ECJ). In this book, both the names have been referred depending on the time of a particular opinion expressed in relation to a particular case.

[47]*Football Dataco* (n 46).

[48]ibid, s 3.2.

[49][2010] EWCA Civ 1380.

[50]As predicted by the evaluation report, First Evaluation of Directive 96/9/EC, para [1.5].

[51]*Infra* chapter 5.

cases suffices to merit copyright protection.[52] Trend observed later shows that publishers opt for copyright protection, and engages in adding value to information that are factual in nature.[53] Therefore, compilers consider copyright protection as a sufficient measure to recover their investments.

It has been observed that standards expected under AOIC resemble the guidelines of the US Supreme Court in *Feist*.[54] Overall, there was footprint of *Feist* decision. Judgement of CJEU has played a pivotal role ensuring that monopoly is averted with relation to factual data. Similar to the jurisprudence developed through *Feist* decision, the CJEU ensured freeing up of information.[55] Availability of information is considered incentive enough for producers to invest towards databases. Moreover, it has been observed that producers are expending their creative energy towards arranging comprehensive databases. This development concerning Article 3 reflects *Feist* jurisprudence.[56] Further, separating database right under Article 7 from Article 3 ensured that protection extended to information of factual nature remains separate from the copyright protection.[57]

Database right under Article 7 was introduced as a measure to incentivize production of database and was more of a counter measure to face the expected negative effects of *Feist* decision. As explained in the evaluation report, not only is database right ineffective in terms of growth, but provisions therein are potentially harmful, ambiguous and uncertain.[58] In the case of *British Horse Racing Board Ltd and Others v William Hill Organization Ltd* (*BHB*) The European Court of Justice (ECJ) has already highlighted anti-competitive effect that the right may bring about with respect to single-sourced databases.[59] Hence, database right may cause more

---

[52]ibid.

[53]*Infra* chapter 5.

[54]ibid.

[55]ibid.

[56]*Infra* chapter 6.

[57]ibid.

[58]Critiques have been concerned about the overall balance between the requirement for the producer and the final version of the database right. Mark J Davison, *The legal protection of databases* (Cambridge University Press Cambridge 2003); Annemarie Beunen, *Protection for databases: The European Database Directive and its effects in Netherlands, France and United Kingdom* (Wolf Legal Publishers Leiden 2007); over-protection of certain areas in the database right with the fear of monopolization for single-sourced databases, Estelle Derclaye, *The Legal Protection of Databases: A Comparative Analysis* (Edward Elgar, Northampton 2008); question of giving property rights to data, Jerome H Reichman and Pamela Samuelson, 'Intellectual Property Rights in data?' (1997) 50(1) V and L Rev 51; about the problems concerning single-sourced databases, P Bernt Hugenholtz, 'Abuse of Database Right: Sole-source information banks under the EU Database Directive' in F. Lévêque & H. Shelanski (eds.), *Antitrust, patents and copyright: EU and US perspectives* (Edward Elgar Cheltenham 2005) 203-217.

[59]Case C-203/02 *The British Horseracing Board Limited v William Hill Organisation Ltd* [2005] ECDR 1; Article 16(3) states the requirement of checking the anti-competitive effect of the database right, Council Directive 96/9/EC.

inconvenience instead of creating an atmosphere of stability for the database producers.[60]

The book concludes on a note that there are footprints of *Feist* on the overall structure of the Directive. Further it was difficult to balance the Directive without having exact knowledge of the requirement and it shows signs of strain.[61] Article 3 has no immediate concern subsequent to CJEU interpretation of AOIC, yet there are concerns associated with Article 7. There is considerable imbalance in the database right which requires immediate attention.[62] The compulsory licensing provision must be brought back to reduce existing concern with monopoly over factual information.[63] Going by the complexities and uncertainties present in database right, one may be inclined to repeal the right from the Database Directive. This is a difficult proposition to execute considering the amount of resistance such action would face from European publishers.[64] There would be further challenges leading to roll back to the days when there was no database right in Europe. The implications would be felt mostly in Common Law jurisdictions.[65] Based on the high number of cases that have already been decided, the proposition of rolling back may increase uncertainty.[66] Therefore, the options of repealing the right and maintaining *status quo* as proposed in the first evaluation report are untenable.[67] It has been suggested that database right may be amended to the structure that was proposed under the first draft proposal pending further empirical evidences suggesting possible requirement.[68]

1.2 Structure of the Chapters

This book is divided into seven chapters excluding the concluding chapter.

Chapter 2: The Argument for a Database Directive in Europe

This chapter essentially acts as a background to this book. It generates the idea of using the *Feist* decision as one of the arguments behind enacting the Database Directive in Europe, and its implication on the overall structure of the Directive.

[60]There is uncertainty in claiming database right for databases and is noticeable in the recent case of *Forensic Telecommunications Services Limited v The Chief Constable of West Yorkshire Police and others* [2011] EWHC 2892 (Ch); [2012] 15 FSR 428 where the claim was not based on database right, instead it was based on database copyright.

[61]*Infra* Conclusion.

[62]*Infra* Chapter 7.

[63]ibid.

[64]First Evaluation of Directive 96/9/EC, para [1.5].

[65]ibid, para [6.1].

[66]ibid, para [6.1].

[67]*Infra* Conclusion.

[68]ibid.

Chapter 3: *Feist*, Not a New Line of Jurisprudence

This chapter questions the argument that *Feist* developed a new-line of jurisprudence in US concerning the protection of factual compilations under copyright. It shows that there was general consensus with the threshold standard and therefore the decision did not generate much surprise. *Feist* merely clarified the existing law relating to copyright protection towards compilations. There was some conflict but was limited to few circuit courts. As a result, it did not cause for any substantial changes in the registration process of compilations at the Copyright Office. There were little inconsistencies with the principles of *Feist*. They have been used consistently by later decisions to raise enough incentives for producers of compilations.

Chapter 4: The Effect of *Feist* in the US Database Market

The objective of this chapter is to show that investment towards database production can continue without a *sui generis* database right. Such right is not a necessary component for producers of databases. The impact of 'sweat of the brow' as an incentive is inconclusive in the US. There was no appreciable concern and sense of urgency with protection of electronic databases amongst publishers. Even, there was a large gap of 5 years before the debate concerning database right started in US. The eight-year long US database debate did not have *Feist* at the centre stage and it was an outcome of a combination of multiple factors.

Chapter 5: Threshold of Author's Own Intellectual Creation

The interpretation of decisions of member states in this chapter suggests that threshold assigned to AOIC is not stringent. There has been a shift in how nations have dealt with the situation subsequent to incorporating threshold standard under the Directive. Compared to the examples of France and Germany considered in this chapter, there was considerable change in the UK. The CJEU's interpretation confirms that it would not be difficult for a producer to reach the threshold of originality under Article 3. Further, CJEU identified type of creativity associated with the said Article meaning that creativity towards creation of contents of a database would not be covered. The interpretation suggests that protection is limited to creativity towards selection or arrangement of existing contents.

Chapter 6: *Feist* standard in the Threshold Assigned to AOIC

Article 3 and its threshold resembles the standard prescribed in the *Feist* case. There is enough indication to suggest that producers may successfully use copyright to protect databases that are comprehensive in nature. While contents remain free, the creativity has been expressed towards arranging the factual contents.

Chapter 7: Uncertainties with Database Right: Negative Interpretation of *Feist*

Article 7 included the aspects that were discarded in the *Feist* case. This chapter demonstrates the uncertainties with the part that covers database right. Article 7 is heavily inclined towards producers, thereby ignoring the possible monopoly situation that exists with single-sourced databases. Other than existing concerns with the current structure of Article 7, cases decided by ECJ confirm that Article 7 may obstruct dissemination of information, which is important for the overall growth of database market in Europe.

Chapter 2
The Argument for a Database Directive in Europe

The enactment of the Database Directive saw a number of arguments. Available copyright protection for databases was not considered adequate in Europe.[1] This was primarily on two grounds. First, there was no express legal provision suggesting that electronic databases were covered under copyright; and second, copyright protection was limited to the original selection or arrangement of contents in a compilation.[2] This meant that the contents were left unprotected. It was further believed that electronic databases for commercial use would be comprehensive and less selective in nature. Therefore, the Database Directive looked to rectify the situation by harmonizing copyright protection for databases in Europe.[3] Contents that remained unprotected under copyright received a new layer of protection through the enactment of database right. Unlike creativity for copyright, database right does not require producers to prove investment to "protect the contents" of their database.[4] Therefore, the Database Directive formed a novel incentive for producers to invest. Although incentive was identified for producers, there was not much evidence to suggest that such incentive was truly required. According to the first evaluation report of Database Directive, economic impact of the database right was unproven.[5] Thus, the justification of having a Directive was challenged with a high degree of seriousness. Besides the argument that copyright would not be an effective incentive for the production of electronic databases, the first draft proposal to the Directive considered the impact of the US Supreme Court decision in *Feist*

[1]Commission, 'Proposal for a Council Directive on the legal protection of databases' COM (92) 24 final (COM (92) 24 final), para [2.2.5].

[2]ibid 30.

[3]ibid 30.

[4]Council Directive of 1996/9/EC of 27 March 1996 on the legal protection of databases [1996] OJ L 77/20 (Council Directive 96/9/EC), art 7.

[5]'DG Internal market and services working paper: First Evaluation of Directive 96/9/EC on the legal protection of databases' (*Commission of the European Communities*, 12 December 2005) available at <http://ec.europa.eu/internal_market/copyright/docs/databases/evaluation_report_en.pdf> (accessed 31 October 2016) (First Evaluation of Directive 96/9/EC), para. [1.4].

I. Gupta, *Footprints of Feist in European Database Directive*,
DOI 10.1007/978-981-10-3981-2_2

Publications v. Rural Telephone Service (*Feist*).[6] The decision led to believe that copyright would not be effective in protecting electronic databases that are comprehensive in nature.[7] This book will only concentrate on the justification of considering *Feist* case as an argument and attempt to identify its footprints on the overall structure of the Directive. Before looking at the *Feist* case and its overall impact in the United States, this chapter gives a background to the arguments that were considered before enacting the database directive in Europe.

2.1 Suggesting Protection for Databases in the First Draft Proposal

Long consultation process for the Database Directive in Europe began with the Green Paper in 1988, and ended with the introduction of the first draft proposal in 1992.[8] Favouring the database right, the proposal highlighted the potential of the database market in Europe. The Commission considered that online databases of European origin included 25% of databases in the world, in comparison to the US share of 56%.[9] This figure was an improvement from figures that existed ten years prior to the proposal. Back then, online databases of European origin only accounted for one-tenth of the size of the US database market.[10] The online information market of Western Europe was valued at 2.4 billion US dollars.[11] In the background of the visible growth an argument for a new incentive in the form of a *sui generis* right is questionable.[12] While the European database market was growing, the inclusion of an additional incentive was suggested to accelerate the rate of production of European databases. The proposal, however, did not connect additional requirement of an incentive with some degree of empirical evidence.[13]

The Commission believed that the European database industry needed to adapt newer technologies to facilitate manipulating and storing large quantities of data to remain internationally competitive.[14] The then existing legal database industry

---

[6]499 US 340 (1991).

[7]COM (92) 24 final, para [2.3.3].

[8]COM (92) 24 final; Commission, 'Copyright and the Challenge of Technology' (Green Paper), COM (88) 172 final (COM (88) 172 final).

[9]The explanatory memorandum referred to the "Panorama of EC Industry 1990", COM (92) 24 final, para [1.1].

[10]ibid.

[11]ibid, para [1.1].

[12]ibid.

[13]Miriam Bitton, 'Exploring the European Union Copyright Policy through the lens of the Database Directive' (2008) 23(4) Berkeley Tech LJ 1411, 1426.

[14]COM (92) 24 final, para [2.1.2].

showed the benefits of storing vast amounts of information electronically, which helped in providing a better and effective service.[15]

The proposal identified 'electronic information services', 'bibliographic databases', 'electronic databases', 'real-time financial information services' and 'full-text databases' as the future of database industry.[16] The delivery media for these services were online American Standard Code for Information Interchange (ASCII) databases,[17] video texts,[18] CD-ROM databases[19] and audio text[20] and broadcasting.[21] Contrary to the observation made in the proposal that these media were hardly competitive at an international level, Reuters a UK based company was dominating the world real-time information market, including currencies, stocks, bond futures and other financial instruments.[22] In fact, Europe was only behind US in the information services sectors with the largest home market in comparison to United States and Japan.[23]

In Europe, nine out of ten databases were only accessible in the language of the member state where such database was produced. Only 52% of those databases were in English. UK production was between 30 and 50% of the total number of ASCII databases produced in the community.[24] With a 15% world-wide share,

---

[15]ibid, paras [1.2] and [1.3].

[16]ibid, para [2.1.4].

[17]"American National Standard Code for Information Interchange, a standard code for the interchange of information between computer systems, data communication systems, and associated equipment. Since it is a standard code (rather than one developed by a particular manufacturer) it allows equipment of different manufacturers to exchange information. It is thus widely used.", John Daintith and Edmund Wright, 'The Facts on File Dictionary of Computer Science' Infobase Publishing, 2004, 11.

[18]"Videotext is a communication medium which can be used for a variety of purposes: games, entertainment, advertising, E-Mail, transactions, information retrieval.", COM (92) 24 final, para [2.1.11].

[19]CD-ROMs has the "ability to record a huge mass of Information on a small compact disc which can be retrieved with a PC…", COM (92) 24 final, para [2.1.14]; "CD-ROM today covers a wide variety of applications, from diagnostic programmes, computer graphics via cartography and full-text encyclopaedias. The size and the fields covered vary greatly from country to country.", COM (92) 24 final, para [2.1.15].

[20]Audio text provides an "interactive access to information and telephone communication services". The user accesses the interactive information service by using the twelve keys on his telephone, COM (92) 24 final, para [2.1.18].

[21]Broadcasting includes "data transmission by radio relay channel, i.e. ground-based TV networks, satellite or FM radio sub carriers, and is an alternative method of supplying electronic information services", COM (92) 24 final, para [2.1.17].

[22]Reuters Holdings 1992 Annual Report and Accounts, (ICC REPORT NO: 091653, December 31, 1992); Charles R McManis, 'Database Protection in the Digital Information Age' (2001-2002) 7(1) Roger Williams U L Review 7, 30.

[23]Commission, 'Report from the Commission to the Council, The European Parliament and the Economic and Social Committee on the Main Events and Developments in the Information Market 1993-1994' (COM (95) 492 final), s 3.

[24]COM (92) 24 final, para [2.1.5].

Europe was lagging behind in the production of CD-ROM databases, while US was the market leader covering almost 56% of world-wide production.[25] The proposal predicted a bright future for the European CD-ROM database industry, since the number of CD titles on databases was expected to grow from 750 in the year 1989 to 6000 by the end of 1992.[26] There was similar expectation with the new delivery media comprising of audio text and broadcasting. The proposal predicted that the revenue of audio text service had the potential to increase by 300–400% with an appropriate regulatory authority in place.[27] Video text service was the only medium that already had a strong foundation with Europe as the market leader.

The Commission feared that the growth and future prospect of the European database industry would face severe threat from the problem of fragmentation that existed due to technical, legal and linguistic barriers in the member states.[28] This problem would ultimately hinder free movement of information services in the community and create further obstacles for the European database industry. Although this problem culminated because of three issues in the member states, as a counter measure, a legal solution was proposed. The Commission believed that the existing legal anomalies would fail to provide enough incentive for database producers to invest towards databases and thus, it would be difficult for Europe to keep up with the requirement of the community and to compete internationally.[29] Moreover, foreign databases can meet the demand of the European and international market to the detriment of the European database industry.[30] Figures and circumstances surrounding the potential European database industry provided the initial reason for proposing the incentive of database legislation.

2.1.1 Database Production and Legal Structure in Europe

The proposal stated that for increasing international competitiveness, database manufacturing should not be limited to the boundaries of the member states. In the backdrop of the linguistic barrier, there was concern with the production of databases that were in English language.[31] Further, the proposal also identified technical

---

[25]ibid, para [2.1.4].

[26]ibid.

[27]The market of audio text was valued at 300 million European currency unit (ECU) in 1989 and was predicted to reach to 1,200 million ECU by 1993, ibid, para [2.1.19].

[28]ibid, para [2.1.3].

[29]The legal issues have been considered in section 2.1.1; ibid, para [1.4].

[30]ibid, para [1.4].

[31]Commercial databases used in business and scientific communities are in English and not in Portuguese, Finnish, Danish or Hungarian, Estelle Derclaye, 'Intellectual property rights on information and market power – comparing European and American protection of databases' (2007) 38(3) IIC 275, 297.

barriers relating to infrastructural problems that were affecting production of databases in Europe.[32]

While the Commission identified legal incentive as a solution to tackle fragmentation, it is possible that such solution would not be ideal under the circumstances. There was lack of reasoning or argument to suggest that incentive via legislation may overcome the problem of fragmentation.[33] For instance, the evaluation report, which will be discussed later, questions the growth of the database market in Europe despite the presence of legislative incentive.[34] This indicates that legislation may not be an ideal solution for problems that existed in Europe. One has to note that at the time of the proposal there was investment towards the legal database industry in Europe, although there were no similar signs of investments in other industries.[35] Therefore the argument that incentive was necessary for the overall growth of the database industry in Europe fits in well. There is, however, a possibility that the development of database industry is to a great extent market driven. The proposal already has stated the immense potential of the database market.[36] An adequate market may act as a far greater incentive for the industry than incentive via legal rights. In fact, the US database market showed steady growth over the years without a special database right.[37] The producers invested in the US despite the fact that there were special incentives in Europe.[38] This indicates that the nature of incentive required for the database industry may be different from just introducing a legal right. A possible approach in the European context would have been to study the nature of incentive for the database industry prior to laying down the right.[39]

On the contrary, it could be argued that the legal incentive was the only alternative to resolve the fragmentation problem. Linguistic barrier may not be removed, since the origin of such barrier is in the diverse culture of the European community.[40] However, if the future demand was with databases accessible in English, the

---

[32]Bitton (n 13) 1424; McManis (n 22) 29-30.

[33]Anyways there was less confidence with legislation in absence of any evidence, Bitton (n 13) 1424.

[34]First Evaluation of Directive 96/9/EC, para [4.2.3].

[35]COM (92) 24 final, paras [1.2] and [1.3].

[36]ibid 2.

[37]There may not be any additional incentives required to fundamentally initiate production of databases. This is clear from the annual reports and production of databases in US, *Infra* Chapter 4.

[38]"Nevertheless, as the figures discussed below demonstrate, there has been a considerable growth in database production in the US, whereas, in the EU, the introduction of "sui generis" protection appears to have had the opposite effect. With respect to "non-original" databases, the assumption that more and more layers of IP protection means more innovation and growth appears not to hold up", First Evaluation of Directive 96/9/EC, para [5.2].

[39]Absence of empirical evidence has always been an issue, Bitton (n 13) 1426.

[40]European Commission, Press Release: Winners of 2015 European Border Breakers Awards (EBBA) for pop, rock and dance music unveiled (Brussels/Groningen, October 14, 2014) available at <http://europa.eu/rapid/press-release_IP-14-1135_en.htm?locale=en> (accessed 30 December 2016).

Commission could have proposed specific incentive instead of creating a legal incentive for all databases.[41] The technical barrier resulted because of infrastructural problems associated with the European market. Digital revolution and the development of internet happened in the US before Europe and helped towards the development of the US economy.[42] In the course of time, development of internet led to the business of e-commerce.[43] These initial developments provided US with a competitive edge over the European database market. There was no such projection in the draft proposal stating how long this advantage of the US market over the European market would have lasted. Therefore, the Commission had a choice between setting up incentives for the European database producers to overcome the initial hurdles or think of something similar to the standard of protection which is available now. Whatever the thinking was at the time of the proposal, the Commission only intended to offer limited protection to producers.[44]

2.1.2 Protecting Electronic Databases

As an incentive to database producers, there was a proposal for two separate levels of protection for databases.[45] According to the Commission, the existing legal barrier resulted because member states protected databases differently.[46] For databases, certain degree of copyright protection existed in most member states, alongside protection under unfair competition law and catalogue rule in some States.[47] In order to curb legal barriers, the Commission warranted copyright as a starting point for harmonizing database law in Europe.[48] As to the option of harmonizing unfair competition law, it was pointed out that the structure of such law was vastly different in the member states with the example of no unfair competition law in the United Kingdom.[49] Under the circumstances it was felt that it would not be worthwhile to only harmonize the law concerning unfair competition for databases without harmonizing the existing law in Europe.[50]

In the background of a potential electronic information market, it was reasoned that existing copyright protection in member states may not be adequate in protecting electronic databases. There was no express provision for protecting such

[41]Major databases should be accessible in English, Derclaye (n 31) 297.

[42]Bitton (n 13) 1424.

[43]McManis (n 22) 29-30.

[44]*Infra* Chapter 7, section 7.1.

[45]COM (92) 24 final.

[46]The catalogue rule was only limited to Scandinavian countries, ibid, para [2.2.10] 16.

[47]ibid 16 and 36.

[48]ibid 36.

[49]ibid 36.

[50]ibid.

databases under copyright law.[51] Even if implicit protection was present, there was considerable uncertainty due to existing differences in originality standard for copyright protection.[52] Under these circumstances, member states would apply different threshold standards before determining copyright protection for a database. Therefore, a particular database may receive protection in one member state, while remaining unprotected in others.[53] The standard of originality with respect to a particular work was an outcome of different levels of creativity in common and civil law jurisdictions.[54] On one hand there was the threshold of sufficient labour, skill or judgement with effective parameters being time spent and effort expended. On the other, originality threshold in civil law jurisdictions required an independent touch in terms of uniqueness attached to the work.[55] The work in question should reflect author's individuality, which means that expending labour and time was not sufficient to merit copyright protection.[56]

In the opinion of the Commission, uncertainty in copyright protection would not incentivize production of electronic databases. Thus, harmonization of available copyright protection for databases was proposed.[57] According to the Article, copyright protection is only afforded to a database, "…for the way the collection has been made, that is, the personal choices made by the author in selecting or in arranging the material and in making it accessible to the user".[58] This harmonization formed the first tier of protection under the Database Directive.[59]

Although harmonization ensured copyright protection for original selection or arrangement of contents in a database, such protection was not extended to the contents themselves. The Commission saw future electronic databases as a

---

[51]The word 'database' was not present in legislations and collection of data was expressly protected in few member states like UK and Spain, ibid, para [2.2.3]; The legislations of the member states based on Article 2.1 and 2.5 (copyright protection to Literary or Artistic Work or as collections) of the Berne Convention may not be same as protecting electronic databases comprising of compilation of data in an online environment, ibid, para [2.2.4].

[52]More detailed analysis about the threshold standards in the member states are in chapter 5, First Evaluation of Directive 96/9/EC, para [1.1].

[53]COM (92) 24 final, para [2.2.5].

[54]ibid.

[55]ibid.

[56]ibid.

[57]This was also in accordance with art 2.5 of the Berne Convention "Collections of literary or artistic works such as encyclopedias and anthologies which, by reason of the selection and arrangement of their contents, constitute intellectual creations shall be protected as such, without prejudice to the copyright in each of the works forming part of such collections", 'Berne Convention for the protection of Literary and Artistic Works', (WIPO) available at <http://www.wipo.int/treaties/en/ip/berne/trtdocs_wo001.html> (accessed 21 December 2008); ibid, paras [3.2.1] and [3.2.2].

[58]ibid, para [3.2.2]; In this context, there is no explanation of the threshold of creativity related to an author and this issue has been analyzed in chapter 5.

[59]Council Directive 96/9/EC, art 3.

comprehensive and extensive resource where the scope of selection may be narrow or negligible.[60] In some instances, there may not be any scope for either selection or arrangement like in the case of a telephone directory arranged in an alphabetic order.[61] While original selection or arrangement in such databases would come under copyright, technically there was nothing concrete to stop downloading of the contents from an electronic database.[62] A particular competitor may not face any hindrance from copying the contents, and re-sell it as a part of his own product.[63] To the detriment of a database producer, there was a possibility that a competitor may be able to copy and reproduce electronic databases at a low cost.[64] Indeed, once contents are accessible, reproduction is possible at a lower cost than cost of production.[65]

The low cost of copying in an electronic environment essentially reflects the 'public goods' problem in a database.[66] Public goods mean that they are non-rivalrous and non-excludable in character.[67] Non-rivalrous means that many people can access the same good, or service, without reducing the value or depleting it,[68] whereas non-excludable is a situation when it is difficult to prevent people from accessing goods or services after they have been released in the public domain.[69] Electronic databases are non-rivalrous because all electronic copies are of the same standard. Many users can use them simultaneously, and the use of one individual does not reduce the value of the database for the subsequent individual.[70] A database is also non-excludable because one may copy after it has been released in the market, and it is difficult on the part of the producer to stop such acts. This situation creates the problem of free-riding as referred in the explanatory

---

[60]COM (92) 24 final, para [3.1.9].

[61]ibid, para [3.2.4].

[62]ibid 28 and 31.

[63]ibid 30.

[64]ibid, para [3.1.11].

[65]ibid, 30.

[66]Robin Elizabeth Herr, *Is the Sui Generis Right a Failed Experiment? A legal and Theoretical Exploration of How to Regulate Unoriginal Database Contents and Possible Suggestions for Reform* (DJØF Publishing Copenhagen, Denmark 2008) 24; Alfred C Yen, 'The legacy of *Feist:* Consequences of the weak connection between Copyright and the Economics of public goods' (1991) 52(5) Ohio St L J 1343, 1365-1373.

[67]Public Goods problem is related to the Intellectual Property Rights aspect, William M Landes and Richard A Posner, 'An Economic analysis of copyright law' (1989) 18(2) J Legal Stud 325, 326; Roger Van Der Bergh, 'The role and social justification of copyright: a "law and economics" approach' (1998) 1 IPQ 17, 20.

[68]Herr (n 66) 24; Van Der Bergh (n 67) 20.

[69]Herr (n 66) 24.

[70]'Information' is an example characterized by non-rivalrous use, Van Der Bergh (n 67) 20.

memorandum.[71] As a consequence of free-riding, the producers would be reluctant to invest towards electronic databases.[72]

The explanatory memorandum did not mention the possibility of using Technological Protection Measures (TPM).[73] For example, the emergence of TPM and strong legal protection like the Digital Millennium Copyright Act (DMCA) in US is good news for database producers who want to protect their content which is not original.[74] It has been however argued that TPM is not a full proof solution and this means that legal sanctions are still required and effort of privatization of goods through TPM is not a perfect solution.[75] Nevertheless, TPM is a possible way to privatize the public nature of databases, which could not have been foreseen at the time of the first draft proposal.

Any one circumventing such protection measure is in violation of the laws governing cybercrime.[76] Even if electronic databases are indeed non-rivalrous, there is the possibility to reduce accessibility. A database producer exclusively controls accessibility in this regard, and the use of TPM may prove effective.[77]

Databases act as a vital commercial tool for dissemination of electronic information. Optimal conditions would encourage investment towards its production.[78] Alongside harmonization of copyright protection, there was a proposal for limited

---

[71]COM (92) 24 final, 28-31.

[72]Arguing for - Intellectual property is ill-suited for eliminating free-riding, Mark A Lemley, 'Property, Intellectual Property and Free Riding '(2004-2005) 83(4) Tex L Rev 1031, 1032; The problem of free-riding may reduce incentives for the producers to invest in creation, resulting which there would be undersupply of public goods; Van Der Bergh (n 67) 20.

[73]On a different note, if two sets of protection are available for the database producer, is there a need for an extra layer of protection in form of a special database right? In the context of US, there is a possibility that TPM will impede dissemination of data, Jane C Ginsburg, 'Creation and Commercial Value: Copyright protection of works of Information' (1990) 90(7) Colum. L. Rev. 1865, 1921-1922; Jessica Litman has given the example of copyright protection to computer software. She expressed that giving meaningful protection to databases would not stop the database publishers from using other means (like TPM) of protection. Litman said that computer software should be an example in this regard, where the publishers are using all possible means (mixing both copyright and trade secrecy) to restrict use even after meaningful copyright protection to computer software. In case of databases of informational work, there may be the repetition of the same story. It is unlikely that publishers will give up the use of TPM, and the possible problem with dissemination will remain, Jessica Litman, 'After *Feist*' (1992) 17(2) U Dayton L Rev 607, 612-613.

[74]Herr (n 66) 181.

[75]Estelle Derclaye, *The Legal Protection of Databases: A Comparative Analysis* (Edward Elgar, Northampton 2008), 25.

[76]For example in the UK, the Computer Misuse Act, 1990, ch 18.

[77]Digital rights management solves public good problem to a great extent. However, it must be noted that paper format databases do not have the above outlined TPM advantage, (IVIR), 'The Recasting of Copyright & Related Rights for the Knowledge Economy' (November 2006) 104, available at <http://ec.europa.eu/internal_market/copyright/docs/studies/etd2005imd195recast_report_2006.pdf> (accessed 10 April 2010).

[78]COM (92) 24 final, 28-31.

protection for the contents of a database if such contents were not already protected under copyright.[79] By envisaging this layer of protection, the Commission proposed the enactment of a special database right against unfair extraction of the contents of a database.

In the background of the risk of copying faced by the producers, the proposed protection should have reflected the impending concern. Instead, the proposal offered limited protection to the contents, thereby questioning the level of concern associated with the production of electronic databases.[80]

2.2 Incentive Argument and Production of Databases

Using incentive as one of the justifications behind enacting an intellectual property right has an American lineage.[81] There is a general understanding that intellectual property legislation balances the problems associated with public goods. In its absence, there would be insufficient incentive to produce vulnerable works that are easily appropriable.[82] Further, the producer has little chance to recover the investment towards such production.

The incentive theory surrounding the copyright protection presupposes that profit motivates an individual.[83] Without copyright protection, production and dissemination of work may not happen at an optimal level due to the possibility of unauthorized appropriation.[84] In the absence of copyright, there may be difficulties in recovering investments made towards the production of a work.[85] Copying in the

[79]ibid, para [3.2.8].

[80]*Infra* chapter 7, section 7.1.

[81]Lemley (n 72) 1031; American story about copyright protection is that it provides economic incentive essential for the creation of new works, Diane Leenheer Zimmerman, 'Copyright as Incentives: Did we just imagine that' (2011) 12 (1) Theoretical Inquiries in Law 29, 30; On the contrary Ralph Brown has said that the Copyright clause in the US Constitution does not say to 'maximize returns to authors and inventors', Ralph Brown, 'Eligibility for copyright protection: a search for principled standards' (1985) 70(2) Minn L Rev 589, 592.

[82]Patent is observed as a reward system, *Miguel Figueroa v United States*, United States Court of Appeals for the Federal Circuit, 05-5144 (October 2006); It was acknowledged that the term protection for copyright was increased by 20 years to provide incentives for creators, *Eldred v. Ashcroft* 537 US 186 (2003), (arguing against) Lemley (n 72) 1031-1033; Shubha Ghosh, 'The Intellectual Property Incentive: Not so a natural as to warrant strong exclusivity' (2006) 3(2) available at <http://www.law.ed.ac.uk/ahrc/script-ed/vol3-2/ghosh.asp> (accessed 17 July 2010).

[83]Herr (n 66) 47; Innovation on the part of the producer is directly proportional to the returns, Stanley M Besen & Leo J Raskind, 'An Introduction to the Law and Economics of Intellectual Property' (1991) 5 J. Econ. Persp. 3, 5; Greater incentives to create intellectual property comes with more extensive intellectual (copyright) protection, Landes & Posner (n 67); Arguing against it, Zimmerman (n 81).

[84]Lionel Bently & Brad Sherman, *Intellectual Property Law* (Oxford University Press, 3rd edn, 2008) 37.

[85]*Supra* (n 83).

digital world will reduce the incentive for an author to create further work so much so that the "millennium of the internet will eliminate the modern day Michelangelo because his services are no longer valued".[86] According to the incentive theory, law of copyright rectifies possible 'market failure' by incentivizing production and stopping undersupply of works. The mere presence of copyright will assure the authors to produce new work.[87] Although commentators have linked the role of copyright in the pre-production stage, there are not enough arguments given in this regard.[88] From the point of creativity, a person creating a work for the very first time may not be aware of copyright protection. His creativity develops from desire and little from copyright. The issue of protection begins at a later stage when there is the realization that the work in question is worth protecting.[89] Contrary to this proposition, in commercial houses conceptualization of a work may start because of the prior knowledge of copyright protection. There is an indication that strong copyright protection is preferable among producers, since they want to widen the scope covering databases to comprise of works and non-copyrighted material.[90] The copyright protection for them seems to be an incentive for future investment towards databases. Therefore, it would be incorrect to relate the influence of copyright protection with the development of any creative work.[91] Those arguing against such contention have not disagreed with the role of copyright at the post-production stage.[92] They have, however, ignored the influence of copyright protection at a pre-production stage for commercial producers.[93]

A database with original selection or arrangement of the contents is a literary work and comes under Article 3 of the Database Directive.[94] The other category of databases recognized under the Directive is non-original as per copyright standard. These databases are protected under Article 7 of the Directive.[95]

Going by arguments mentioned above, an author may be inspired out of creative pleasure to produce a database, which is original according to the standard

[86]David Balaban, 'The Battle of the Music Industry: the distribution of Audio and Video Works via the internet, music and more' (2001-02) 12(1) Fordham Intell Prop Media & Ent L J 235, 240.

[87]Arguing against copyright as an incentive to creativity, Zimmerman (n 81) 35–42.

[88]See generally, ibid.

[89]This assertion connects to the argument posed by Zimmerman pointing that the painter or an artist would not be in a position to know that someone else would read the book or hang the painting, Zimmerman (n 81) 43–48.

[90]Working programme of the Commission in the field of copyright and neighbouring rights. Follow-up to the Green Paper. COM (90) 584 final, 17 January 1991, 18 (COM (90) 584 final).

[91]This means relating either the extrinsic or the intrinsic factor in the premise of 'any creative work' is faulty and it is connected to the person involved in making the work, See (n 83) – (n 89).

[92]The premise of the argument is that existence of the copyright does not ensure more creative work and thus, includes the pre-production stage; see Zimmerman (n 81).

[93]ibid.

[94]Council Directive 96/9/EC, art 3.

[95]ibid.

prescribed in the Directive.[96] This is, however, not the situation with non-original databases, which are not original in copyright sense. As a result there can be no creative pleasure in producing them.[97]

In the absence of creative pleasure in the production of non-original databases, it is difficult to identify incentives that are present for a database producer.[98] These databases will be produced with the intention of maximizing profits. Therefore, logically, incentive is required, which will ensure protection of the investment made by the producer.[99] Database production may suffer without such initiative, thereby identifying a theoretical need of enacting a database right for databases that are non-original by copyright standard.[100]

Although incentive may work as an impetus for certain category of authors, it is difficult to conclude that such incentive will increase production. There is no reason to believe that production will continue in the absence of a market.[101] It is inconceivable to think that commercial producers would ignore the market and only invest because of the availability of copyright protection.[102] The uncertainty with production may remain even after introducing the incentive.

2.2.1 Perspective of Producers at Proposal Stage

The starting point of incentive for electronic databases was primarily based on copyright.[103] Differences in the threshold standard of originality were identified as a

---

[96]The standard of originality has been discussed in chapter 5.

[97]In the context of public dissemination, there is a tendency to overlook "author's incentive to spur the creation of fact-works". The sheer "importance and utility of fact-works justify greater incentives for their creator", Denise R Polivy '*Feist* applied: Imagination protects, but perspiration persists – the bases of copyright protection for factual compilation' (1997-98) 8(3) Fordham Intell Prop Media & Ent L J 773, 777-778.

[98]Although for some poets creativity has a greater value than monetary incentives, the same is unlikely for "prosaic compositions", Ginsburg (n 73) 1908; It may be the case that database producer will produce databases if there is a market for it. There may not be any additional incentives required to fundamentally initiate production of databases. This is clear from the annual reports and production of databases in US, infra chapter 4, section 4.1; This proposition is contrary to the thought that these works (compilation of facts) may require a prompt to their production, Jane C Ginsburg, 'No "Sweat"? Copyright and the Protection of Works of Information after *Feist v Rural*' (1992) 92(2) Colum L Rev 338, 341.

[99]Following the argument that intellectual property in purely business sense acts as an incentive, Zimmerman (n 81) 30.

[100]Council Directive 96/9/EC.

[101]It has been observed later in the book that commercial databases are mostly driven by the market requirement, *infra*, section 4.3.1.

[102]The production of databases continued in US in absence of database legislation. It means market has a role to play other than the fact that there is enough incentive to continue production. *Infra* chapter 4.

[103]COM (92) 24 final, para [2.2.5].

problem for the production of electronic databases and were harmonized to ensure an atmosphere of certainty for the producers.[104] Although there are no explicit reasons given in the proposal on questions of law relating to harmonization of copyright protection, the role of copyright in incentivizing production is identified from the opinions of the stakeholders.[105] Prior to the proposal, the stakeholders were asked two questions in relation to copyright protection of databases. The questions were firstly, about whether databases with copyrighted contents should receive copyright protection, and secondly, whether the copyright protection should apply, and extend to databases, which contain data available in the public domain.[106] In response, the stakeholders overwhelmingly preferred copyright protection for databases comprising of copyrighted contents.[107] There was no interest shown for the enactment of a new database right.[108] They also suggested that copyright protection should be made available for databases comprising of both copyrighted works, and non-copyrighted data.[109] The argument that database producers did not fully comprehend the scope of database right and hence opted for copyright protection is incorrect.[110] It is difficult to support such proposition, since majority of the producers involved in the business of database production voted for copyright protection.[111] Producers were at the best position to understand the consequences of the database right, which proposed to protect the contents of their database. Contrary to the support for copyright, there was no comparable support for the enactment of database right.

2.2.2 *The First Evaluation Report and Question of Incentive*

The first official performance report of the Database Directive primarily focused on the assessment of policy goals behind the introduction of the new database right in Europe, although the title of the report suggests evaluation of the database directive.[112] Broadly, the evaluation report considered whether there has been an increase in investment towards production of databases and whether growth rate of the European database industry has increased after the introduction of the database

---

[104]ibid 30.

[105]COM (88) 172 final, 208.

[106]ibid.

[107]COM (90) 584 final, 18.

[108]George Metaxas, "Protection of databases: quietly steering in the wrong direction?" (1990) 12 (7) EIPR 227-228.

[109]COM (90) 584, 18.

[110]Derclaye (n 75) 44.

[111]ibid.

[112]First Evaluation of Directive 96/9/EC, para [2.1].

right.[113] The report investigated whether beneficiaries under the new legislation have actually produced more databases than they would have done in the absence of database legislation.[114] For the reasons mentioned above, the report consulted the results of an online survey addressed to the European database industry, and the empirical evidence generated from Gale Database Directory (GDD). The online survey was sent to 500 European database companies and organizations involved in e-business. They comprised of publishers, suppliers of data and information, database manufacturers and distributors. Out of 500 companies covered by the survey, only 101 responded.[115] GDD was the second source other than the survey. At the time of the report, GDD was the only available database that provided statistical information on growth of database industry in the world.[116]

The online survey considered the level of investment towards the production of databases. In the survey, 49% of the respondents believed that the level of investment increased by more than 20% after 1996. While 37% said that the investments were between 0–20%, 15% believed that it has remained same or actually decreased. The increase in investments has been mainly towards improving information technology and staff development.[117]

The second part of the report focused on the actual evolution of database sales to measure the impact of Database Directive.[118] European Association of Directory and Database Publishers (EADP) claimed significant increase in supply of information after the enactment of the Database Directive. In the opinion of EADP, the difference between the number of databases produced and the amount of information delivered through databases should have been recognized.[119] The evaluation report conceded that measuring the number of databases might not be the only way to assess the evolutionary nature of the sale of databases. Supply of information could be a possible alternative.[120] However, EADP neither provided any empirical evidence, nor did they propose the methods to be used to quantify and measure information delivered through databases.[121] In the absence of other empirical evidence, the impact of Database Directive, especially the database right, had to be measured by the number of databases produced.

GDD measured the size of the database industry in terms of database entries in the directory. According to the directory, the number of European databases in 2004 was 3095 when compared to 3092 in 1998. This number increased from 3092 in

113 ibid.

114 ibid.

115 ibid, para [1.3].

116 ibid.

117 ibid, para [4.2.2].

118 ibid, para [4.2.3].

119 ibid.

120 ibid.

121 ibid.

1998 to 4085 in 2001, but recorded a decline in 2004.[122] Although GDD was consulted, the report introduced important caveats about the empirical evidence used to judge the performance of the Directive. For instance, there was no clear indication about the parameters for recognizing a database before their entry was recorded in the GDD. There was a possibility that the wide scope of the definition of database under the Database Directive was not well represented in the directory.[123] Thus, the GDD report was considered as a rough estimate of the performance of the database market in Europe.[124] In the context of the 'fall' in the number of databases in 2004 as compared to 2001, the EADP argued that the fall does not represent decrease in sale of database, since the level of supply of information via databases has not decreased. There was no evidence given in support of this argument. Further, EADP claimed that there was a change in delivery of databases from stand-alone product to portal based applications, thereby providing a single point access to many databases.[125] The fall in the number of databases resulted because of a transition in the medium of delivery of information from magnetic tapes, diskettes, and CD-ROM, to single point access portal. GDD has failed to consider this aspect and, therefore, their report was incorrect in the context of the European database market.[126] The report conceded that there was considerable uncertainty with the figures given in the GDD and further empirical evidence must be consulted before taking any firm policy measures.[127] However, the report did say that database right did not have any proven economic impact on the production of databases in Europe.[128] One of the recommended policy measures was to repeal the database right from the Database Directive.[129]

In the first draft proposal it was expected that by virtue of the database right, European markets were expected to compete with the US market.[130] Therefore, it is questionable as to how the European market would compete without producing more databases. The report observed that introduction of the database right was to stimulate database production.[131]

The report questioned the incentive of a database right even though there may have been a theoretical need to incentivize production of non-original databases. It did not question the increase in investment towards production of databases. In fact,

[122]ibid, para [4.2.3].

[123]"It appears entirely possible that certain compilations such as newspapers, magazines and electronic programme guides, which would fall within the scope of the Directive, have not been counted as a database entry in the GDD statistics", ibid.

[124]ibid.

[125]ibid; For example Westlaw, a portal based application, forms a single point of access to many databases.

[126]ibid, para [4.2.3].

[127]ibid.

[128]ibid, para [1.4].

[129]ibid, para [1.5].

[130]COM (92) 24 final, para [1.1].

[131]First Evaluation of Directive 96/9/EC, para [1.4].

Table 2.1 Investments of the European database industry

Area of investment in database industry	Percentage of investment (%)
Information technology	(85.1)
Staff to feed data into a database	(69.3)
Staff to run a database	(65.3)
Marketing/advertising of a database	(64.4)
Staff to collect data	(63.4)
Acquisition of data	(62.4)
Licences	(58.4)
Office space	(35.6)
Other	(21.8)

Source Commission services' online survey (August–September 2005) in First Evaluation of Directive 96/9/EC, 17

the online survey conducted as a part of the report reflected increase in investments.[132] Table 2.1 represents the structure of investment.

About 88% of respondents in the online survey believed that investment increased by 20% or more.[133] Table 2.1 shows sectors where investment has been made by the European database industry. Each category represents the sum total of investments (percentage) made by the respondents in that particular category. For instance, 85.1% of investment in information technology was the total percentage of all investments made by the respondents towards information technology. Two major areas have been information technology and information technology staff. An increase in investment should be encouraging from the point of enacting the database right.

Although the figures record an increase in investments, there is considerable apprehension with such conclusion. Only 101 (20%) of the companies replied to the survey, representing a fraction of the total number of companies involved in the business.[134] Among 101 companies, 80% said that there has been increase in investment, which makes eighty companies out of a total of 500.[135] The argument of increase in investment has been based only on the reply of (80 out of 500) 16% companies. This makes statistic less credible.[136] Although there is a trend of increased investment towards databases, the figures do not give an explicit picture. It is difficult to comprehend the reason behind such poor response from companies

[132]ibid, para [4.2.2].

[133]ibid, para [4.2.2].

[134]Total number of companies in the survey was 500; ibid, para [4.2.2].

[135]ibid.

[136]There has been criticism about the size of the sample used and critique said that the conclusion of the report should not be treated seriously, Derclaye (n 31) 297.

in a matter that is so important for the future of database right.[137] Companies should have been much more pro-active in their response if database right was an incentive for them.

There has been criticism of the report because the empirical evidence reflects position of one database i.e. GDD.[138] Under these circumstances, the evidence is limited and may not be an actual representation of the number of databases produced in Europe.[139] The report stated that the number of databases was equivalent to pre-Directive levels.[140] This may give impression that there was no production between 1996 and 2004. In reality, however, Table 2.2 represents a different situation.

Subsequent to the incorporation of database right in 1998, there was steady increase in the number of databases, and by 2001, a growth of 25% was noticeable in the European database industry.[141] After 2001, however, production fell to the pre-Directive level.[142] If incentive of database right played a role in the rise of 25%, such incentive did not have similar effect when numbers were decreasing. Therefore, the incentive worked differently in the period of six years (1998–2004). The EADP said that decrease in media like magnetic tapes, diskettes and CD ROMS led to the disappearance of some of the databases.[143] New media should have developed, even if the old media disappeared due to technological change. In fact, database right was introduced for the delivery of information through various new media in the electronic age.[144] Despite shortcomings of the empirical evidence, this report provides an insight on the application of incentive theory and confirms that incentives may not always work.[145]

Reference to numbers to establish a certain argument is something that has not happened on previous occasion. At the time of the proposal, the explanatory memorandum highlighted the immense potential of European database industry with the help of numbers.[146] The assessment of the potential market was not based on supply of information.[147] Following a similar logic, numbers can determine the performance if similar method had been followed at the time of assessing potential.

---

[137]Similarly there was a gap of five years after the decision of *Feist* in the US and the debate for enacting legislation for protecting databases only started in 1996. The gap essentially means less concern on the part of the publishers, *Infra* section 4.2.

[138]Derclaye (n 31) 275 and 297.

[139]The Evaluation Report introduced certain caveats detailing the limitation of the study, First Evaluation of Directive 96/9/EC, para [4.2.3].

[140]ibid, para [4.2.3].

[141]The numbers increased from 3092 to 4085, which was an increase of almost 1000 databases; In 1998 member states started to incorporate the database right in their national laws.

[142]The fall was from 4095 to 3095, i.e. about 1000 databases.

[143]First Evaluation of Directive 96/9/EC, para [4.2.3].

[144]COM (92) 24 final, para [1.3].

[145]*Supra* section 2.2.

[146]*Supra* (n 18) - (n 21).

[147]ibid.

Table 2.2 Database production in "West Europe" (1992–2004)

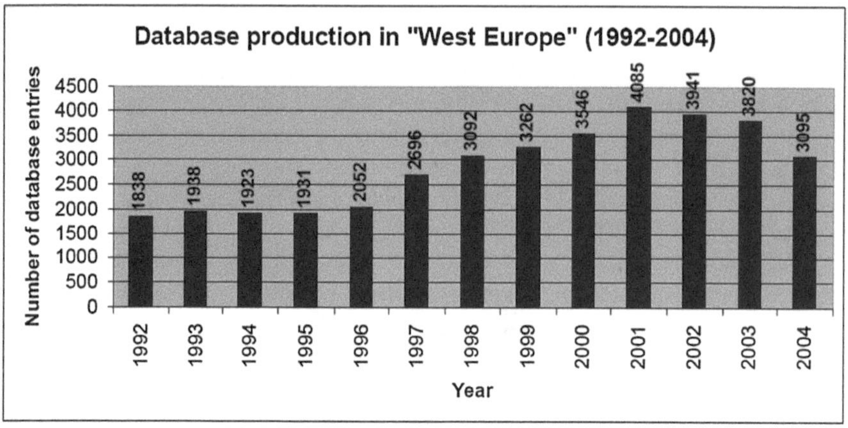

Source The Gale Directory of Database 2005, Vol. 1, Part 2 in First Evaluation of Directive 96/9/EC, 19

Although the exact number of databases produced in Europe is questionable, the report indicates the trend that European market did not react to the incentive of database right.

The explanatory memorandum to the first draft said that the "…Directive aims to address both the creative and economic aspects of the protection of databases".[148] Protection of investment through the enactment of the database right is an economic right.[149] In an implicit way, the report questioned the economic evidence that led to believe that database right was a necessary economic incentive for producers. Commentators have said that the exact requirement of database legislation was not clear, since there was no evidence of piracy preceding such legislation.[150] Economic justification behind the enactment of database right was not fully developed, since empirical evidence was not consulted prior to the enactment of database right.[151] Further, justification of the database right was an economic one and validity of such justification was in the empirical evidence.[152] There was no incidence of market failure or any conclusive evidence to suggest the requirement

[148]COM (92) 24 final, para [4.2.6].

[149]Council Directive 96/9/EC, art 7.

[150]Bitton (n 13) 1432.

[151]ibid; Mark Powell, 'The European Union's Database Directive: An International Antidote to the side effects of Feist' (1996-97) 20(4) Fordham Int'l LJ 1215, 1225; Mark J Davison, *The legal protection of databases* (Cambridge University Press Cambridge 2003) (n 75), 6-7; Pamela Samuelson, 'Should economics play a role in copyright law and policy' (2003-04) 1(1-2) Univ of Ottawa L T J 1, 14.

[152]P Drahos, *A Philosophy of Intellectual Property* (Dartmouth, Aldershot, 1996) 7; Davison, (n 151) 6-7.

of database right. Hence, its introduction was purely speculative in nature.[153] Absence of economic evidence prior to enacting the Directive is reflected on the structure of the database right. It has been suggested that the prime intention of the database right was to locate substantial investment to merit protection. This approach has excluded the intention of database maker. Moreover, there is no need for the database maker to show any market failure or "potential danger in recouping investment".[154] A database maker only needs to show that extraction has been substantial. Thus, the Directive allows for less stringent threshold and protection of "mundane collection of information".[155] This is contrary to the position taken by the explanatory memorandum where the economic impact on publishers was considered.[156] Thus, economic evidence in formation of the database right and further economic links in the subsequent application of database right were both absent.

The objective of the database right was "to create a climate in which investment in data processing can be stimulated" by way of protecting contents of a database against misappropriation.[157] In the background of this objective, it is interesting to note that economic consideration was not the rationale behind the formation of database right.[158] This contention is particularly interesting since reading of the Recitals makes it clear that the Directive followed the economic analysis of informational goods.[159] Recital 8, 10 and 11 reflects upon the economic aspects involved in the Directive. In particular, database right and corresponding Recitals indicate that justification behind adopting such right was purely economic.[160] The

[153]"EU accepted …the underlying economic assumptions of proponents of database protection and assumed that with no legal protection producers will have no incentive to produce databases", Bitton (n 13) 1411 and 1426.

[154]Guido Westkamp, 'Protecting Databases Under US and European Law- Methodical Approached to the Protection of Investments between Unfair Competition and Intellectual Property concepts' (2003) 34(7) IIC 772, 785, 793.

[155]ibid.

[156]COM (92) 24 final, 25.

[157]ibid.

[158]This non-consultation of economic evidence must have been in the context of the current structure of the Database Directive. The explanatory memorandum, attached to the first proposal did develop the empirical research and economic evidence concerning the possibility surrounding the European database market in the information age. It was provided as a pre-text to harmonizing protection of databases, ibid, para [1.0].

[159]Council Directive 96/9/EC; "Strong economic motives underpinned the adoption of Database Directive", Maurizio Borghi and Maria Lilla Montagnani, 'Promises and Pitfalls of the European Copyright Harmonisation' in David Ward (ed.) *The European Union and the Cultural Industries* (2007 Ashgate Publishing) 13; Derclaye (n 75) 39.

[160]J Philips, *Databases, the Human Rights Act and EU law* in J Griffiths and U Suthersanen (eds), *Copyright and Free Speech, Comparative and International Analyses,* (Oxford University Press, 2005) 411; Derclaye (n 75) 40.

purpose of database right was to garner economic benefits, but there was no substantive empirical evidence that suggested imminent problems.[161]

As database right was enacted without any economic evidence, it would have been difficult to know the requirement constituting structure of such right. Therefore, it must have been a challenge to estimate the overall balance in such legislation.[162] For the purpose of investment, it was difficult to predict the incentive required for a particular database producer.[163] There is an inherent difficulty in balancing incentive to correct possible market failure.[164] For instance, prior economic consultations have taken place in the EU for framing appropriate rules for copyright protection of computer programs.[165] At the point of inception, economic evidence could have possibly estimated requirement of the incentive of a novel database right.[166] The database right is thus prone to suffer from overall imbalance.[167]

We have come across various reasons and arguments that were cited at the time of enacting the Directive. There was also a quick reference to the decision of US Supreme Court in *Feist Publications v Rural Telephone Service*.[168] The evaluation report stated that US did not react to the decision of US Supreme Court in *Feist*. Nevertheless, Europe went ahead with the enactment of database right.[169]

---

[161]Bitton (n 13) 1426.

[162]Estelle Derclaye's work looks at the issues of over protection and under protection in relation to Database Directive, Derclaye (n 75).

[163]To know the optimal level of protection is a difficult proposition, Van Der Bergh (n 67) 32; Incentive theory does not tell much about the "structure of intellectual property" i.e. the requirement, other than stating that intellectual property rights should be as "strong as possible", Ghosh (n 82) 97.

[164]Arguing that not enough economic analysis is done for the purpose of policy making in the field of intellectual property law, Samuelson (n 151).

[165]This has been said in the context of Article 6 of the Software Directive, Council Directive 1991/250/EEC of 14 May 1991 on the legal protection of computer programs [1991] OJL122/1; This Article permits de-compilation of the computer program code for the purposes of achieving interoperability among programs, Samuelson (n 151); A substantial empirical research shows that increase in copyright protection does not automatically mean the increase in number of work produced. Raymond Shih Ray Ku & others, 'Does Copyright Law promotes creativity? An Empirical analysis of Copyright's Bounty' (2009) 62(6) Vand L Rev 1667, 1694.

[166]There is no previous example of the database right in the world, Anna Koo, 'Database Right decoded' [2010] 32(7) EIPR 313, 313.

[167]Davison (n 151).

[168]Feist Publications (n 6).

[169]First evaluation of Directive 96/9/EC, para [2.4].

2.3 Feist Decision as an Argument for Protection of Databases

The *Feist* decision was identified in the explanatory memorandum as an emergence of "... new-line of jurisprudence" that "...rejects the 'sweat of the brow' criteria and requires originality in the copyright sense".[170] Further, electronic databases, and to some extent, databases in paper-format will be excluded from the purview of copyright protection failing the test of originality.[171] This non-protection would be "...regardless of the skill, labour, effort or financial investment expended in their creation".[172] It was believed that in commercial context, electronic databases must be comprehensive in order to be useful. On the ground of comprehensiveness, it would be difficult for those databases to meet the requirement of originality based on selection or arrangement of the contents.[173]

In the back drop of concern expressed in the explanatory memorandum, one needs to understand the structure of an electronic database. An electronic database typically comprises of three components: contents, logical schema that describes the contents and their relationship with each other, and a database management system, which helps in searching for information in the database.[174] There are two kinds of selection mechanism possible in an electronic database. The first one may be adopted at the point of collecting the data. A second type of selection or arrangement is possible, while presenting the information to a user.[175] At the initial stage, the primary objective is to make databases commercially viable and the maker intends to make the contents comprehensive to raise usefulness of an electronic database. Therefore, for comprehensive databases, selection is not expected at the initial stage, however, it depends on the type of the database in question.[176] At the second stage of making an electronic database, database maker follows selection or arrangement to present the collected data in an informative way. This is an important stage where the maker gets the opportunity to show creativity with respect to an electronic database. Selection and arrangement at a logical schema stage, and the structure representing connections between the logical schema and the database management system should come under the scope of copyright threshold.[177] Selection or arrangement at the logical stage provides an opportunity

---

[170] COM (92) 24 final, para [2.3.3].

[171] ibid.

[172] ibid.

[173] ibid.

[174] Herr (n 66) 28-30; See generally for the structure of a typical database, Wesley L. Austin, 'A Thoughtful and Practical Analysis of Database Protection under Copyright Law, and a Critique of *Sui Generis* Protection' (1997) 3 (1) J of Tech L & P.

[175] This assertion is based on the working of databases like Westlaw and LexisNexis.

[176] *Infra* section 6.4.

[177] L Ray Patterson, 'Copyright overextended: a preliminary inquiry into the need for a federal statute of unfair competition' (1991-92) 17(2) U Dayton L Rev 385, 394.

for the user to select and access information.[178] This is contrary to the belief that there is no selection or arrangement on the part of the database producer and working of a database depends on the selection of the user.[179] Selection or arrangement mechanism is compulsory for an electronic database to function.

The explanatory memorandum makes it clear that removal of 'sweat of the brow' will disincentivize database producers.[180] Depending on the size of a database, process of collection may involve substantial investment. Since protection under copyright extends only towards creativity in selection or arrangement of the contents, a database comprising of factual information may be used by any second comer. There is lack of incentive for the database maker if the second comer obtains the valuable contents without incurring any legal liability.[181] 'Sweat of the brow' was ideally placed in this situation, since protection extends to the contents, thereby providing enough incentive for producers.[182] According to the 'sweat of the brow' theory, a second compiler must expend similar effort in collecting the same factual information contained in the first compilation.[183] Therefore, in absence of creativity through selection or arrangement of the contents, the first compiler may protect the collection by virtue of the expended effort.[184]

There have been comments about the role that *Feist* had played in bringing about the database right in Europe. For instance, the Head of the Unit in the Directorate General for Copyright Policy suggested that '...apparently [the Commission] decided to introduce a *sui generis* right in the draft [proposal] after reading [the *Feist*] decision'.[185] It has been suggested that the database right was enacted in Europe as a remedial measure further to the apprehension that *Feist* decision will disincentivize production of databases.[186] Other than the *Feist* decision there was *Van Daele* in the Netherland.[187] The *Van Daele* case concerned the copyrightability of a dictionary in Dutch language. In this case, the plaintiff Van Daele, alleged infringement in the act of copying keyword entries in the dictionary of the plaintiff. Although this decision was before the *Feist* decision, similar to *Feist,* the Dutch Supreme Court said that there was no originality in a compilation of 'factual

---

178 *Infra* section 4.3.2.

179 Patterson (n 177).

180 COM (92) 24 final, para [3.1.9].

181 ibid 25.

182 ibid, para [3.1.9].

183 Detailed argument on sweat of the brow theory see *Infra* chapter 3.

184 ibid.

185 Daniel J Gervais, 'The protection of databases' (2007) 82(3) Chicago-Kent Law Review 1109, 1119.

186 ibid; Derclaye (n 75). The author also cited Van Daele as the other reason for incorporating the *sui generis* right (database right) in the Directive.

187 With reference to the US Copyright Law, factual information is also referred as "fact-works" meaning works, which compile and communicate factual information, Robert A Gorman, 'Fact or Fancy? The Implications for Copyright-The Twelfth Annual Donald C Brace Memorial Lecture' (1982) 29 (6) Journal of the Copyright Society 560, 561.

information'. Such compilation only becomes original by virtue of selection expressing the personal view of the maker.[188] One can notice that the urge to act was even greater after *Feist,* since *Van Daele* was decided prior to *Feist.* The explanatory memorandum has only referred to *Feist* decision, and such reference indicates a distinct argument for enacting the database right.[189] This sense of urgency relates to functioning of the European market, although *Feist* decision merely reflected the position of US. It is indicative of the fact that irrespective of jurisdictions, *Feist* decision was believed to hold the key to the future of electronic databases.[190] In Europe, lack of uniformity in copyright protection and the difference in threshold of originality was an additional concern.[191] The Commission expressed, "if [harmonization] is not done quickly, there is a risk that member states may legislate expressly in widely differing ways…"[192] The thought of member states legislating differently may have been the reason to act immediately after the *Feist* decision.[193]

There was however not enough evidence to suggest that immediate action in form of an incentive was required to curb the possible negative effect of the *Feist* decision.[194] The evaluation report has said that unlike Europe, US did not initiate any process for the enactment of database legislation.[195] Therefore, it is questionable whether there was immediate requirement. Despite having no immediate requirement, one has to consider that the objective of the European database industry was to compete internationally, especially with the leading US database industry.[196] The background of *Feist* decision may have provided the required initiative to proceed with database legislation in the EU.[197] Production of databases has been a platform for comparing competitive strengths of Europe and US.[198] Gaining competitive edge over US was an issue and has been stated in many of the official communications of the European Commission.[199]

---

[188]Romme/Van Dale Lexicografie, B.V., Hoge Raad der Nederlanden [HR] [Supreme Court of The Netherlands], 4 January 1991, *translated in* Protecting works of facts: Copyright, Freedom OF Expression and Information LAW, app. I 93-96.

[189]COM (92) 24 final, para [2.3.3].

[190]Gervais (n 185).

[191]COM (92) 24 final, para [2.2.5].

[192]ibid 16.

[193]Estelle Derclaye has suggested in her book that *sui generis* right was enacted because there was no uniform law protecting investments in member states, Derclaye (n 75) 45; This corroborates the fear of the Commission that member states may legislate differently.

[194]In the context of US database market, *Infra* chapter 4.

[195]First Evaluation of Directive 96/9/EC, para [2.4].

[196]*Supra* section 2.1.

[197]ibid; COM (92) 24 final, para [2.3.3].

[198]The first evaluation report compared the production of databases in Europe to the production of databases in US, First Evaluation of Directive 96/9/EC, para [2.4].

[199]COM (88) 584 final, 207; COM (92) 24 final, 7.

Europe followed a pro-active step by enacting a database right that had no precedent in the world market. It becomes important to assess the uniqueness attached to the *Feist* decision in US and the impact of *Feist* on production of databases.

2.4 Two-Tier Structure of Database Directive

Four years after the proposal, the Database Directive was enacted in the year 1996 with a two-tier protection for databases.[200] In the Database Directive, the word 'database' means "a collection of independent works, data or other materials arranged in a systematic or methodical way and individually accessible by electronic or other means."[201] The definition of database has been criticized for creating a broad horizon and unnecessary vagueness.[202] However, in the case of *Fixtures Marketing Ltd v. Organismos Prognostokon Agonon Podosfairou*, ECJ confirmed that the definition of database is meant to be broad so as to cover future databases in any form.[203] According to Recital 13, "this Directive protects collections, sometimes called 'compilations', of works, data or other materials which are arranged, stored and accessed by means which include electronic, electromagnetic or electro-optical processes or analogous processes".[204] Although scholars have been critical of the definition of a database under the Directive, there is little confusion at the time of applying this definition.[205]

Article 3 and 7 represents a two-tier protection under the Directive. Article 3 of the Database Directive states that:

> in accordance with this Directive, databases which, by reason of the selection or arrangement of their contents, constitute the author's own intellectual creation shall be protected as such by copyright. No other criteria shall be applied to determine their eligibility for that protection. The copyright protection of databases provided by this Directive shall not extend to their contents and shall be without prejudice to any rights subsisting in those contents themselves.[206]

---

[200]Council Directive 96/9/EC.

[201]ibid, art 1(2).

[202]Davison (n 151) 100; Juan Carlos Fernandez-Molina, 'The legal protection of databases: current situation of the international harmonization process' (2004) 56 (6) Aslib Proceedings 325, 327; Jacqueline Lipton, 'Databases as Intellectual Property: New Legal Approaches' (2003) 25 (3) EIPR 139, 141.

[203]Case C-444/02 *Fixtures Marketing Ltd v Organismos Prognostikon Agnon Podosfairou (OPAP)* [2005] ECDR 3; CJEU in the case of Case C 30/14 *Ryanair Ltd v PR Aviation BV*, [2015] ECLI:EU:C:2015:10; CJEU in the case of Case C 490/14 *Freistaat Bayern v Verlag Esterbauer GmbH,* [2015] ECLI:EU:C:2015:735.

[204]Council Directive 96/9/EC.

[205]Derclaye (n 75) 54-66; Davison (n 151) 70-73; The application of the definition has been consistent, *infra* section 5.3.

[206]Council Directive 96/9/EC, art 3.

This protection is meant for databases that are original by reason of selection or arrangement of the contents. The threshold to merit copyright protection is the AOIC, which will be discussed in detail in the later chapters.[207]

The rights and infringement applicable for database right are prescribed under Article 7.[208] According to this Article, database producers can prevent 'extraction' and 're-utilization' of the whole or substantial parts of the database evaluated either 'qualitatively' or 'quantitatively'. The database producer must show 'substantial investment' made either qualitatively or quantitatively towards 'obtaining', 'verifying' or 'presenting' the contents of the database.[209] The terms quantitative and qualitative have not been explained in the Database Directive. Further, authors have questioned the utility of this distinction, since there is an overlap with the 'qualitative' criterion, which is required to merit copyright protection.[210] The ECJ, in three cases, has given some insights to the meaning attached to quantitative and qualitative assessment. According to ECJ, quantitative assessment refers to quantifiable sources and qualitative assessment refers to sources that are non-quantifiable, such as intellectual effort or energy stated under Recitals 7, 39 and 40 of the Database Directive.[211]

Other than extraction and re-utilization, the Directive has been silent about terms like 'substantial', 'obtaining', 'verifying' and 'presenting'. The word 'substantial' has not been defined in the Directive and its scope has been discussed in subsequent chapters.[212] 'Obtaining' has not been defined either and is highly contentious in relation to the word 'creating'.[213] Meaning attached to verification can be identified through several ECJ decisions.[214] It includes substantial costs, which are used to

[207]*Infra* chapter 5.

[208]Council Directive 96/9/EC.

[209]ibid art 7.

[210]ibid art 7(1); Davison (n 151) 83-89; English translations of viewpoint of Matthias Leistner (Qualitative as a supplementary criterion); Van Eechoud (Doubts whether qualitative has independent significance; Hagen (Qualitative could be used as a safety net if quantitative is not sufficient, Annemarie Beunen, *Protection for databases: The European Database Directive and its effects in Netherlands, France and United Kingdom* (Wolf Legal Publishers Leiden 2007), 106-107.

[211]C-46/2, *Fixtures Marketing Ltd v. Oy Veikkaus Ab*, [2005] ECDR 2; C-338/02, *Fixtures Marketing Ltd* v. *Svenska Spel AB* [2005] ECDR 4, 49; *Organismos* (n 203).

[212]There is an additional issue of spin-off databases and the investment made in this regard. No clear indication existed about the protection offered to spin-off databases prior to the decision in *The British Horseracing Board Limited (n* Case C-203/02, *The British Horseracing Board Limited v William Hill Organisation Ltd* [2005] ECDR 1); The ECJ said that spin-off databases may still be protected based on separate substantial investment other than the investment in creating; for the issue of spin-off databases and its inherent contradictions, Estelle Derclaye, "Databases Sui Generis Right: Should We Adopt the Spin Off Theory?" (2004) 26 (9) EIPR 402; Mark J. Davison and P. Bernt Hugenholtz, 'Football Fixtures, Horseraces and Spin Offs: The ECJ Domesticates the Database Right' (2005) 27(3) EIPR 113.

[213]*British Horseracing Board Limited* (n 212).

[214]*Oy Veikkaus* (n 211); *Svenska Spel* (n 211); *Organismos* (n 203) & *British Horseracing Board Limited* (n 212).

ensure reliability and monitor accuracy after obtaining the contents for the database.[215] ECJ said presentation means substantial costs made towards the function of processing information i.e. selection, arrangement and individual accessibility.[216]

For the purpose of the Directive, extraction means "permanent or temporary transfer of all or substantial part of the contents of a database by any means and in any form".[217] The database right holder must provide authorization "… when on-screen display of the contents of a database necessitates the permanent or temporary transfer of all or a substantial part of such contents to another medium".[218] Re-utilization means making available all or substantial part of the contents of a database by way of distributing copies. Distribution can take place by renting the database, transmitting it online, or by any other forms of transmission.[219] Protection to databases under the database right is for 15 years. The requirements relating to Article 7 have been discussed later.[220]

[215] *Svenska Spel* (n 211) 49.

[216] *Oy Veikkaus* (n 211); *Svenska Spel* (n 211) & *Organismos* (n 203).

[217] Council Directive 96/9/EC, art 7(2) a.

[218] ibid recital 44.

[219] ibid art 7(2) b; As discussed before the meaning attached to extraction and re-utilization has similarities attached to the terms of reproduction and rights of communication to public. ECJ in *British Horseracing Board* said that both direct and indirect extraction could constitute infringement of extraction, *British Horseracing Board Limited* (n 212) 12-15. In a more recent case in Case C-545/07 *Apis-Hristovich EOOD v Lakorda AD* [2009] ECDR 13; ECJ has substantially explained the meaning attached to extraction, and how extraction may happen in the context of a database. Similarly in Case C-304/07 *Directmedia Publishing GmbH v Albert-Ludwigs-Universität Freiburg* [2008] ECR I-7565 ECJ developed the principle of extraction in the context of on-screen consultation. As to re-utilization ECJ in C-203/02 said that re-utilization may be both direct and indirect. However, the meaning associated with indirect re-utilization is still not very clear, Beunen (n 210) 168.

[220] *Infra* chapter 7.

Chapter 3
Feist, Not a New-Line of Jurisprudence

It was believed that *Feist* decision replaced 'sweat of the brow' argument for providing copyright protection to factual compilations.[1] Removal of sweat of the brow theory from the ambit of copyright protection was held detrimental for future production of databases.[2] This chapter shows that *Feist* decision was not unique and it re-iterated existing copyright law in US. *Feist* tried to resolve the conflict relating to the threshold of originality in limited circuits. The threshold standard stated for copyright protection was not a surprise for the US Copyright Office. Further, the guidelines of *Feist* decision have been consistently followed in decisions dealing with the question of copyrightability of factual compilations.

3.1 *Feist* Guidelines

Feist case questioned the copyrightability of a telephone directory and primarily said that factual compilations must be original to merit copyright protection.[3] Originality could only be an outcome of creativity, and should be associated with the selection, co-ordination or arrangement of the contents in a compilation.[4] In this case, Rural provided telephone service to the communities in Kansas. As per the State regulation, Rural published a telephone directory constituting the names and addresses of its subscribers. Feist was in a similar business and specialized in

[1]Commission, 'Proposal for a Council Directive on the legal protection of databases' COM (92) 24 final (COM (92) 24 final), para [2.3.3].
[2]ibid, para [3.1.9].
[3]*Feist Publications v Rural Telephone Service*, 499 US 340 (1991), 348; *Nimmer on Copyright: A Treatise on the Law of Literacy, Musical and Artistic Property and the Protection of Ideas*, Vol 1, para 2.01 [A]-[B] (issue 75-5/2008, 80-12/2009, 63-4/04, 82-8/2010-Pub. 465); Robert C Denicola, 'Copyright in Collections of Facts: A theory for the protection of nonfiction literary works' (1981) 81(3) Colum L Rev 516, 525.
[4]ibid.

I. Gupta, *Footprints of Feist in European Database Directive*,
DOI 10.1007/978-981-10-3981-2_3

area-wide telephone directories covering larger geographic range. They extracted portions of Rural's directory without consent. This was after Rural had refused to license white pages covering 11 different telephone service areas. After the extraction was complete, Feist altered the listings according to their requirement, although many of the listings were identical to the original listing published by Rural. As a result, Rural claimed copyright infringement of their telephone directory. The United States District Court for the District of Kansas held that white pages directory of Rural was copyrightable, and hence there was clear copyright infringement.[5] When Feist appealed, Court of Appeal for the Tenth circuit affirmed the judgement of the District Court.[6] The US Supreme Court, however, reversed the judgement on Constitutional and Statutory grounds. According to the Supreme Court, white pages directory did not meet the requirement of originality under the statutory provision of US Copyright Law or under the US Constitution.[7]

The US Congress enacts copyright law, based on the power vested by the US Constitution. According to Article I, § 8, clause 8 of the Constitution, the US Congress may enact legislation "To promote the Progress of Science and useful Arts, by securing for limited times to Authors and Inventors the exclusive right to their respective Writings and Discoveries".[8] In the *Feist* decision, the US Supreme Court stressed that originality was a Constitutional requirement, and terms like 'authors' and 'writings', had been considered in previous cases.[9] The Supreme Court referred to *The Trade-Mark Cases* and *Burrow-Giles Lithographic Co. v. Sarony* (*Burrow-Giles*). These two cases, while defining Constitutional terms like authors and writings, "…made it unmistakably clear that these terms presuppose a degree of originality".[10]

The Trade-Mark Cases were a composition of three cases: *United States v. Steffens, United States v. Wittemann and United States v. Johnson.*[11] They were under one group as a single appeal case before the US Supreme Court. The subject matter of *Trade-Mark Cases* was counterfeiting of trade-marks. This case

---

[5]*Rural Telephone Service Co. v. Feist Publications*, 737 F. Supp. 610 (D. Kan. 1990).

[6]*Feist Publications* (n 3) 344.

[7]ibid, 345-354; "Originality is a statutory, as well as a constitutional requirement" *Nimmer on Copyright*, Vol. 1, para 1.06 [A] (issue 85-8/2011 Pub 465).

[8]*Nimmer on Copyright*, Vol 1, para 1.02 (issue 74-11/2007 Pub. 465).

[9]"Authors" and "Writings" in Article I, § 8, cl. 8 of US Constitution; "Requirement of originality is more generally regarded as due to this use of the term "authors" in a subsequent phrase of the Copyright Clause.", *Nimmer on Copyright*, Vol 1, para 1.03 [B] (issue 85-8/2011); On the point that originality is a Constitutional requirement, Patterson & Joyce, 'Monopolizing the Law: The Scope of Copyright Protection for Law Reports and Statutory Compilations' (1989) 36(4) UCLA L. Rev 719, 759.

[10]*The Trade Mark Cases* 100 US 82 (1879) and *Burrow-Giles Lithograph Co v Sarony* 111 US 53 (1884); *Feist Publications* (n 3) 345-354; This proposition finds support in the work of Brian Dahl and he says that the use of the 'sweat of the brow' theory works against the requirement of originality under the US Constitution, Brian A Dahl, 'Originality and creativity in reporter pagination: a contradiction in Terms'? (1989) 74(4) Iowa L Rev 713, 720–721.

[11]*The Trade Mark Cases* (n 10), 94.

commented on the Constitutional scope of writings, in the context of trademark, invention or discovery.[12] In the *Trade-Mark Cases*, the Supreme Court said that writings, in order to be protected, must be an outcome of creativity, and fruits of intellectual labour.[13] This view finds support and criticism in the works of scholars. In the opinion of Nimmer, a work needs modicum of intellectual labour to come under copyright protection and "...clearly constitutes an essential Constitutional element".[14] Likewise Elizabeth Saunders suggested that the Constitution on its face did not say about originality as a pre-requisite for copyright protection but the 'word' implies such requirement. The word in this context was 'authors'.[15] However, there were others who thought that *Feist* ignored historical evidence about the requirement of creativity. This was because, the Supreme Court did not state the reason behind the proposition that US Constitution mandates level of creativity as something pre-requisite to copyright protection. There was no explicit assertion on the parameters required to meet such standard of creativity. Moreover, by referring only to *Trade-Mark Cases*, *Feist* decision completely ignored United States Copyright Law prior to the nineteenth century, where Courts and commentators viewed originality in the context of independent creation.[16]

Similar to the *Trade-Mark* cases, the Supreme Court referred to the decision in *Burrow-Giles*.[17] In this case, the question before the US Supreme Court was the copyrightability of a photograph of Oscar Wilde. It was alleged that *Burrow-Giles Lithograph* did not take prior permission before marketing lithographs of the photograph. Burrow-Giles claimed that a photograph would not come either under the Constitutional requirement of authors and writings, or under statutory provision of copyright law. One has to remember that the US Copyright Act of 1870, which was considered in the case, explicitly included photograph as a subject matter under copyright.[18] While deciding the matter, the Supreme Court said ordinary photographs might be an outcome of a mechanical process, but not the photograph in

[12]ibid.

[13]ibid.

[14]*Nimmer on Copyright*, Vol 1, para 1.08 [C] (issue 60-4/03 Pub 465).

[15]Elizabeth M Saunders, 'Copyright protection for compilations of Fact: Does the originality standard allow protection on the basis of industrious collections' (1987) 62(4) Notre Dame L Rev 763, 764.

[16]George Ticknor Curtis, A Treatise on the Law of Copyright: Books, Dramatic and musical composition, letters and other manuscripts, engravings and sculptures (A Maxwell and Son 1847) 171 and Eaton S Drone, A Treatise on the Law of Property in Intellectual Productions in Great Britain and the United States: Embracing Copyright in Works of Literature and Art, and Playwright in Dramatic and Musical Compositions (Little, Brown 1879) 198-99 and based on case decisions in Emerson v. Davies, 8 F. Cas. 615, 619 (C.C.D. Mass. 1845) (No. 4436) and Gray v. Russell, 10 F. Cas. 1035, 1037-38 (C.C.D. Mass. 1839) (No. 5728) in Jennifer R Dowd, 'A selection view on history: *Feist Publications, Inc v Rural Telephone Service Co.*' (1992-1993) 34 BCL Rev 137, 154-157.

[17]*Burrow-Giles Lithograph* (n 10).

[18]U.S. Copyright Act 1870, 16 Stat. 198.

question. The intellectual capacity of the author in selecting the right ambience for a photograph was considered relevant in this case.[19] Author was defined as someone "…to whom anything owes its origin" and that the scope of copyright, is limited to "original intellectual conceptions" of an author.[20]

Other than the Constitutional requirement of originality, the US Supreme Court in *Feist* considered the US Copyright Acts of 1909 and 1976. With reference to section four of the Copyright Act of 1909, copyright protection in accordance with the above outlined Constitutional requirements, was only available to "…all writings of an author".[21] This copyright protection was only for "the copyrightable components of the work".[22] While elucidating 'all writings of an author' in the context of the 1909 Act, the Supreme Court held that the Act had only talked about originality, which differentiates between copyrightable and non-copyrightable components in a particular work.[23] *Feist* decision suggested that Section 4 of the 1909 Act, represented clearly the elements that may be copyrightable.[24] However, it seems that issues as to copyrightability of factual compilations and the way to seek copyright protection was not explicitly clear under the 1909 Copyright Act. Although section 4 considered Constitutional terms like authors and writings, it was not explicitly clear whether such writings should be original.[25] The preciseness, which was absent in the 1909 Copyright Act, was rectified in the 1976 Copyright Act. *Feist* case referred to certain changes made to the actual wordings of the 1909 Act. In place of "…all writings of an author" under Section 4 of the 1909 Act, it talks about "…original works of authorship".[26] The 1976 Act, however, said that it was only clarifying existing law.[27] Similarly, § 102(b) of the 1976 Act, replaced section 3 of the 1909 Act, and identified specific elements for which there was no copyright protection. § 102(b), among other things, stated that copyright protection does not extend to discoveries and ideas.[28]

There was an additional problem with the application of Section 5 of the 1909 Copyright Act. This section listed category of works that could be registered under copyright and included works like directories. Following such section, one may

[19] *Feist Publications* (n 3) 347.

[20] ibid; The Supreme Court defined author in Constitutional sense and established that authorship is the indispensable element of originality, *Nimmer on Copyright*, Vol 1, para 1.06 [A] (issue 85-8/2011).

[21] Copyright Act of 1909, s4.

[22] ibid, s3.

[23] *Feist Publications* (n 3) 351.

[24] ibid.

[25] ibid.

[26] ibid, 354–358.

[27] 'House Report No. 94-1476 (US Copyright Act, 1976)' (*US House of Representatives*) available at <http://www.copyright.gov/history/law/clrev_94-1476.pdf> (accessed 27 November 2016) 51.

[28] ibid.

construe that the category of works referred under section 5 were copyrightable per se without the requirement of originality.[29]

The *Feist* decision also considered the 1976 Copyright Act. Further to the requirement of originality, the 1976 Act specifically states that a factual compilation is original, if the contents (pre-existing materials, data or facts) have been "... selected, co-ordinated or arranged in such a way that the resulting work constitutes an original work of authorship".[30]

After considering originality as a Constitutional and Statutory requirement, the US Supreme Court in *Feist* connected this requirement to the issue of copyrightability of the directory in question. In the process, the Court dealt with two questions. The first one was in relation to copyrightability of facts, and the second question considered copyrightability of factual compilations.[31]

As to the first question, the US Supreme Court held that facts could never be copyrightable, since facts do not originate from an act of authorship.[32] Facts in the context of the case were only discoverable and creation of facts was not possible.[33] It has been suggested that the decision in *Feist* is faulty in this respect. There are facts that "clearly owe to discrete acts of human originality".[34] For instance, the example of Equifax, which is a credit rating provider. One needs to however carefully examine the Equifax example. Equifax charges subscription fees from the users.[35] For the furtherance of the database comprising of user records, Equifax collects and gathers financial information from banks and other financial institutions.[36] This method hardly makes them creator of data as they are only engaged in collecting facts. As per *Feist* decision, they have only discovered facts and hence

---

[29]*Feist Publications* (n 3) 352; In *Miller v Universal City Studios, Inc* 650 F.2d 1365 (5th Cir 1981) 1370, the problem associated with the application of section 5 of the 1909 US Copyright Act was stated.

[30]Copyright Act, 1976, § 101; In the sense of copyright, *Feist Publications* (n 3) 356; *Mills Music Inc v. Synder* 469 U.S. 153 (1985); William Patry, 'Copyright in Compilation of Facts (or Why the "White Pages" Are Not Copyrightable)' (1990) 12(4) Com. & Law 37, 64.

[31]*Feist Publications* (n 3).

[32]*Feist Publications* (n 3) 347; *Nimmer on Copyright*, Vol 1, para 2.11 [A] (issue 68-12/05 Pub. 465).

[33]ibid; this impediment would be against the policy of freeing up of information, as they are building blocks for future production and the "same is true of all facts—scientific, historical, biographical, and news of the day" *Feist Publications* (n 3) 348. Similarly in *Miller* (n 29) 1369 the court said that these information "...may not be copyrighted and are part of the public domain available to every person." There is a totally different view point concerning originality and about the decision in *Feist*. According to that view, originality is a redundant criterion to provide property rights and ultimately such threshold distorts market and affects production, Mark Sherwood-Edwards, 'The Redundancy of Originality' (1995) 6(3) Ent L R 94; This proposition is questionable, since even after the decision in *Feist* the US market grew considerably.

[34]Justin Hughes, 'Created Facts and the flawed ontology of Copyright Law' (2007-2008) 3(1) Notre Dame L Rev 43, 45.

[35]Equifax, available at <http://www.equifax.com/home/en_us> (accessed 10 February 2010).

[36]ibid.

there can be no authorship attributed to Equifax.[37] In reality, data concerning personal information is officially 'created' once. A person's registration with the birth office is the first step when his name is officially entered in the list of names and further on is added with the corresponding address (with the Council) of his residence.[38] In course of time, the address may change but the Council updates data every time. This data remains in the public domain depending on the choice of the person.[39] Organizations are merely engaged in collecting or gathering of information. In short, they never create the data. Any additional information added by the organizations after the collection may apparently seem as creation of data. In reality, these creations of individual data may fall short of the originality standard comprising of selection or arrangement.[40] For example, in case of Banks, the additional information created by them is account number and banking transactions. While these data may be creation in the course of financial transactions, they are unlikely to be original in copyright sense. Moreover, if there is acknowledgement of creativity in these data then there may be problem of accessibility at a later stage.[41]

Under any circumstances, persons engaged in discovering facts may not be considered as maker or originator of such factual data.[42] Thus facts "...do not trigger copyright because [they lack creativity in the absence of a maker or originator, and]...are not 'original' in Constitutional sense".[43] Therefore, there can be no copyright protection for facts contained in the telephone directory considered in the *Feist* decision.

As to the second question, the US Supreme Court said that factual compilations might possess requisite originality to merit copyright protection.[44] The Court had the option of upholding originality through the process of selection or arrangement of contents, or through 'sweat of the brow' or industrious collection approach.[45] According to the US Supreme Court, misinterpretation of section 5 of the 1909 Act led to the development of 'sweat of the brow' theory, which was corrected by the 1976 Copyright Act.[46] It has been said that the presence of 'sweat of the brow' was

---

[37]*Feist Publications* (n 3) 347.

[38]This is a standard procedure in the United Kingdom.

[39]This is similar to the situation of a telephone directory where an individual has the option to opt out from his name appearing in the Directory, *Infra* section 6.4.1.

[40]*Feist Publications* (n 3) 347.

[41]*Supra* (n 33).

[42]*Feist Publications* (n 3) 347; *Nimmer on Copyright*, Vol 1, para 2.03 [E] (issue 79-8/2009 Pub. 465); Denicola (n 3) 523.

[43]*Feist Publications* (n 3) 347; *Nimmer on Copyright*, Vol 1, para 2.03 [E] (issue 79-8/2009 Pub. 465) 563.

[44]*Feist Publications* (n 3) 348.

[45]Previously in *Baker v Seldon* 101 US 99 (1879), the US Supreme Court implicitly rejected the 'sweat of the brow' doctrine by denying copyright protection to a book-keeping system. While giving the judgment, the court held that the industrious effort on the part of the claimant is praiseworthy, but under the Law, there is no contemplation of rewarding them for such labour.

[46]*Feist Publications* (n 3) 355.

because of unquestioned acceptance of English case precedent in the US Copyright system.[47] With the adoption of the 1976 Act, correct picture has been represented and 'sweat of the brow' has little place in the US Copyright Law.[48]

It is evident, however, that the 1976 Act was unable to solve the misconception, since subsequent to the 1976 Act, cases were decided based on the 'sweat of the brow' argument.[49] Although the 1976 Act said 'originality' and 'authorship' as the keystone of copyrightability, it did not define such terms.[50] It has been argued that, the adoption of 'sweat of the brow' goes against public policy and the first amendment protection for free speech.[51] Contrary to the above proposition, there is counter argument to the theory that 'sweat of the brow' is against public benefit. The act of permitting use of contents from one compiler to another, removes the incentive for the first compiler to engage in data gathering. Therefore, 'sweat of the brow' doctrine is favoured in protecting computer databases.[52] Likewise, it has been suggested that interpretation of creativity requirement under the 1976 Act is incorrect and goes against the original intention of the framers.[53]

Among the possible options, the US Supreme Court upheld originality requirement through the process of selection or arrangement of contents in a compilation.[54] Further by way of this process of selection or arrangement, a directory consisting of facts could still meet the Constitutional and Statutory requirement of originality.[55] In that case the choices made regarding the selection or arrangement of the contents must entail a minimal degree of creativity.[56] Through

---

[47]Patry (n 30) 66.

[48]ibid.

[49]*Feist* decision is an example in this regard.

[50]*United Telephone Company of Missouri v. Johnson publishing* 855 F 2d 604 (8th Cir 1988); "The phrase "original works or authorship," which is purposely left undefined [in 1976 Act], is intended to incorporate without change the standard of originality established by the courts under the present [1909] copyright statute.", 'House Report No. 94-1476 (US Copyright Act, 1976)' (*US House of Representatives*) available at <http://www.copyright.gov/history/law/clrev_94-1476.pdf> (accessed 27 November 2016); Saunders (n 303) 766; Ginsburg (n 141) 1895.

[51]Michael J Haungs, 'Copyright of factual compilations: Public policy and the First Amendment' (1990) 23(3) Colum J L & Soc Probs 347, 357.

[52]Jack B Hicks, 'Copyright and computer databases: Is traditional compilation Law adequate?' (1987) 65(5) Tex L Rev 993, 1025-1027.

[53]Russ Versteeg, 'Sparks in the Tinderbox: *Feist*, "Creativity", and the legislative history of the 1976 Copyright Act' (1994-1995) 56(3) U Pitt L Rev 549, 557-572. The author highlighted the concern about the high level of creativity requirement in the future copyright decisions. The *Feist* court has already said that the level of creativity should be minimal.

[54]*Feist Publications* (n 3) 347.

[55]*Harper & Row Publishers Inc and the Reader's Digest Association v Nation Enterprises and the Nation Associates, Inc*, 471 US 539 (1985) 547.

[56]*Nimmer on Copyright*, Vol 1, para 2.11 [D] (issue 80-12/2009); Denicola (n 3) 523.

selection or arrangement, there exists an opportunity to include sufficient amount of creativity, which is different from discovering pre-existing facts.[57]

The US Supreme Court suggested that justifying copyright protection to factual compilations based on 'sweat of the brow' theory would be faulty. This theory provides copyright protection as a reward for the labour expended in a factual compilation.[58] Copyright argument based on 'sweat of the brow' extends protection beyond selection or arrangement of the contents and would provide protection to facts. The second compiler would "...not [be] entitled to take one word of information previously published", instead, the second compiler needs to expend independent effort for finding the same information contained in the first factual compilation.[59] This argument was against the fundamental axiom that copyright cannot be extended to facts or ideas.[60] In Constitutional sense, if facts were not protected under copyright, then there was nothing original in a factual compilation except the possible original selection or arrangement of the factual contents.[61] The US Supreme Court, in not considering 'sweat of the brow' theory, took account of the necessary Constitutional requirement of 'authors' and 'writings'.[62]

While explaining level of creativity satisfying the requirement of originality, the US Supreme Court said that minimal creativity was sufficient. The case contemplated that a vast majority of factual compilations would be creative enough 'no matter how crude, humble or obvious' the creativity might be.[63] Further, the originality standard does not require novelty and a particular work might still be original, even if such work closely resembles a different work.[64] Copyright protection in a factual compilation, however, was limited to the originality in selection or arrangement, and under any circumstances does not extend to the facts.[65] Thus, the protection afforded was thin and any subsequent compiler was free to copy the underlying facts except the original, precise selection or arrangement of the first compiler.[66] The *Feist* decision provided numerous guidelines that require detailed attention.

---

[57]*Feist Publications* (n 3) 347.

[58]'Sweat of the brow' in the background of US cases, *Infra* section 3.2 and 3.3.

[59]*Feist Publications* (n 3) 353; criticizing *Jeweler's Circular Publishing Co. V. Keystone Publishing Co.*, 281 F 83 (CA2 1922); Using "sweat of the brow" theory "...would impede progress by requiring compilers to continually collect raw data anew", Denise R Polivy '*Feist* applied: Imagination protects, but perspiration persists—the bases of copyright protection for factual compilation' (1997-98) 8(3) Fordham Intell Prop Media & Ent L J 773, 800.

[60]*Feist Publications* (n 3) 353; *Miller* (n 29) 1372.

[61]*Feist Publications* (n 3) 353.

[62]It is beyond the scope of this book to assess whether the Supreme Court in *Feist* has rightly referred to the US Constitution. In addition, it will not be analyzed whether the Supreme Court should have limited the originality criterion as a statutory requirement.

[63]*Feist Publications* (n 3) 345.

[64]ibid.

[65]ibid 349.

[66]ibid (n 3) 347.

3.1.1 Originality and the US Constitution

With reference to the Constitutional aspect in *Feist* decision, scholars said that "by grounding its opinion in the copyright clause of the Constitution, rather than in the copyright statute, the Court appeared to foreclose the possibility that Congress would repair damage in *Feist* by amending the copyright law".[67] Rejection of 'sweat of the brow' theory on Constitutional ground was not considered necessary.[68] By referring to the US Constitution, the US Supreme Court ensured that enactment of future database legislation based on the 'sweat of the brow' principle would not be possible pursuant to the Copyright Clause of the US Constitution.[69] In other words, future legislation relating to the protection of factual databases must originate outside the ambit of the Copyright Clause. Therefore, reference to the Constitution did not restrict such legislation per se.[70] It may be argued that by referring to the US Constitution in *Feist*, the US Supreme Court wanted to keep copyright and protection of 'facts' separate. The Court used a great sense of foresight and this step was essential to prevent any confusion that may result in deciding the threshold of originality.[71] There may have been other reasons behind the Constitutional reference. Creating a Constitutional barricade may prevent the US Congress from adopting a biased approach in the future.[72] Through *Feist*, the Supreme Court ensured freeing up of factual data and left them outside the scope of copyright protection. The decision was path-breaking in the sense that it foresaw the need for freeing up of information, which formed the building blocks, in the

[67]Robin Elizabeth Herr, *Is the Sui Generis Right a Failed Experiment? A legal and Theoretical Exploration of How to Regulate Unoriginal Database Contents and Possible Suggestions for Reform* (DJØF Publishing Copenhagen, Denmark 2008) 24, 165; Similarly Jessica Litman, 'After *Feist*' (1992) 17(2) U Dayton L Rev 607.

[68]"The *Feist* decision's dicta regarding Constitutional requirements neither dictates sweeping changes in the current state of copyright law, nor pre-emptively precludes Congressional alteration of the original requirement", Michael B. Gerdes, 'Getting Beyond Constitutionally Mandated Originality as a Prerequisite for Federal Copyright Protection' (1992) 24(4) Ariz St L J 1461, 1477.

[69]ibid; Herr (n 67) 165; Whereas there have been comments to suggest that the US Congress is still competent to use the Copyright clause to decide on the copyrightability of a particular work, Jane C Ginsburg, 'No "Sweat"? Copyright and the Protection of Works of Information after *Feist v Rural*' (1992) 92(2) Colum L Rev 338, 375.

[70]It has been suggested that database legislation may be enacted by following the Commerce clause instead of the copyright clause.

[71]ibid.

[72]Arguing on the possibility of lobbying pressure on the US Congress, Polivy (n 59) 791; Similar contention has been raised by Marci A Hamilton, Marci A Hamilton, *Database Protection and the Circuitous Route Around the United States Constitution* in Charles EF Rickett & Graeme W Austin *International Intellectual Property and Common Law World* (Hart Publishing, 2000) 34.

ensuing digital age.[73] Thus, on Constitutional ground *Feist* was unique, in terms of a case that took preventive measures.

3.1.2 The Threshold for Protecting Compilations

Both constitutionally and statutorily, *Feist* decision contended that a minimal amount of creativity through selection or arrangement of contents makes a factual compilation original.[74] Although level was minimal, the decision did not explain sufficient level of creativity. The decision of *Feist* has been criticized in the context of originality. It has been argued that *Feist* de-valued authorship component, since in relation to originality, the US Supreme Court said that "a work may be original even though it closely resembles other works, so long as the similarity is fortuitous, not the result of copying".[75] This proposition in *Feist* is contrary to the US Copyright Act, which says that copyright protection is only afforded to original works of authorship.[76]

The US Supreme Court contemplated that majority of compilations would be able to meet the requirement of creativity set up in the *Feist* decision.[77] One has to remember, however, [that] "…Rural expended sufficient effort to make the white pages directory useful, but insufficient creativity to make it original."[78] Therefore, even though the level of creativity requirement was not stringent, it should always be higher than the level of creativity expended by Rural. It is obvious that there is only one way of arranging the contents of the directory in question, i.e. alphabetically, and the Supreme Court observed that the selection of Rural "…could not be more obvious".[79] Although the creativity standard proposed in the *Feist* decision is not stringent, such standard exists, and a directory will fail the creativity standard, if the act of selection or arrangement of facts is mechanical or a routine process.[80] This makes the level of creativity case specific. As long as there is more than one way of selecting or arranging contents, such selection or arrangement should pass the *Feist* grade.[81] It has been proposed that the "greater number of combination of

---

[73]"The Court thus seems to have envisioned the challenges and technological advances that were to come. The origins of the jurisprudence inherent in *Feist*, therefore, necessarily lie in twentieth century achievements, rather than those of the nineteenth century". Miriam Bitton, 'Protection for Informational Works after *Feist Publications, Inc v. Rural Telephone Service Co* (2011) 21(3) Fordham Intell Prop Media & Ent L J 611, 625.

[74]*Feist Publications* (n 3) 363-364.

[75]ibid 345; Leo J Raskind, 'Assessing the Impact of Feist' (1992) 17(2) U Dayton L Rev 331, 334.

[76]ibid.

[77]*Feist Publications* (n 3) 345.

[78]ibid 359.

[79]*Feist Publications* (n 3) 362.

[80]ibid.

[81]The book will attempt to observe the level of creativity in future American cases concerning databases, *infra* section 3.3.

data, the more likely the selection of any particular combination will be deemed minimally creative".[82]

Further, the US Supreme Court said that originality does not require novelty.[83] Therefore, a compiler may have a selection or arrangement used by previous compilers.[84] The second compiler, however, should not copy but use independent creativity towards such selection or arrangement. Thus, standards of creativity are less stringent and most factual compilations should be able to pass the test.[85] One must, however, consider that even with this creativity requirement, a certain category of factual compilations would remain unprotected under copyright.[86] This is because selection or arrangement in these factual compilations is obvious and mechanical.

Despite suggesting that creativity standard was not stringent, the US Supreme Court introduced an important caveat in the *Feist* case. Protection of factual compilations was limited to original selection or arrangement because facts remain non-copyrightable.[87] In other words, the available protection is relatively thin in nature.[88] With thin protection in place, a subsequent compiler may copy the facts and use them for his compilation, excluding the precise way of selection or arrangement.[89] This freedom to copy gives the subsequent compiler an advantage over the original compiler.[90]

Going by the *Feist* decision, it is relatively easy to get copyright protection for factual compilations.[91] However, such protection is essentially limited. One can observe that the US Supreme Court left factual compilations unprotected in two ways, i.e. where minimal level of creativity is absent and where the copyright protection is only extended to the selection or arrangement of the contents. Further,

[82]Ginsburg (n 69) 347; This has been said in the context of the case decision in *Kregos v Associated Press* 937 F2d 700 (2d Cir 1991). The Court calculated 167,980 possible combinations to choose from when a person compiles a nine category pitching form from a pool of twenty statistical categories. The minimal creativity in this context satisfies the *Feist* criterion.

[83]*Feist Publications* (n 3) 345.

[84]ibid.

[85]ibid.

[86]ibid (n 3) 345.

[87]ibid 344.

[88]ibid 349.

[89]In this context, apparently Justice O'Connor has accepted 'free-riding' as a policy enshrined in the US Constitution, Ginsburg (n 69) 349. Justice O'Connor said in the context of the dissenting comment of Brennan, J in *Harper & Row Publishers* (n 55) 589 that it may seem unfair when one can use much of compiler's labour without compensation. However, this is "essence of copyright" and "a Constitutional requirement", *Feist Publications* (n 3) 349; There is the argument that *Feist* has grossly neglected the incentive role of copyright, Ginsburg (n 69) 350; However, there is an issue about the role of copyright in incentivizing production. It relates to the proposition that the creation of work does not possibly depend on the existence of copyright protection, *Supra* section 2.2.

[90]*Feist Publications* (n 3) 349.

[91]ibid 358.

a second compiler is free to use the facts in a competing work.[92] Although in some cases factual compilations are not entitled to copyright protection or even entitled to limited protection, they are nonetheless expensive to produce.[93] In most cases, there would be investments undertaken by compilers. Future investment in databases may suffer because of less copyright protection.[94]

3.2 *Feist* and the Existing Law in US

Before the *Feist* decision, there was certain difference of opinion existing in various circuits concerning the copyrightability of factual compilations.[95] The conflicting judgements resulted because of the difference in the threshold of originality.[96] *Feist* thus tried resolving conflicting position among various circuits in the US.[97] By removing 'sweat of the brow', *Feist* restored uniformity in the standard of originality for copyright protection of compilations.[98] Nevertheless, "…decision taken in the *Feist* case was not earth shattering from a theoretical perspective".[99] Ralph Oman, who was the Registrar of Copyrights said that "the Supreme Court [actually] dropped a bomb" in the form of *Feist* decision.[100] On the other hand "…seemingly genial nature of the [*Feist*] decision" has been observed and the overall decision should not have been an outright shock.[101] There was further opposition to the idea that *Feist* was a decision that brought about a new law. It was suggested that "after all, it did not establish a new originality paradigm as such, but only ended a long division among federal circuits concerning the protection under copyright of factual compilations".[102] Further, "the results of *Feist* are hardly remarkable, although it

[92]ibid 349.

[93]The US Supreme Court identified the effort expended by Rural, *Feist Publications* (n 3) 364.

[94]COM (92) 24 final, para [2.3.3].

[95]John Tessensohn, 'The Devil's in the Details: The Quest for Legal Protection of Computer Databases and the Collections of Information Act' (1997-98) 38(3) IDEA Intell Prop L Rev 439, 443; *Feist* case was a review of originality requirement in US, Hasan A Deveci, 'Databases: Is *sui generis* a stronger bet than copyright?' (2004) 12(2) IJLIT 178, 187-188.

[96]Even though there was confusion and disparity, in *Feist* the Supreme Court pointed out that the 1976 US Copyright Act clearly suggests originality must be based on selection or arrangement, Herr (n 67) 158-159.

[97]*Feist Publications* (n 3).

[98]As observed before, prior to *Feist* decision, cases decided on the basis of sweat of the brow, had no tenuous link between creativity and originality. A compilation, under the "sweat" theory would be original, if it was not copied and resulted from effort; Herr (n 67) 162; Polivy, (n 59) 782.

[99]Herr (n 67) 165.

[100]Copyright Office and Copyright Royalty Tribunal Report Status to House Panel, 41 Pat Trademark & Copyright J (BNA) No. 524 (April 18, 1991) in Herr (n 67) 166.

[101]Daniel J Gervais, '*Feist* goes global: A comparative analysis of the notion of originality in copyright law' (2002) 49(4) Journal of Copyright Society of the US 949, 950.

[102]Herr (n 67) 166.

rejected precedents" practiced in minority of circuits.[103] Therefore, one needs to observe how far the decision in Feist has led to a new-line of jurisprudence.

The use of 'sweat of the brow' doctrine relating to copyright protection of factual compilations surfaced in the case of *Jeweler's Circular Publishing Co. v. Keystone Publishing Co (Jeweler)*.[104] This case, involving a directory consisting information of trade-marks of jewellery and kindred trades accepted the argument of 'sweat of the brow' as a basis for copyright protection. Kay L said that originality should not be a point of concern or a requirement to merit copyright protection, where a person has expended labour, while compiling facts that existed in the public domain.[105] Therefore, copying of facts would amount to copyright infringement in the absence of independent investment of time.[106] Subsequent decisions have held that "... original compilations of names and addresses is copyrightable even though individual names and addresses are in public domain and not copyrightable".[107] Following the *Jeweler* case, the ninth circuit also considered 'sweat of the brow' in *Leon* et al. *v. Pacific Telephone & Telegraph Company* (*Leon*).[108] The defendant Leon rearranged the contents of a numerical directory and published the same. It was held that he has infringed copyright in an alphabetically arranged telephone directory containing names, addresses and telephone numbers, since there was no independent effort on his part.[109] *Jeweler* and *Leon* were considered as precedents in subsequent cases where 'sweat of the brow' argument was held valid.[110]

If the above cases were decided based on 'sweat of the brow' argument, there were other circuits that considered creativity towards selection or arrangement as a requirement to merit copyright protection. It is appropriate to consider the US Supreme Court decision in *Harper & Row Publishers Inc. and the Reader's Digest Association v. Nation Enterprises and the Nation Associates, Inc.* (*Harper*), which was later referred in the *Feist* decision.[111] This case involved copyright infringement of the memoirs of President Ford. Other than the original expression,

---

[103]David O Carson, 'Copyright protection for factual compilations after *Feist*: A practioner's view' (1992) 17(3) U Dayton L Rev 969, 971.

[104]281 F 83 (CA2 1922); The theory of 'sweat of the brow' in US traces back to old English precedent and the theories modern expression lies in the Jeweler case, Haungs (n 51) 351.

[105]*Jeweler's Circular Publishing* (n 104) 88.

[106]*Orgel v. Clark Boardman Co.*, 301 F 2d 119 (1962); Robert A Gorman has said 'sweat of the brow' as equivalent to "original fact gathering"- meaning, the issue of independent requirement of labour, Robert A Gorman, 'Copyright protection for the collection and representation of facts' (1963) 76(8) Harv L Rev 1569, 1584.

[107]*Charles E. Schroeder and Marion S. Schroeder v. William Morrow and Company and George Banta & Co* 566 F 2d 3 (7th Cir 1977) para [6].

[108]91 F 2d 484 (1937).

[109]ibid.

[110]*Charles E. Schroeder* (n 107); *Illinois Bell v. Haines and Company* 905 F 2d 1081 (7th Cir 1990) 1086.

[111]The Supreme Court in this case did say that compilations of pure facts may be copyrightable but did not say anything further about how such test should be developed, *Harper and Row Publishers* (n 55) 547.

the memoirs contained historical facts and memoranda during the reign of the President. The Court held that verbatim use of 300 words by the defendant constituted copyright infringement by virtue of the original "…selective description and portrait of public figure" in the memoirs.[112] There was no protection for facts in the work[113] unless it bears "…stamp of author's originality."[114] Further, facts or ideas as such were not copyrightable, since there was a "…greater need to disseminate factual works than works of fiction or fantasy".[115] In similar judgements the originality argument based on selection or arrangement of the contents was present.[116] For instance, in the second circuit decision of *Dennis W. Eckes and James Beckett v. Card Prices Update and Suffolk Collectables* (*Dennis W. Eckes*) the issue of selective judgement was in relation to the selection of 5000 premium cards from a guidebook consisting of 18,000 baseball cards.[117] The Court rejected the 'sweat of the brow' argument and held that the plaintiff had "…exercised selection, creativity and judgement' by determining the premium list".[118] Likewise, the 11th circuit in *Southern Bell Telephone v. Associated Telephone*[119] dealt with the question of copyright infringement in the act of copying individual listing and advertisements off a yellow pages directory. The directory in question displayed the logo of 'walking fingers' and there was additional reference to the term 'yellow pages'.

According to the 11th circuit, although facts were not copyrightable, a compilation consisting of facts may merit copyright protection due to original selection or arrangement of the factual contents.[120] There was sufficient creativity "…in preparing artwork and layout, and in the selection, compilation and arrangement of the information contained therein".[121] The ninth circuit similarly in *Fred L. Worth v. Selchow &. Righter Company* (*Fred L. Worth*) decided on copyrightability of a book consisting of alphabetic arrangement of facts. Similar to other judgements, the

[112]ibid.

[113]ibid.

[114]ibid.

[115]ibid; This has been previously said by Robert A Gorman, He said, "our law, as reflected in the terms of our copyright statutes and the language of our courts, emphasizes the greater need to disseminate the contents of fact works in contrast to the contents of works of artistic or literary fancy", Robert A Gorman, 'Fact or Fancy? The Implications for Copyright-The Twelfth Annual Donald C Brace Memorial Lecture' (1982) 29(6) Journal of the Copyright Society 560, 561.

[116]*Harper House, Inc. v. Thomas Nelson, Inc* 889 F 2d 197 (9th Cir 1989); *Dow Jones & Company Inc. v. Board of Trade of the City of Chicago* 539 F Supp 190 (1982); *Dennis W. Eckes and James Beckett v. Card Prices Update and Suffolk Collectables* 736 F 2d 859 (2d Cir 1984) 863; *Southern Bell Telephone v. Associated Telephone* 756 F 2d 801 (11th Cir. 1985) 809; *Fred L. Worth v. Selchow &. Righter Company* 827 F2d 569 (9th Cir 1987).

[117]*Dennis W Eckes* (n 116) 863.

[118]ibid.

[119]*Southern Bell Telephone* (n 116) 809.

[120]ibid.

[121]ibid.

Court held that facts or ideas could not be original work. There was no infringement, since the defendant did not copy the exact arrangement of the claimant's book. To prove infringement in a factual work, there must be evidence of bodily appropriation of the original expression.[122] Thus, factual compilation receives limited protection.[123] The above cases need further analysis to understand the uniqueness and principles associated with the *Feist* decision.

3.2.1 Principles of Feist *in Previous Cases*

There are comparable cases that indicated the principles laid down in the *Feist* decision. In the *Harper* case it was decided that a second compiler can copy facts freely as long as he can separate such facts from the original expression.[124] Thus, in a compilation comprising of work and factual information, copyright protection is limited to the creative expression of author. Even the scope of protection decided in *Feist*, i.e. thin copyright protection for factual compilations, was present in the *Fred L Worth* and *Harper* cases. For instance, the *Fred L Worth* case upheld thin protection by stating that copyright infringement in a factual compilation was possible only in case of bodily appropriation of the original expression.[125] Therefore, the second compiler may extract factual information from the first compilation except the original expression of the author. In other words, the second compilation may be very similar to the first one but should not be the same. This implies that creativity requirement for the second compiler is not stringent, which is in accordance with *Feist* decision.[126] One can also observe the modicum of creativity requirement based on selection or arrangement. For instance, in *Southern Bell*, there was sufficient creativity in the layout of yellow pages directory.[127] Such threshold signifies minimal level of creativity, which was later re-iterated in *Feist* decision. The decision in *Southern Bell* indicates that even if creativity is 'humble', such creativity may be sufficient for the purpose of copyright protection.[128] Thus, creativity threshold in prior cases suggests that majority of the compilations would come under the purview of copyright protection. The proposition that majority of

---

[122]*Fred L. Worth* (n 116).

[123]Similarly in the case of *Harper House* (n 116) the Court of Appeal said that organizer/compilation with mostly un-copyrightable facts, should be provided with extremely limited protection; Thomas P Arden, *The conflicting treatments of compilations of facts under the United States and United Kingdom copyright laws* (1992) 3(2) Ent L Rev 43.

[124]*Harper and Row Publishers* (n 55) 547.

[125]*Fred L. Worth* (n 116).

[126]*Feist Publications* (n 3) 362.

[127]*Southern Bell Telephone* (n 116) 809.

[128]It has walking fingers logo and the reference of the term yellow pages, *Southern Bell Telephone* (n 116).

compilations may receive copyright protection was later affirmed in the *Feist* decision.[129]

All of the above outlined cases have notably answered two questions: compilation as a subject matter under copyright, and the required originality threshold in factual compilations.[130] The first question did not create any confusion, since compilations do receive copyright protection in the US. For instance, the 1909 Copyright Act has explicitly included compilations as a subject matter under copyright law.[131]

The second question relating to threshold for factual compilations is complex and there exists a clear division. Courts relying on 'sweat of the brow' doctrine have primarily based their decisions on the 1909 Act.[132] As far as the interpretation of 1909 Act is concerned, the courts held that an independently created compilation should suffice the originality threshold for copyright protection.[133] From the *Jeweler* and *Leon* case one can observe that originality means and requires that a work must not be copied, and that independent effort is present when the compiler engages in the collection of factual information from the public domain.[134] Thus, if compilations were not copied, courts following 'sweat of the brow' argument justified that those compilations could certainly be protected under copyright.[135]

On the other hand, courts denying 'sweat of the brow' argument decided originality in factual compilations based on selection or arrangement criterion. Their argument was based on the 1976 Copyright Act, which explicitly states that copyright protects only the "...original works of authorship".[136] It means that a particular work is original if its origin can be traced back to an author.[137] After the passage of the 1976 Copyright Act, some of the circuits have stated that the concept of originality has not changed. They argued that this Act primarily followed the previous Copyright Act of 1909 and therefore, the rationale of 'sweat of the brow' continues to exist in the US Copyright Law.[138] Copyright protection may be

---

[129] *Feist Publications* (n 3) 345.

[130] *Supra* section 3.2.

[131] US Copyright Act, 1909, s5.

[132] For example *Jeweler's Circular Publishing* (n 104) *and Leon* (n 108).

[133] ibid.

[134] *Jeweler's Circular Publishing* (n 104) 88; Leon (n 108).

[135] Further evidence shows that after the passage of the 1976 US Copyright Act, telephone companies chose to claim copyright protection in directories in a more hospitable jurisdiction. This is said in the context that 1976 Act brought about the correct form of originality instead of the application of 'sweat of the brow' theory, Shira Perlmutter, 'The Scope of Copyright in Telephone Directories: Keeping Listing Information in the Public Domain' (1991) 38(1) Journal of the Copyright Society 1, 1-4.

[136] Copyright Act, 1976, §102.

[137] *Feist Publications* (n 3) 347.

[138] *Hutchison Telephone Directory v. Fronteer Directory Company* 770 F 2d 128 (8th Cir 1985) 131; *Rand McNally & Company v. Fleet Management Systems Inc.* 591 F Supp 726 (ND Ill 1983) 737 on the basis of *Charles E. Schroeder* (n 107).

granted to original work of authorship in a particular compilation but previous decisions based on 'sweat of the brow' justified copyright protection to information existing in the public domain.[139] The decisions indicate a fair share of cases that were decided based on 'sweat of the brow' argument, alongside the application of the selection or arrangement criterion.

Cases based on 'sweat of the brow' theory, however, have been limited to four circuit courts.[140] Therefore, majority of circuit courts have adhered to selection or arrangement criterion before offering copyright protection to factual compilations.[141] Moreover, circuit courts involved in judgements following the 'sweat of the brow' argument had reasoned selection or arrangement requirement in later decisions.[142] For instance, the second and ninth circuit decisions in *Dennis W. Eckes* and *Fred L. Worth.*[143]

Although the guidelines given in *Feist* had always existed in the US, it is undeniable that the alternative option of 'sweat of the brow' existed in the minds of scholars, commentators and limited circuit courts.[144] There are contradictory opinions as to the uniqueness associated with *Feist* decision. In the opinion of Paul Goldstein, in case of *Feist*, few had expected the reasoning, although most expected the result. "It came as a surprise for us who had thought that, outside the narrow field of photographs and art reproductions, originality meant only that the copyright claimant had not copied from another source".[145] He further added that "apart from scattered dicta, this is pretty much new law".[146] In similar terms, Marci Hamilton said that the decision in *Feist* was not surprising, but interesting because of the way it has been expressed by Justice O'Connor. Marci Hamilton said repeated reference to the Constitutional requirement of originality was unnecessary, as the same outcome would have resulted by following the statutory provisions. Further, she argued there was little need to decimate the age old historical background of 'sweat of the brow' theory, and the case could have been decided easily by referring telephone directory comprising of white pages as not copyrightable.[147] From both the opinion of Hamilton and Goldstein one must conclude that the decision was not

---

[139]ibid.

[140]The circuit courts have been 2nd, 7th, 8th and 9th. In the rush to offer incentives in the directory cases, the courts have foregone the concepts of ideas, facts and information, Shira Perlmutter, (n 135) 1–3.

[141]Polivy (n 59) 780–781.

[142]In case of exhaustive selections, copyright "…somewhat uncomfortably used to protect the underlying effort, time and expense ('sweat of the brow') rather than fanciful expression that it typically protects", Gorman (n 115) 571.

[143]*Dennis W Eckes* (n 116) 863 & *Fred L. Worth* (n 116).

[144]ibid.

[145]Paul Goldstein, 'Copyright' (1990-91) 38(3) Journal of the Copyright Society 109, 118–119.

[146]ibid 118–119.

[147]Marci A Hamilton, "Justice O'Connor's opinion in *Feist Publications Inc v. Rural Telephone Service Co*: An Uncommon Though Characteristic Approach" (1990-91) 38(2) Journal of the Copyright Society 83, 86–89.

surprising. This shows that the guidelines set by *Feist* was not unique or unprecedented, although in the opinion of the scholars, Constitutional approach was surprising.

Similar to Hamilton, Jennifer Dowd said that the US Supreme Court could have reached to the same conclusion without entirely dislodging ‘sweat of the brow’ theory.[148] This was because the theory existed in the US Copyright Law for a long time and there was a historical background to such existence. The US Supreme Court could have said that “*Feist* did not borrow anything other than un-copyrightable facts”.[149] Hence, such action on the part of *Feist* was not actionable.[150] Borrowing without spending independent labour is against the fundamental idea of the ‘sweat of the brow’ theory.[151] According to this theory, the same facts may be collected after expending similar effort as the previous compiler.[152] Posing a different argument, William Patry said that the US Supreme Court should have given careful consideration to the 1976 US Copyright Act, which clearly dislodges ‘sweat of the brow’, and not the decades of bad law and commentary. The “apparent use of claims of copyright in the white pages not to vindicate intellectual property rights, but rather to eliminate competition for yellow pages advertisers”.[153]

The above arguments and counter arguments do not reflect a sense of surprise with the results of *Feist*, and makes it clear that the criterion based on originality existed prior to *Feist*. The US Supreme Court only confirmed such presence, since *Feist* clarified the already existing correct option.[154] Therefore, it would be incorrect to interpret the reasoning in *Feist* as a new-line of jurisprudence in the field of copyright law.[155] The unanimous decision of Supreme Court in *Feist* is not something unique and unprecedented.

Dependence on the ‘sweat of the brow’ theory was beginning to fade away in the context of factual compilations.[156] This signifies the presence and application of the theory to a certain extent. Such dependence, however, started to phase out owing to the correct interpretation of the existing law.[157] Long before *Feist* and starting around the 1980s, there was enough indication to suggest that selection or arrangement in factual compilation was the only way to merit copyright protection.[158] Thus, *Feist* did not provide guidelines that were new.

---

[148]Dowd (n 16) 154–157.

[149]ibid.

[150]ibid.

[151]*Feist Publications* (n 3).

[152]*Jeweler's Circular Publishing* (n 104) 88–89.

[153]Patry (n 30) 37 and 40.

[154]*Feist Publications* (n 3).

[155]This was the argument posed in the first draft proposal, COM (92) 24 final, para [2.3.3].

[156]*Supra* section 3.2.

[157]*Feist Publications* (n 3).

[158]*Dennis W Eckes* (n 116) 863 & *Fred L. Worth* (n 116).

3.2.2 Registration of Compilations Subsequent to Feist

The registration requirements for copyright protection of factual compilations would give an indication of the prevailing situation before and after the *Feist* decision. In this context, the practice at the US Copyright Office has been considered.[159] Although the registration of a copyrighted work is voluntary, compulsory registration is required to initiate a lawsuit concerning infringement of a US copyrighted work.[160]

The US Copyright Office published a report in 1997 that considered the requirement of database legislation in US.[161] The report observed the practice concerning the registration of factual compilations and the effect that *Feist* had on the registration process. In the pre-*Feist* era, before registration under copyright, the Copyright Office permanently required a compilation to meet the originality threshold.[162] 'Sweat of the brow' was used as an argument for registering compilations until 1980s, but "…beginning in 1987, the office began to question copyrightability of works where 'sweat of the brow' was the only basis for registration".[163] By 1989, the Copyright Office stopped entertaining 'sweat of the brow' argument for all compilations except for telephone directories.[164] As a result, the Copyright Office issued guidelines and compilations failed copyright registration, if they did not "…represent a modicum of selection and/or arrangement authorship".[165]

The report said that, "…*Feist* decision did not have a major impact on the Copyright Office's registration process for compilations".[166] *Feist* actually clarified and provided a clear representation that henceforth, there will be no copyright protection for factual compilations based on 'sweat of the brow' argument.[167] The Copyright Office held that even after *Feist*, most compilations would remain protected.[168] Only telephone directories, which were somewhat protected under the

[159]"…Registration is a legal formality intended to make a public record of the basic facts of a particular copyright", 'US Copyright Office', available at <http://www.copyright.gov/circs/circ01.pdf> (accessed 27 November 2016).

[160]'US Copyright Office' available at <http://www.copyright.gov/help/faq/faq-general.html#automatic> (accessed 10 Jan 2011).

[161]'US Copyright Office: Report on Legal Protection for Databases: August 1997' available at <http://www.copyright.gov/reports/db4.pdf> (accessed 27 November 2016). ('US Copyright Office: Report on Legal Protection for Databases: August 1997').

[162]ibid.

[163]ibid.

[164]ibid.

[165]ibid.

[166]ibid.

[167]ibid.

[168]ibid.

'sweat of the brow' argument, would be strictly scrutinized under the *Feist* criteria.[169]

The report did not show appreciable concern with the *Feist* decision. This position of the US Copyright Office is clear from the above narration. Even before *Feist*, most of the compilations would fail to satisfy the registration requirement if they had only relied on 'sweat of the brow' argument.[170] On the contrary, compilations must show originality based on modicum of creativity towards selection or arrangement of the contents.[171] These propositions were exactly represented in the *Feist* decision and even in cases decided before *Feist*.[172] Almost a decade before *Feist*, there was clear indication that selection or arrangement was the decisive factor for registration under copyright.[173] The acceptable threshold for copyright protection of a factual compilation reflects understanding of the law that prevailed in the 1980s.[174]

Before the *Feist* decision, the Copyright Office registered a narrow structure of factual compilation based on the 'sweat of the brow' argument. These registrations were limited to telephone directories.[175] Among all factual compilations, the only doubt that existed with telephone directories was because of conflicting judgements in different circuit courts.[176] However, despite the persisting doubt, the Copyright Office considered registration not only on the basis of 'sweat of the brow' argument, but also on selection or arrangement criterion.[177] No immediate preference was given to 'sweat of the brow' argument over selection or arrangement of contents. This practice of the US Copyright Office shows, and also proves that *Feist* only provided some stability in the narrow range of telephone directories, and largely reinstated the aspects already known for the purpose of registration under copyright.

3.3 Cases Following Principles of *Feist*

This section observes the arguments in cases that were decided after *Feist*. Inconsistencies at the stage of applying the principles of *Feist* would create uncertainty for producers and deter further investment towards database.

In the fifth circuit decision of *Hodge E Mason v. Montgomery Data Inc.* (*Mason*), copyright protection subsisted in the compilations of maps.[178] *Mason*

---

[169] ibid.

[170] ibid.

[171] *Feist Publications* (n 3).

[172] *Supra* section 3.2.

[173] ibid.

[174] *Supra* section 3.2.

[175] 'US Copyright Office: Report on Legal Protection for Databases: August 1997' (n 161).

[176] *Supra* (n 140) and section 3.2.

[177] 'US Copyright Office: Report on Legal Protection for Databases: August 1997' (n 161).

[178] *Hodge E Mason v Montgomery Data Inc.*, 967 F2d 135 (5th Cir 1992).

started working on Real Estate Ownership maps from 1967, and collected materials available in public domain. These maps pictorially defined size and other features of land within the Montgomery County, United States. *Mason* had to overcome inconsistencies at various stages of compilation, which existed in the sources. He claimed to have used substantial amount of judgement and discretion to select features that were published in final version of the maps. *Mason* also alleged that the defendant had infringed the copyright in maps describing Geographical Indexing System. The fifth circuit upheld infringement of copyright, since the map was creative enough to meet the *Feist* requirement of originality.[179] Further, the fifth circuit held that the District Court erred in applying the Doctrine of Merger. This doctrine was applicable in the event of an idea and its expression, which were inseparable and there will be no copyright protection for the work in question. Before applying such doctrine, the District Court should have "focus on whether the idea is capable of various modes of expression".[180] Therefore, the first task was to identify the idea that the work expresses followed by separation of the idea from expression of the author. By comparing maps created by *Mason* and his competitors, the Court concluded that the map in question could be expressed in various ways.[181] Although *Mason* and his competitors used the same idea, they used different parameters in relation to placement, size and dimensions of numerous surveys, tracts, and other features. Evidence from other licensed surveyors also indicated that the difference between the map of *Mason* and other mapmakers existed because of "selection of sources, interpretation of those sources, and discretion in reconciling inconsistencies among the sources; and skill and judgement in depicting the information".[182] In the process of such selection, skill and judgement of the mapmaker (*Mason*) was involved.

The Court also settled a contentious issue that maps must seek to depict information accurately. This means that there are no two ways of describing a map. The Court held that "conflicts among the sources and limitations inherent in the process of representing reality in pictorial map form required [Mason] to make choices that resulted in independent expression".[183] By extending copyright protection, there is no question of granting monopoly to Mason because other mapmakers can express the same idea in a different way.[184] This means that the extent of accuracy depends on how the sources are interpreted and inconsistencies are removed.

According to few commentators, this case reflected the inconsistencies while applying the principles of *Feist*.[185] It has been argued that creation of maps would

---

[179]ibid 139.

[180]ibid.

[181]ibid.

[182]ibid 140.

[183]ibid.

[184]ibid.

[185]Application of *Feist* decision, Tracy L Meade, 'Ex-post *Feist*: Applications of a landmark Copyright decision' 2(1) J Intell Prop L 245 (1994–1995).

involve the application of the 'sweat of the brow' theory. "Holding ...creativity in constructing maps arose from verifying pre-existing maps generated by the U.S. Geological Survey" amounts to an industrious effort that *Feist* case discarded.[186] Commentators have compared this case with the fourth circuit's decision in *United States Payphone, Inc. v. Execs. Unlimited, Inc.*[187] In the *Payphone* case, the Court accepted that the guide produced as a "...result of hundreds of hours of reviewing, analyzing, and interpreting state tariffs and regulations of the fifty states and the District of Columbia" would come under copyright.[188] Similar inconsistencies are observed in *Publication International ltd v Meredith Corp* decided by the seventh circuit where there was an overlap between *Feist* and 'sweat of the brow' argument. The Court said that, "a compilation's originality flows from the efforts of industrious collection by its author".[189]

In *Key Publications, Inc. v. Chinatown Today Publishing* (*Key Publications*), the copyrightability of a Chinese yellow pages directory was discussed.[190] The directory listed business in accordance with the requirement of the Chinese community. At the time of designing the directory, *Key Publications* left out businesses which, in their opinion, would not continue for long. The second circuit in this case held that the act of selection and individual judgement constitutes sufficient creativity that led to the formation of the directory. This was original enough to merit copyright protection. Selection meant "exercise of judgement in choosing, which facts from a given body of data to include in a compilation".[191] After examining the originality in selection, the Court considered the arrangement followed in the directory.[192] Although similar classified directories had used some of the categories used by the directory in question, remaining categories were not common and they were of special interest to the Chinese-American community. The categories, moreover, were irrelevant for the purpose of the decision. Even the arrangement

[186]ibid.

[187]18 USPQ 2d 2049 (4th Cir 1991).

[188]ibid 2050.

[189]88F 3d 473 (7th Cir 1996) 480.

[190]945 F2d 509 (2d Cir 1991); There was similar conclusion in the case of *Nester's Map & Guide Corp v. Hagstorm Map Co.* 796 F Supp 729 (EDNY) 1992. This case involved a taxi-driver guide in New York City, where the claimant Nester listed the cross streets, which were useful and most important. Moreover, he assigned approximate street address numbers to the cross streets and avoided the actual street numbers. The selection was based on his knowledge and experience. In this case, the court held that there was sufficient originality in the selection mechanism; similarly, in a case concerning compilations of nouns in *Lipton v Nature Co* 71 F 3D 464 (2d Cir 1995), the court upheld the creativity and informed judgment of the claimant, Lipton. In this case, there was selection from numerous variations of fifteenth century text and manuscripts. Furthermore, the claimant translated the words from Middle English to modern English.

[191]*Key Publications* (n 190) 513.

[192]The 2nd circuit said arrangement "refers to the ordering or grouping of data into lists or categories that go beyond the mere mechanical grouping of data as such, for example, the alphabetical, chronological, or sequential listings of data" ibid.

followed was original and not purely mechanical.[193] There was sufficient creativity "...in deciding which categories to include and under what name".[194]

Again, in *CCC Information Services Inc. v. Maclean Hunter Market Reports Inc.* (*Maclean*), the Red Book of Maclean consisting of prices of used cars was held copyrightable.[195] Maclean was involved in publication of a red book that included valuations of used cars. The valuation decisions did not depend on historical market prices, quotations, averages; neither did they originate from mathematical formulae or statistics. On the contrary, editors of Maclean predicted these valuations based on their professional expertise and various other informational sources. The alleged infringement was against the defendant who was also engaged in the business of providing information about used cars. The Court held that the compilation of Maclean indicated enough creativity in selection or arrangement to meet the Feist standard.[196]

The 11th circuit decision in *BellSouth case* involved the question of copyrightability of a yellow pages directory.[197] Bellsouth considered geographic area to determine the scope of yellow pages. The directory maintained a closing date for any changes that were required in the listing. Based on the *Feist* judgement the Court held that selection or arrangement including geographic area and closing date were excluded from copyright protection.[198] Moreover, it was usual for a factual compilation to follow a closing date and geographic area for a yellow pages directory. The claimant also adopted marketing techniques to generate listings in the directory. In the opinion of the Court, these selective mechanisms do not constitute sufficient originality to attract copyright protection. They were not an act of authorship, but "merely techniques to discover facts".[199] As a result, there was no copyright protection for the directory in question.

A second circuit decision in *Victor Lalli Enterprises Inc. v. Big Red Apple Inc.* (*Victor Lalli*) questioned copyrightability of horseracing information charts.[200] The claimant was engaged in producing gambling charts. All other publishers, including the defendant, used the same grid of rows and columns that provided past results and lucky numbers for a particular race. The Court held that the claimant arranged factual information in a purely functional grid where there was no opportunity to show required amount of creativity to satisfy the *Feist* condition.[201]

---

[193]ibid.

[194]*Key Publications* (n 190).

[195]44 F 3d 61 (2d Cir 1994).

[196]ibid 67.

[197]*BellSouth Advertising & Publication Corp v Donnelley Information Publishing Inc.* 999 F2d 1436 (11th Cir 1993).

[198]ibid 1441.

[199]ibid.

[200]936 F 2d 671 (2nd Cir 1991).

[201]ibid 673.

The decision of the 11th circuit in *Warren Publications, Inc v. Microdos Data Corp* (*Warren Publishing*) involved a directory of cable systems.[202] Warren Publishing published an annual cable directory throughout US. They alleged copyright infringement in connection to one of these volumes of cable and information services. Microdos, on the other hand, marketed compilation of facts relating to cable systems in computer software format. Warren Publishing claimed copyright protection in the selection or arrangement of the aforementioned volume. As a part of the arrangement mechanism, Warren Publication listed the relevant information under the heading of 'principal community'.[203] To avoid duplication they cross-referenced the 'principal community' heading with the headings under other communities.

At the preliminary stage, the District Court found enough creativity to satisfy the requirement of Feist, although the 11th circuit reversed such judgement.[204] The 11th circuit held that Microdos did not copy any of the original selection, co-ordination or arrangement of the directory in question, since the selection or arrangement followed in those cable directories had no minimal creativity attached to them.[205] Selection mechanism followed in case of the directory in question was non-existent, since the listing was all-inclusive. Further, cable operators in each system did the primary selection and thus, claim of originality only rested on the 'arrangement' followed in the directory.[206] *Warren* attempted to make the directory commercially useful. According to the Court, this approach was a "...mere discovery of an organizing principle, which [was] dictated by the market [and], not sufficient to establish creativity."[207] Thus, Warren Publishing failed to make the *Feist* grade in terms of creativity.

In comparison to factual compilations, there have been fewer questions raised on the copyrightability issue of compilations comprising of works. The second circuit in the case of *Stuart Y Silverstein v. Penguin Putnam* (*Silverstein*) questioned the creativity required in selection or arrangement of poems.[208] The Court cited *Feist* to

---

[202]'Cable System' was defined by the claimant *Warren Publications* as 'an entity composed as one or more communities that are offered the same service by the same cable system owner at the same prices' offering'; The Directory in itself was a comprehensive guide giving information on cable systems and included names, address of cable system providers, number of subscribers', the channels offered, the price of service and so on and so forth, *Warren Publications* 115 F3d 1509 (11th Cir 1997); *BellSouth Advertising* (n 197) 1511-1513.

[203]*Warren Publications* (n 202) 1511.

[204]ibid 1520.

[205]ibid.

[206]ibid 1517-1520; "Although courts should, and typically do, analyze selection and arrangement separately, then tend to find both or neither selection and arrangement to be creatively original", Polivy (n 59) 817; courts tend to use disjunctive reading at the time of assessing selection, co-ordination or arrangement in a compilation. This is the observation in the case of *National Business Lists, Inc. V. Dun & Bradstreet* 552 F Supp 89 (N D Ill 1982); William Patry, 'Copyright in Collection of Facts: A Reply' (1984) 6 Comm & Law 11, 30.

[207]*Warren Publications* (n 202) 1520.

[208]368 F 3d 77 (2nd Cir 2004).

observe the standard of creativity and expected sufficient indication of selection.[209] *Silverstein* in this case, was engaged in compiling poems written by the American poet Mrs. Dorothy Parker. Mrs. Parker did not include poems written by her in the three volumes of poetry published during her lifetime. Later on, Penguin publishers included those poems in their latest publication. Further to this publication, *Silverstein* claimed copyright infringement based on original selection or arrangement of the poems in his own compilation. For the claimant, the sources of these poems have been old newspaper and magazines. The category of uncollected poems and selection mechanism in this regard was not considered original to *Silverstein*. Mrs. Parker herself decided to leave some poems out of her lifetime collection. Moreover, copyedits performed by *Silverstein* were trivial in nature.[210] There was no indication of any substantial change that took place in the published book.[211] It seemed that the work of the claimant was a mere reproduction of Mrs. Parker's original work.

There have been various instances where the guidelines of *Feist* decision have been interpreted by subsequent cases. The following section observes possible inconsistencies that may have occurred, while following such guidelines.

3.3.1 Threshold of Protection

The above outlined three cases: *Mason*, *Key Publications* and *Maclean* confirmed that a factual compilation by virtue of selection, arrangement or personal discretion can meet the standard of *Feist*. In *Mason*, prior selection of sources that led to the final version of maps played a very important role.[212] Without selection and use of personal discretion, the compilation would have been an obvious representation of information available in the public domain. Similarly, in the *Key Publications* case, personal discretion seems to hold the key, which separated the compilation from purely mundane work of selecting and arranging all business listings for a yellow pages directory.[213] Expert opinion was considered sufficiently creative in *Maclean*. Prediction, an outcome of individual discretion, helped in deciding the price forecast of cars.[214] The above outlined cases did not clearly state the amount of selection necessary to meet the *Feist* standard.[215] The decision in *Feist*, however,

---

[209]ibid.

[210]Silverstein (n 208).

[211]The claimant said that copyediting changes related to punctuation, titling, or formatting but they were not particularly visible.

[212]This reference will be drawn when discussing the relationship of *Feist* with *Dataco*.

[213]*Key Publications* (n 190).

[214]44 F 3d 61 (2d Cir 1994) 67.

[215]It is equally true that *Feist* itself did not say about the amount of creativity and will be decided on a case-by-case basis.

only suggested non-copyrightability of the practice of including entire list of subscribers in a telephone directory.[216] Thus, one observes an inextricable link between selection process and involvement of creativity.

The cases further provide varied interpretations of the threshold of creativity. There is, however, a certain degree of commonality in all three cases. The context of these cases indicates that claimants have not excelled in terms of creativity to merit copyright protection. For instance, in the *Key Publications* case, the claimant left out certain businesses.[217] Such decision did not result from extensive prior research or calculation. The claimant left out short-term business houses, based on personal discretion and experience. Similarly, in the case involving maps, the claimant did not re-draw the maps to show creativity, but compared and selected consistent features within the existing structure.[218] As in the *Maclean* case, comparing various forecasts of market prices involves a greater level of creativity. Experts did not calculate the predictions, but instead based their decisions on existing informational sources.[219] In all of the above cases, a certain amount of creativity is present, but there is no requirement of novelty. Therefore, the outlined cases follow *Feist* requirement of modicum of creativity.

In *Bell South* and *Victor Lalli* cases, the issue of 'rigidity' came to the forefront.[220] The claimants worked within the confinement of a rigid structure: *Bell South* within the standard requirements of a yellow pages business directory; whereas *Victor Lalli* within the pre-conceived functional grid of a gambling chart. The entire structure in *Bell South* case followed was typical to a yellow pages business directory at that time. Moreover, businesses in the directory were included based on the preferences of customers. Hence, the listing was a prerogative of the customer instead of the claimant. The techniques used for marketing did not amount to authorship but merely discovered facts.[221] Hence, there was no originality in selection or arrangement of contents. Further, in *Victor Lalli*, no opportunity for the claimants to go beyond the rigid structure was provided. Charts used in this case did not give the option to exercise creativity. The claimants had to restrict themselves to the requirement of the grid.[222] Therefore, this compilation was devoid of minimal creativity required to merit copyright protection.

When personal discretion and judgement are used, it is likely that creativity would match the *Feist* standard. This approach is visible in cases like *Mason*, *Key Publications* and *Maclean*.[223] Their selections were not purely mechanical or

---

216 *Feist Publications* (n 3).

217 *Key Publications* (n 190).

218 *Hodge E Mason* (n 178).

219 44 F 3d 61 (2d Cir 1994).

220 Working within the purely functional grid offering no opportunity for variation, Meade (n 185) 264.

221 *BellSouth Advertising* (n 197) 1446.

222 936 F 2d 671 (2nd Cir 1991).

223 *Supra* section 3.1.

obvious, unlike in *Bell South and Victor Lalli*. For example, there are different ways of compiling a Chinese business directory besides selection or arrangement, as was followed by the claimant.[224] Representation made through any compilation would be obvious where the selection or arrangement is limited by choice.

In accordance with the *Feist* decision, it is suggested that purely mechanical processes cannot give rise to creativity. Although majority of compilations will come under copyright protection, there are certain categories that may remain unprotected.[225]

There is a similarity between compilations comprising of works and compilations representing factual information.[226] In the *Silverstein* case, the claimant compiled the poems that he came across in magazines and newspapers.[227] These were the poems left by Mrs. Parker, and as such, there was no adoption of a selection method. The claimant did not select by using his personal discretion and judgement. In the context of the requirement of creativity, the Court adopted the threshold of personal judgement.[228] Such threshold is unlikely to be stringent in nature due to the connection with the *Feist* decision.[229] There have been similar observations made in cases of compilations comprising of factual information.[230]

Other than creativity through selection mechanism, the claim of copyright may rest on creative work related to the copyrighted material in the compilation. In this particular case, the claim of copyright protection was with reference to copyedits required for the collection of poems. Although trivial copyediting was not sufficient, something creative would have triggered copyright protection.[231] Therefore, there may be original contribution through the act of copyediting. It is unlikely that the standard of creativity is stringent in this regard.[232]

---

[224] *Key Publications* (n 190).

[225] *Feist Publications* (n 3) 345.

[226] In spite of the possible similarity in terms of selection requirement, there are differences between the two kinds of compilations. In a factual compilation, no one will claim copyright infringement in contents and hence, a compiler may claim copyright protection as long as a modicum of creativity is present in selection or arrangement. Whereas a licence is required to use the copyright works in the compilation.

[227] 368 F 3d 77 (2nd Cir 2004).

[228] The issue of personal judgement/experience is also observed in *Maclean* case, 44 F 3d 61 (2d Cir 1994).

[229] *Feist Publications* (n 3).

[230] *Supra* section 3.1.

[231] Corrections to text including punctuation or spelling may constitute trivial changes, *Matthew Bender & Co. v. West Publishing Co.*, 158 F.3d 674, (2d Cir. 1998).

[232] ibid.

3.3.2 Extent of Consistency

Inconsistencies are evident in the decisions of *Key Publications*, *BellSouth* and *Warren Publishing*.[233] These inconsistencies relate to the issue of subjective and objective selection method and the application of *Feist's* standard. Subjective elements identify the 'person' in the work, and elements in a work that can be attributed to the person. The person making such selection uses his own discretion and includes or excludes data at the stage of compiling a database. Following an objective criterion, there is conscious exclusion of data from the compilation that meets the objective criteria.[234] In *Key Publications*, the compilation was copyrightable as the producer selected particular businesses. He increased the value of the compilation by adopting selections according to the requirement of the Chinese-American community. He used personal discretion, although that was subsequent to recognizing market demand of yellow pages directory in the Chinese community.[235] Commentators have suggested that selection process in *Key Publications* was not truly subjective, since the 'decision was the result of purely functional considerations'.[236] The claimant merely provided the consumers with a directory that 'included only relevant and useful data'.[237] Contrary to this decision, *Warren Publishing* was penalized because selection was market driven and the arrangement followed in the cable directory was according to the specific need of consumers.[238]

As far as the decisions in *Key Publications* and *BellSouth* are concerned, the difference between the two is based on the facts of the case. There is no subjective evaluation, while selecting geographic area and cut off date for the directory.[239] In contrast, the claimant in *Key Publications* used subjective evaluation at the time of deciding the businesses for his directory.[240] Therefore, the two cases are different in the context of the subjective evaluation. However, the question of market influence affecting the subjective selection remains. In the context of *Key Publications*, it has

---

[233]It has been suggested that "selection and arrangement is a test of subjective authorship", Jane C Ginsburg, 'Creation and Commercial Value: Copyright protection of works of Information' (1990) 90(7) Colum. L. Rev. 1865, 1896, and *Feist* said that selection and arrangement constitutes originality; On a different note, it is evident that post-*Feist* cases have maintained that only "a narrow category of works in which the creative sparking is utterly lacking" will not receive copyright protection, *Feist Publications* (n 3) 359.

[234]Bitton (n 73) 631.

[235]*Key Publications* (n 190).

[236]Bitton (n 73) 634; Moreover, there was similar exclusion of residential rate customers in the BellSouth telephone directory similar to the issue of exclusion in *Key Publications*, Ethan L Wood, "Copyrighting the Yellow pages: Finding originality in factual compilations" (1993-94) 78(5) Minn L Rev 1319, 1334.

[237]ibid; there was caution about how the issue of functionality has been used Meade (n 185) 262.

[238]115 F3d 1509 (11th Cir 1997).

[239]999 F2d 1436 (11th Cir 1993).

[240]Polivy (n 59) 813.

been argued that market driven functional consideration led the compiler to adopt an objective instead of a subjective selection because the compiler had "no real choice in making such decisions".[241] One must understand that the decisions taken in *Key Publications* were both objective and subjective in nature. A compiler cannot possibly forego his personal judgement, even after knowing the market demand. The market demand may give an idea but the compiler needs to express the idea by using his personal discretion and creativity.[242] In fact, this is an inevitable outcome in cases of factual compilations, since compilers, under all circumstances will take into account the market requirement.[243] Production of factual compilations is entirely for commercial reasons and the decision of production is primarily based on the requirement and utility of the information.[244] In the course of making compilation useful for the readers, the publisher gets the opportunity to be creative.[245]

It is inconceivable to deny copyright protection on the ground of usefulness. This practice would leave majority of factual compilations outside the purview of copyright protection.[246] Moreover, the US Supreme Court contemplated that most compilations would remain protected even after the *Feist* decision.[247] The directory in *Feist* was useful but demonstrated insufficient creativity to meet the originality requirement.[248] Further, the case did not say explicitly about the non-copyrightability of useful directories. As long as the publishers "…embody an element of subjective judgement, compilations can respond to market needs and still be held creatively original".[249] Functionally dictated compilations, however, without manifesting creative selection or arrangement are in principle not copy-

[241]Bitton (n 73) 634.

[242]*Key Publications* (n 190).

[243]Authors of most compilations would base their compilation on audience requirement. Alan L Durham, *Speaking of the World: fact, opinion and the originality standard of copyright* (2009) 33 (3) Arizona State Law Journal 791.

[244]*Infra* section 4.3.

[245]Compilations must be effective for the readers and this means the user requirement, and the usefulness of such compilation should be taken into account, Justice O'Conner in *Feist* citing Nimmer said: "author typically chooses which facts to include, in what order to place them, and how to arrange the collected data so that they may be used effectively by readers", *Feist Publications* (n 3) 340.

[246]Durham (n 243) 155.

[247]ibid.

[248]*Feist Publications* (n 3) 363.

[249]Polivy (n 59) 833; For example the arrangement was original in the *Key Publications* (n 190); In the opinion of Benjamin Thorner, "the idea that functional writings are unprotectable by copyright is wrongheaded as it hampers creators' incentives to profitably bring their goods to the public", Benjamin B. Thorner, 'Copyright protection for Computer Databases: the threat of *Feist* and a Proposed Solution' (1997) 5(1) VA J L & TECH 27.

rightable.[250] Therefore, functionally dictated compilations manifesting creative selection or arrangement stand a good chance to merit copyright protection.

The decision of *Warren Publishing* was based on the distinction of fact and expression. In the Court's opinion, a market-policy adopted was a fact because such policy was embedded in the market.[251] In the context of informational works, Jane Ginsburg has commented on the fallacy of using fact/expression distinction. She said:

> with respect to low authorship works, the fact/expression distinction thus is inherently flawed: its grudging measure of protectability undermines its own goals by diminishing incentives to produce informational works.[252]

Ginsburg probably meant that there is little expression in databases comprising of informational works and therefore, there is no need to differentiate between facts and expressions in such works. The distinction may still be necessary in informational works where complementary value has been added by the publisher, alongside the factual information.[253] As observed in Westlaw or LexisNexis databases, the complementary selective information is mixed with factual information, which makes the distinction of fact/expression necessary for the second work.[254]

On a different note, using the argument of purely deterministic and obvious criteria may be a better way of explaining the judgement in *Warren Publishing*.[255] There are a limited number of ways of arranging the information in a cable directory.[256] A second comer in the context of the directory must adhere to the rigid structure followed by the first publisher. Thus, Warren Publishing did not have sufficient room to show creativity in arranging the information in the cable directory.[257] Due to the rigid structure the arrangement was devoid of creativity.

This chapter shows that the *Feist* decision was not unique and a new-line of jurisprudence did not emerge subsequent to the decision. US Copyright Office did not face any appreciable changes in the process of registering factual compilations under copyright. Further, cases subsequent to *Feist* decision proved that the

---

[250] Jerome H Reichman and Pamela Samuelson, 'Intellectual Property Rights in data?' (1997) 50(1) V and L Rev 51.

[251] 115 F3d 1509 (11th Cir 1997).

[252] Ginsburg (n 233) 1915.

[253] *Infra* section 4.3.

[254] www.westlaw.com and www.lexisnexis.com; This trend is also observed in the annual report of Reed Elsevier, ibid.

[255] 115 F3d 1509 (11th Cir 1997).

[256] This situation was similar to the *Feist* case involving telephone directory, *Feist Publications* (n 3).

[257] Furthermore the cable directory in question was not electronic in nature, thereby limiting the possibility of selection or arrangement as it happens in case of an electronic database, *supra* section 2.3.

threshold of protection remained similar to the standard expressed in *Feist*. There were no substantial inconsistencies to raise concern among the producers. Therefore, the *Feist* decision did not cause any appreciable change in the threshold of originality unlike the concern expressed in the explanatory memorandum to the first draft proposal.[258]

---

[258]COM (92) 24 final, para [2.3.3].

Chapter 4
The Effect of *Feist* in the US Database Market

The explanatory memorandum contemplated the 'gap' that *Feist* was likely to create, since 'sweat of the brow' as a reason to provide copyright protection to compilations was removed.[1] It was believed that such removal would result in less incentive for producers engaged in the production of databases.[2] This chapter observes this concern as expressed in the explanatory memorandum in the background of the US database market where the *sui generis* database right is not present. It concludes on a note that 'sweat of the brow' had a questionable role in incentivizing database production.[3] There was less uncertainty with *Feist* decision and investment continued to flow towards production of electronic databases.[4] Further, the prolonged database debate in US did not result from *Feist*.[5] The debate resulted largely because of other factors.

4.1 'Sweat of the Brow' as an Incentive for Database Production

There have been criticisms about expectations that existed with the US Copyright Law. It has been said that database companies were under false assumption that prior to *Feist* decision, US Copyright Law provided compre hensive protection for the structure and contents of a database.[6] It was believed

[1]Commission, 'Proposal for a Council Directive on the legal protection of databases' COM (92) 24 final (COM (92) 24 final), para [2.3.3].
[2]ibid, para [3.1.9].
[3]*Infra* section 4.1.
[4]*Infra* section 4.3.
[5]*Infra* section 4.4.
[6]W Mathew Wayman, 'International Database Protection: A multilateral Treaty solution to the United States' Database Dilemma' (1996–97) 37(2) Santa Clara L Rev 427, 431 and Baila Celedonia, 'From copyright to copycat: Open season on data?', Publishers Weekly Aug 16 1991, 34; Neeta Thakur, 'Database protection in the European Union and the United States: the European Database Directive as an optimum global model' (2001) 1 IPQ 100, 104.

I. Gupta, *Footprints of Feist in European Database Directive*,
DOI 10.1007/978-981-10-3981-2_4

that comprehensive databases in US would receive protection under 'sweat of the brow' theory.[7]

In terms of production of databases, GDD showed an upward trend during 1979–1991.[8] In the year 1979, database production of North America was almost equal to the production of the rest of the world.[9] By the middle of 1985, figures recorded an increase to 2000 and by 1991 increased to 4424.[10] In 1991, North American production was twice as much in comparison to the rest of the world.[11] Going by the figures it is apparent that there was less concern among producers, which needs further analysis.

4.1.1 Extent of Impact on Producers

There was an apparent impression that the presence of 'sweat of the brow' argument with respect to copyright protection incentivized production of databases.[12] As a result, one could possibly argue that the GDD report reflected an increase in number.[13] This argument, contradicts the GDD report referred during the evaluation of performance of the Database Directive in the EU.[14] If we go by numbers, even after *Feist* decision, database industry grew considerably in US.[15] With 'sweat of the brow' as the source of positive incentive, outright rejection of the same in *Feist* should have led to a negative effect on the future of US database

[7]Jane C Ginsburg, 'Copyright, Common Law and *sui generis* protection of databases in the United States and Abroad' (1997–1998) 66(1) U Cin L Rev 151, 151; Cynthia M Bott, 'Protection of Information Products: Balancing Commercial Reality and the Public Domain' (1998–99) 67(1) U Cin L Rev 237, 246.

[8]Martha E. Williams, 'The State of Databases Today: 2004', Gale Directory of Databases 2004 1 (1) in Robin Elizabeth Herr, *Is the Sui Generis Right a Failed Experiment? A legal and Theoretical Exploration of How to Regulate Unoriginal Database Contents and Possible Suggestions for Reform* (DJØF Publishing Copenhagen, Denmark 2008).

[9]ibid; GDD was the same source referred to in first evaluation report concerning Database Directive.

[10]Martha E. Williams, 'The State of Databases Today: 2005', Gale Directory of Databases 2005 in Herr (n 8).

[11]ibid.

[12]Estelle Derclaye, 'Intellectual property rights on information and market power – comparing European and American protection of databases' (2007) 38(3) IIC 275, 291.

[13]Herr (n 8) 162.

[14]'DG Internal market and services working paper: First Evaluation of Directive 96/9/EC on the legal protection of databases' (*Commission of the European Communities,* 12 December 2005) available at <http://ec.europa.eu/internal_market/copyright/docs/databases/evaluation_report_en.pdf> (accessed 31 October 2016) (First Evaluation of Directive 96/9/EC), para [4.4].

[15]'Intellectual property and the National Information Infrastructure: The Report of the Working Group on Intellectual Property rights' (*United States Patent and Trademark Office*, 8 January 2007) available at <https://www.uspto.gov/web/offices/com/doc/ipnii/ipnii.pdf> (accessed 30 November 2016).

industry.[16] However, GDD indicates that there was no visible negative effect, instead the US database industry prospered.[17]

One needs to observe whether database production in US maintained a steady growth from 1985 to 2004, which coincides with the first evaluation report. To have a clear understanding, the entire period has been divided into three parts. The first period is from 1985 to 1991, which also happens to be prior to the *Feist* decision. Subsequent to the *Feist* decision, and leading up to the enactment of database right in Europe (1991–1996), is the second period. The final period of 1996–2004 is after the enactment of database right in EU until the publication of the first evaluation report. During the first period, the database industry grew from two thousand to four thousand and twenty four.[18] The figure rose to more than six thousand by 1996 and exceeded eight thousand by 2004.[19] In the 20 years (1985–2004), for each period, there was a steady growth of more than two thousand database entries.

Going by the numbers, the idea that application of 'sweat of the brow' theory provided assurance to producers who were concerned about their predicaments in a world surrounded by internet was faulty.[20] One must acknowledge that 'sweat of the brow' argument with respect to copyright was receiving support from some of the circuit courts in US.[21] Although 'sweat of the brow' might have provided support, the problem of insecurity and safeguarding investment was a natural concern linked with development of electronic dissemination in the information society.[22] For instance, a report published by the US Congress Office of Technology Assessment in 1986 contemplated the risk of investment towards compilation of a database.[23] There

---

[16] In spite of the hostile attitude of the 2nd and the 9th Circuits' towards copyright protection to factual compilations (*Fred L Worth v Selchow & Richter Co* 827 F.2d 569 (9th Cir 1987) and *Financial Info Inc. v Moody's Investors Service* 808 F. 2d 204 (2nd Cir 1986), "… an abundance of online databases was made available to customers in the states of New York and California", Jessica Litman, 'After *Feist*' (1992) 17(2) U Dayton L Rev 607, 611.

[17] First Evaluation of Directive 96/9/EC; In around year 2000 there were about 31 American companies engaged in the creation of informational databases in comparison to 6 European companies, Mortiner B Zuckerman, 'The Times of Our Lives' (1999) 127 U.S. News & World Report 68,70 in Daniel R Valente, *Feist Overruled? Database Protection in the Next Century* (2000) 17(7) The Computer Lawyer 20, 20.

[18] Martha E. Williams, 'The State of Databases Today: 2005', Gale Directory of Databases 2005 in Herr (n 8) 162.

[19] First Evaluation of Directive 96/9/EC, para [1.1].

[20] Alfred Yen has suggested that the situation of free-riding is not as bad as it seems. "Some compilers will recover their development costs even if copyright is eliminated … Indeed, it is quite likely that the production of many creative compilations needs no further encouragement or that the production of many ordinary compilations requires additional incentives", Alfred C Yen, 'The legacy of *Feist*: Consequences of the weak connection between Copyright and the Economics of public goods' (1991) 52(5) Ohio St L J 1343, 1374–1375; COM (92) 24 final, para [2.3.3].

[21] *Supra* chapter 3 (n 140).

[22] If we refer to the first draft proposal of the Database Directive, concern relating to the protection offered to electronic databases was highlighted throughout, COM (92) 24 final.

[23] US Congress Office of Technology Assessment, 'Intellectual Property Rights in an Age of Electronics and Information' (April 1986) available at <http://www.princeton.edu/~ota/disk2/1986/8610/8610.PDF> (accessed 30 November 2016) 97.

were concerns with the issue of free-riding and the level of protection available for compilations in a more advanced state of technology.[24] Therefore, the link between presence of 'sweat of the brow' and production of databases is doubtful.[25]

4.1.2 Use of Technical Measures

The technologies to protect databases were already in place even before Feist. For instance, publishers used to control access and monitor customer usage and this was prevalent with large number of online databases.[26] Technological Protection Measures (TPM) was effectively used for protecting electronic databases.[27] Although the use of TPM may not provide total security to the contents, there was little evidence to suggest that database producers on a large scale have failed to protect their investments.[28] Estelle Derclaye suggested that TPM has limitations.[29] In the opinion of Kenneth Dam, however, 'self-help systems' like TPM may be immensely useful in protecting contents. Moreover, there may be legislations to support the self-help systems from the vulnerability of cybercrimes. For instance, DMCA in the US.[30] Ejan Mackaay spoke about alternate means of 'fencing'. In his opinion, "a variety of fencing techniques are known, including such unexpected ones as marketing practices and elaborate contractual arrangements and further ones may be discovered as entrepreneurial ones".[31]

There is a mixed response concerning the use of TPM. It is possible that someone could finally get hold of a database in an unauthorized manner.[32]

---

[24]ibid.

[25]*Supra* section 4.1.

[26]This is in agreement with the view of Jessica Litman. Litman (n 16) 611; Similar to the contention of Litman, Paul T Sheils and Robert Penchina have said that database publishers already had well settled licensing agreements in place through which the licensor could restrict the use of the information, including prohibition on the copying, redistribution and re-publication of information, Paul T Sheils and Robert Penchina, 'What's all the fuss about *Feist*? The sky is not falling on the intellectual property rights of online database proprietors' (1991–1992) 17(2) U Dayton L Rev 563, 572.

[27]ibid.

[28]Litman (n 16) 611.

[29]Derclaye (n 12) 197.

[30]Kenneth W Dam, 'Self-help in the digital jungle' in Rochelle C Dreyfuss and others (eds), *Expanding the boundaries of Intellectual Property: Innovation Policy for the Knowledge Society* (Oxford University Press, first published 2001) 104–111; Patrica Akester, 'Survey of Technological Measures for protection of Copyright' (2001) 12(1) Ent L Rev 36, 39; Similarly in the EU the 2001/29/EC Directive includes the anti-circumvention policies. In the UK, the EU Directive provisions are included in the CDPA of 1988 through sections 296-299.

[31]Ejan Mackaay, 'The Economics of Emergent Property Rights on the Internet' in P Bernt Hugenholtz (ed), *The future of Copyright in a Digital Environment* (Kluwer Law International London 1996) 25.

[32]Derclaye (n 12) 197.

Although this possibility exists, remedies to this act of circumvention are covered under various formats of Computer Misuse legislations.[33] Even with an incentive in place, the problem of unauthorized access would persist.

Although there may be some concern with databases in paper-format, such databases would have negligible impact in the electronic age. An additional argument may be put forward based on the reasoning that databases could be in paper-format. While this could be a valid argument, the explanatory memorandum only supported the incentive of 'sweat of the brow' for production of electronic databases.[34] Although the final Directive covers databases in both formats, major databases are likely to be electronic in nature.[35]

It was less likely for *Feist* to have possibly disincentivized database business.[36] It indicates that perhaps there was limited concern among stakeholders with no sign of extensive uncertainty. Limited concern was observed in the period subsequent to *Feist* when there was little initiative on the part of publishers to enact database legislation in US.[37]

There is no definite indication about requirements of any special incentive for the production of electronic databases.[38]

4.2 Five Years After *Feist*

There have been suggestions that *Feist* had a 'drastic consequence' on the protection of future databases and on the database industry. There was fear of misappropriation of contents, underproduction of databases and market failure.[39] In the opinion of Bruce Lehman there was increasing concern that valuable factually-oriented databases would go unprotected.[40] Reporting in the Wall Street Journal, Wade Lambert raised the consequences of *Feist* on the lucrative yellow page industry that generated advertising revenue of $8 billion.[41] One of them have been quoted saying that

---

[33]*Supra* section 2.1.2.

[34]COM (92) 24 final.

[35]Council Directive of 1996/9/EC of 27 March 1996 on the legal protection of databases [1996] OJ L 77/20 (Council Directive 96/9/EC).

[36]Cases subsequent to *Feist* suggested that the threshold can be easily met, *supra* sections 3.2 and 3.3.

[37]This would be further analyzed in the next section in relation to the gap of five years after *Feist*.

[38]Going by numbers argument, *supra* section 2.2.2.

[39]Dennis S Karjala, 'Misappropriation as a third Intellectual Property Paradigm' (1994) 94(8) Colum L Rev 2594, 2596-2598; Michael Schwarz, 'Copyright in compilations of facts: Case Comment' (1991) 17(5) EIPR 178, 182.

[40]Bruce Lehman 'Intellectual Property and the National and Global Information Infrastructures' in Egbert J Dommering and P Bernt Hugenholtz, *The future of Copyright in a Digital environment* (Kluwer Law International London 1996) 103.

[41]Wade Lambert, 'Yellow pages reuse is found not violate Copyright" (September 24, 1991) The Wall Street Journal (Eastern Edition) New York, B1.

> ...in the aftermath of *Feist* and its progeny, database providers, finding their databases inadequately protected against misappropriations, began pressuring Congress to enact legislation that would provide them the protection they had under the 'sweat of the brow' doctrine.[42]

The Report of US Commerce Department in 1994 predicted that subsequent to *Feist* there would be less incentive to produce informative databases.[43] However, in the following year they retracted from their statement and stressed on the requirement of dissemination of information.[44] Michael Klipper, who later became one of the major proponents of database legislation in US, observed that *Feist* would have some kind of adverse effect in the production of factual compilation.[45] This would be disastrous in an information society purely because these facts, were customized, delivered and compiled in an understandable format for the purpose of reference.[46] In terms of originality, informative compilations may fall short of *Feist* standard because of obviousness in selection or arrangement, but the utility of such compilations were beyond doubt.[47] The proponents of American database legislation thought that negative effect would throttle and disincentivize further productions of valuable compilations. It would be disastrous on the electronic information industry and the US economy. The standard of *Feist* leaves automated databases and factual compilations unprotected. Moreover, the available protection measure under misappropriation, law of contract and unfair competition may not help in creating sufficient incentive.[48]

While there were people who believed that *Feist* would cast a negative effect on the production of non-original databases, there were others who were not very certain about the ill-effects of *Feist*. In the opinion of Jessica Litman, there was "little fear that the [database industry would] be withering away".[49] Further, there were other effective measures and the industry would have surely adjusted with the post-*Feist* world.[50] Similar to Litman, others said that the issue of drastic consequences was greatly exaggerated. According to Vice President of the Information Industry

---

[42]J Ryan Mitchell, 'If at *Feist* You Don't Succeed, Try, Try Again: An Evaluation of the Proposed Collections of Information Piracy Act' (1999) 78(4) Neb L Review 901, 902.

[43]Dept. of Commerce, U.S. Industrial Outlook 1994, at 25-1 in Debra B Rosler, 'The European Union's proposed Directive for the legal protection of databases: A new threat to the free flow of information' (1995) 10(1) High Tech L J 105, 133.

[44]ibid.

[45]Michael R Klipper and Meredith S Senter, *The facts after Feist: The Supreme Court addresses the Issue of the Copyright ability of factual compilations* in Jon A Baumgarten (ed) '*Fact*' *and Data Protection After Feist* (Prentice Hall Law & Business, New Jersey 1991); In contrast early twentieth century onwards US database market dominance over UK in relation to database production was clearly evident, Gary Lea, 'In defence of originality' (1996) 7(1) Ent L Rev 21, 23.

[46]ibid.

[47]Klipper and Senter (n 45).

[48]Philip H Miller, 'Life after *Feist*: Facts, the First Amendment and the Copyright status of automated databases' (1991-1992) 60(3) Fordham L Rev 507, 533-534.

[49]Litman (n 16) 611.

[50]ibid.

Association in Washington DC, *Feist* would ensure mixed results for the industry. Most compilations should come under the threshold that *Feist* created. Further, there could be possible concern with the extent of protection afforded to factual compilations.[51] There were others who thought that the effect of *Feist* was not immediately clear. It was suggested that future negative effect of *Feist* should be covered, but to the extent of providing only the required incentive to database producers.[52] The gap that *Feist* would create was not clear.[53] It was believed that properly drafted licensing agreements will help the proprietors of databases to stop unauthorized copying.[54] Moreover, remedies under misappropriation and unfair competition would continue to be an effective weapon in the hands of proprietors.[55]

If *Feist* was a decisive cause for new database legislation, initiative for such legislative process should have begun in US long before than it actually got started. The first American attempt to introduce database legislation was in the year 1996.[56] The large gap of five years in the background of the threat perception has not been discussed at greater length in most of the writings.[57] There have been claims to suggest that after *Feist*, database industry had requested legislative approach to correct the negative effect.[58] This statement does not synchronize with the time of first legislative proposition, and thus questions the 'gap' of five years. There was, however, a white paper published under the Clinton administration on "Intellectual Property and the National Information Infrastructure", which did discuss about a prospective international *sui generis* protection on databases.[59] The question of inordinate delay in the American database debate needs further analysis.

---

[51] Steve Metalitz, '*Feist* and the Information Industry' (June/July 1991) 17(5) Bulletin of the American Society for Information Science 11–12.

[52] David O Carson, 'Copyright protection for factual compilations after *Feist*: A practioner's view' (1992) 17(3) U Dayton L Rev 969, 969-970.

[53] Stanley Lai, 'Recent Developments in Copyright, Database Protection and (On-line) licensing' (1999) 7(1) Int'l J of L & Information Technology 73, 86-87.

[54] Sheils and Penchina (n 26).

[55] ibid.

[56] US Copyright Office, 'Report on Legal Protection For Databases: August 1997'; Miriam Bitton 'A New Outlook on the Economic Dimension of the Database Protection Debate' (2006-07) 47(2) IDEA Intell Prop L Rev 93, 96; " Domestic threat of database exploitation poses the greatest risk to the US database industry", Wayman (n 6) 466.

[57] The lack of protection became especially apparent after the Supreme Court ruling in *Feist*", Charles Brill, 'Legal Protection of Collection of Facts' (1998) 2 Computer L Rev & Tech 1, 59.

[58] "In response, the industry has been working to push through Congress a database protection bill ..." Russell G Nelson, 'Seeking Refuge from a Technology Storm: The Current Status of Database Protection Legislation after the Sinking of the Collections of Information Anti-Piracy Act and the Second Circuit Affirmation of *Matthew Bender & (and) Co. v. West Publishing Co. Recent Development*' (1998-99) 6(2) J Intell Prop L 453, 456.

[59] 'Intellectual property and the National Information Infrastructure: The Report of the Working Group on Intellectual Property rights' (*United States Patent and Trademark Office*, 8 January 2007) available at <https://www.uspto.gov/web/offices/com/doc/ipnii/ipnii.pdf/> (accessed 30 November 2016).

The people who represented the publishers later in the American database debate also proposed that *Feist* would have disastrous effect. There would be less incentive for database producers. As a result, production of informative databases would suffer.[60] While this situation reflects the need for urgent action, there was no visible activity in the period of five years immediately after the *Feist* decision.

The US Supreme Court's reference to the US Constitution was unexpected at some quarters and the publishers could take this plea.[61] It may be argued that the Constitutional reference in *Feist* was something which surprised the publishers, and it was not expected at that time. One must however note that from the point of originality, reference to the Constitution is not something unique. The Constitutional aspect, as discussed in the previous chapter, has been referred in the other Supreme Court decisions.[62] Some reciprocal action on the part of publishers was expected if the Constitutional aspect was the biggest concern. It relates to the general issue surrounding incentives for producers and their investments towards the production of electronic databases. The obstacle of the Constitution should have ensured more activity in the background of the claim that incentive was required for database producers. However, there seems little evidence that the concern was real. Further, the concern expressed with the removal of 'sweat of the brow' is also doubtful.[63] Even before the *Feist* decision, the 'sweat of the brow' argument for the purpose of copyright protection of compilations was on the verge of exit.[64]

4.3 Amount of Investment Towards Databases in US

This section questions the impact of *Feist* with the objective to understand whether *Feist* stopped or disincentivized the investment process in electronic publishing. As an example the case of Reed Elsevier an Anglo-Dutch conglomerate and one of the largest publishing houses has been considered.[65] They also have substantial

[60]Klipper and Senter (n 45).

[61]*Supra* section 3.2.

[62]*The Trade Mark Cases* 100 US 82(1879) and *Burrow-Giles Lithograph Co v Sarony* 111 US 53 (1884), cases referred to in the *Feist* decision.

[63]*Supra* section 4.1.

[64]*Supra* section 3.2.

[65]Elsevier is the world's leading provider of scientific and medical information and serves scientists, health professionals and students worldwide. The Science & Technology business is the world's leading science journal publisher, producing over 200,000 new research articles in some 1,100 journals every year, with Science Direct, its flagship electronic solution, accessed by over 11 million users, 'Annual Report and Financial Statements 2008' available at <http://www.relx.com/annualreport08/business/Pages/elsevier.aspx> (accessed 30 November 2016); Reed Elsevier was one of the chief proponents of database legislation in US. Other than Reed Elsevier, Thomson advanced their interests for database legislation. In fact, Reed Elsevier was seen as a company leading the debate on database legislation in US; Laura D'Andrea Tyson and Edward F. Sherry, 'Statutory Protection for Databases: Economic and Public Policy Issues', (unpublished report for

business interests towards production of databases in US.[66] The excerpts selected from the annual reports relate to level of investment and ascertains any point of concern after *Feist*. One of the obvious questions is whether concern posed as a result of *Feist* would reflect in the annual report of a company.[67] As a legal requirement, any issue that affects the shareholders due to change in business policy must be stated in the annual reports. An example in this regard would help to clarify the issue. Around 1993, the investment of Reed Elsevier was broadly towards four sectors: Scientific & Medical, Professional, Business and Consumer. Report covering Medical Publishing stated that profit of the company declined by over 50% in the background of uncertainty surrounding the US pharmaceutical market. Reed Elsevier met with unprecedented challenges because of the proposed US Governmental healthcare reform legislation.[68] Due to this legislative initiative, clients of Reed Elsevier had to severely cut down on their promotional and marketing expenditure resulting which there was a substantial drop in the revenue and profit of Reed Elsevier.[69] Further to substantial drop in revenue, Reed Elsevier re-structured its business.[70] This example shows an instance of how proposed change in law affected the business of the publishing company. Therefore, the consulted annual reports may reveal issues relating to *Feist*, which might have affected the investment in electronic publishing.

These reports will indicate the strategy of companies about their investments towards supply of information.[71] This has direct relation to the issue of factual compilations, since facts are essentially informative.[72] To meet the objective, the Annual Reports of Reed Elsevier from the year after *Feist* till 1999 have been considered. The year 1999 coincides with the European Database Directive. It was enacted in 1996, and by the end of 1998, most of the European member states incorporated the Directive in their national legislations. By 1999, any negative effect of not having protection similar to EU would have been perceived in US.

(Footnote 65 continued)

the Information Industry Association, 1997); Siva Vaidhyanathan, *Copyrights and Copywrongs: The Rise of Intellectual Property and How it Threatens Creativity* (NYU Press 2003) 167; Patti Waldmeir, 'Who should own the raw facts?: Database Legislation: Courts must balance the rights to private property and to public access' Financial Times (London, 22 May 2002) 19; Mathew Swibel, 'Defending the Database' (31 March 2004) available at <http://www.forbes.com/2004/03/31/cz_ms_0331beltway.html> (accessed 3 January 2010).

[66] *Infra* section 4.3.1.

[67] Davison cited excerpts from some of these reports to comment about the strategies of publishers, Mark J Davison, *The legal protection of databases* (Cambridge University Press Cambridge 2003), 261-263.

[68] H.R. 191: American Consumers Healthcare Reform Act of 1993. This bill never became law.

[69] 'Reed Elsevier annual report 1993' available at <http://www.reed-elsevier.com/investorcentre/reports%202007/Pages/1992-2001.aspx> (accessed 10 December 2010) (Reed Elsevier annual report 1993).

[70] ibid.

[71] Davison (n 67) 261-263.

[72] ibid.

4.3.1 Investment Towards Database Business

The 1992 Report talks about enormous acquisition opportunities of national companies in US and continental Europe.[73] It highlighted that Reed Reference Publishing (RRP), which was a major subsidiary of Reed Elsevier, accounted for 80% of revenue and published over five hundred titles. RRP acquired National Register Publishing (NRP) in 1991 and subsequently publications of this company improved significantly. The 1993 Annual Report noted investment towards future database publishing industry by acquiring Congressional Information Service (CIS). CIS was a leading compiler of US historical and governmental data such as legislation, committee hearings, regulations, foreign policy and statistics. This report highlighted the performance of NRP under RRP. It stated that the publishing company has actually developed as a global database publisher, exceeding all expectations. Thus, there was encouragement towards developing similar products.[74] 1994 was an important year, since Reed Elsevier acquired LexisNexis, which was a leading publisher in US providing online information services.[75] Similar to RRP, the success story continued with the launch of new products in both paper and electronic format. By that time, Reed Elsevier already acquired CIS, with the successful launch of electronic versions of their databases. There was an all-round improvement with substantial growth and revenue generation from electronic publishing. In the wake of commercial internet, the 1995 report highlighted the need to create a convenient and effective niche for customers.[76] Acquisition of LexisNexis in 1994 showed benefits within a year. Thus, "... LexisNexis, which in its first full year of ... ownership, exceeded ...profit expectation".[77] US were identified as an advanced information market with an increasing need for quality information.

Half of the sales of Reed Elsevier came from the US.[78] The performance of RRP was within expectation, since it introduced its online prime directory products on LexisNexis service. The future of RRP was bright as the company concentrated on delivering electronic databases using LexisNexis platform. 1996 highlighted the phasing stage of printed to electronic media and the encouraging growth structure

---

[73] 'Reed Elsevier annual report 1992' available at <http://www.reed-elsevier.com/investorcentre/reports%202007/Pages/1992-2001.aspx> (accessed 10 December 2010). (Reed Elsevier annual report 1992).

[74] 'Reed Elsevier annual report 1993 (n 69).

[75] 'Reed Elsevier annual report 1994' available at <http://www.reed-elsevier.com/investorcentre/reports%202007/Pages/1992-2001.aspx> (accessed 10 December 2010). (Reed Elsevier Annual Report 1994).

[76] 'Reed Elsevier annual report 1995' available at <http://www.reed-elsevier.com/investorcentre/reports%202007/Pages/1992-2001.aspx> (accessed 10 December 2010). (Reed Elsevier annual report 1995).

[77] ibid.

[78] ibid.

of the company.[79] The Report indicated the inherent value of publishing. It indicated the capacity of the good infrastructure to handle competition from other publishers. In the wake of commercial internet and database publishing the RRP was re-organized, and NRP was merged with the LexisNexis service.

Reed Elsevier invested heavily towards electronic publishing in US where, unlike Europe, there is no database right.[80] The sign of investment indicates enough confidence among publishers in the absence of legislation.[81] This confirms that any additional special incentive may not be required where there is a market for databases. It has been suggested that publishers were confident about protecting electronic databases.[82] Such contention is consolidated by the reports of Reed Elsevier.[83] Further, no hesitation is noticed in any of the investments towards electronic publishing, unlike the negative concerns expressed by those who feared the negative effect of *Feist*.[84]

The above outcome was also controlled by the types of databases that Reed Elsevier was involved with at the time of the report. These are also the types of databases that they are presently producing for the international audience. The databases mentioned aforesaid were full-text materials and were unlikely to be affected as a result of the *Feist* decision. For instance, the CIS database compiled US historical and governmental data such as legislation, committee hearings, regulations, foreign policy and statistics.[85] These were not factual data arranged in a mundane way, which was disallowed by the US Supreme Court in *Feist* decision.[86] Reed Elsevier on the other hand was dealing with full-text materials, which were arranged and selected in a way to merit copyright protection.

The above reports spanning over five years is indicative of the level of investments in US, and business confidence in the market subsequent to the *Feist* decision. Reed Elsevier did not refer to any obstacles in the transition to online dissemination services. As a result, one observes the acquisition of LexisNexis for 1 billion pound sterling, which was one of the major full-text online legal and news information providers in US.[87] In subsequent years, LexisNexis acted as a backbone to many of the subsidiaries to launch electronic databases.[88] There was no detrimental effect of *Feist* unlike the situation where Reed Elsevier suffered because

[79]'Reed Elsevier annual report 1996' available at <http://www.reed-elsevier.com/investorcentre/reports%202007/Pages/1992-2001.aspx> (accessed 10 December 2010).

[80]There was prolonged debate relating to the idea of having a database right in US, *Infra* section 4.4.

[81]Miriam Bitton, 'Exploring the European Union Copyright Policy through the lens of the Database Directive' (2008) 23(4) Berkeley Tech LJ 1411, 1424.

[82]*Supra* section 4.1.

[83]Reports spanning from 1993–1996.

[84]*Supra* sections 4.1 and 4.2.

[85]Reed Elsevier annual report 1993 (n 69).

[86]*Feist Publications v Rural Telephone Service*, 499 US 340 (1991).

[87]Reed Elsevier Annual Report 1994 (n 75) 4 and 14.

[88]Reed Elsevier annual report 1995 (n 76).

of proposed legislative changes in US.[89] Overall, United States was a lucrative destination for publishing business comprising of electronic and paper-format database. Although the effect of the *Feist* decision was directed at electronic databases, it was a decision that decided the copyrightability of a telephone directory in paper-format.[90] Dissemination of information in electronic format ensured transition from paper-format databases.[91] Thus, the negative effect apprehended was mostly in relation to databases in electronic format.

With reference to databases in paper-format, it was believed that anyone can misappropriate factual contents.[92] The effect of *Feist* on databases in paper-format would mean less incentive for producers. It was observed in the 1994 Annual Report that Reed Reference Publishing (RRP), a major subsidiary of Reed Elsevier, continued their success story with the launch of new products both in paper and electronic format.[93] A new product in paper-format indicates that the apprehended negative impact of *Feist* may have been misconceived. This negative effect apprehended is subject to the type of database. Despite the transition to electronic dissemination system, investment towards paper-format databases shows the existence of a possible market even though there is less protection offered in terms of TPM, which is naturally assigned to the structure of electronic databases. Other than the signs of investment, there are instances of publication of yellow pages directories in paper-format. Cases subsequent to *Feist* decision reflected that publishers successfully claimed copyright protection for their databases in non-electronic format.[94]

4.3.2 *Effective Business Policy and Utility of Legislation*

Other than reports above, two further Annual Reports of Reed Elsevier have been consulted to assess free-riding problem in the electronic age. The consultation of annual reports has been restricted up to the time when Howard Cobble introduced the second database bill in 1998.[95] This was also the time when the European Database Directive was incorporated by most member states.[96] These reports will

[89]*Supra* section 4.3.

[90]*Feist Publications* (n 86).

[91]COM (92) 24 final.

[92]*Supra* section 4.2.

[93]Reed Elsevier annual report 1992 (n 73).

[94]*Supra* section 3.3.

[95]'Reed Elsevier annual report 1997' available at <http://www.reed-elsevier.com/investorcentre/reports%202007/Pages/1992-2001.aspx> (accessed 10 December 2010). (Reed Elsevier annual report 1997).

[96]First Evaluation of Directive 96/9/EC, para [4.1.1].

possibly indicate any underlying challenges for the US database industry, since there was an already existing database protection in Europe.

The two reports did not show any appreciable concern with investment, but stressed on the importance of creating new business models to generate revenue in the electronic age. Even after *Feist* decision there were no visible complaints made by the publishers to the US Congress. It reflects that to some extent the existing protection measures were adequate in one of the biggest revenue generating industry.[97] Further, the 1997 Annual Report considered the utility of value added information and services, which were most likely to attract copyright protection, and would not require separate database legislation.[98] There were also opinions suggesting non-requirement of database legislation. Producers, in case of scientific databases, were going to invest with or without protection.[99] According to Stephen M Maurer, even if existing databases were freely copied, the producers invest in them because there were a number of existing 'self-help' methods.[100] Some of them include bilateral agreements, online contracts, inserting copyrighted materials within facts, etc. Although it was difficult for competitors to comprehensively copy a database, the threat of unauthorized access and downloading remained.[101]

The reports indicated no definite concern of losing investment or negative growth because of the EU database right.[102] If legislation were not a primary condition for investment, then existence of EU database legislation would not have a negative impact on US database industry. Acquisitions and investments continued in the US subsidiaries where, unlike Europe, no special protection is available. Nothing in the reports shows that the problem of free-riding, affected both investment and profitability of the company.[103] There seems to be a structural change in business policy that needs further analysis.

---

[97]William Patry, 'The Enumerated Powers Doctrine and Intellectual Property: An Imminent Constitutional Collision' (1999) 67(2) The Geor Wash L R 359, 386.

[98]Reed Elsevier annual report 1997 (n 95).

[99]Stephen M Maurer and Suzanne Scotchmer, 'Database protection: Is it Broken and Should we fix it' (1999) 284 Science, 1129–1130.

[100]Stephen M Maurer, 'Raw Knowledge: Protecting Technical databases for science and industry' (14-15 January, 1999) available at <http://www2.sims.berkeley.edu/courses/is296a-3/s99/database.pdf> (accessed 25 November 2010).

[101]Raymond T Nimmer and Patricia A Krauthaus, 'Information as Property Databases and Commercial Property' (1993–94) 1(1) IJLIT 1.14; There are pitfall and effectiveness of adopting unfair competition to protect databases, Paula Baron, 'Back to the future: Learning from the past in the Database Debate' (2001) 62(2) Ohio St L J 1, 7.

[102]Council Directive 96/9/EC.

[103]Having said that there was the case of *ProCD v Zeidenberg* 86 F3d 1447(7th Cir 1996) involving copying of telephone directories off a CD ROM. *Zeidenberg* extracted the contents and released them on the internet at a lesser cost. For ProCD the cost of the compilation was extensive. The case was decided on the basis of a licensing clause in the CDROM.

The reports mentioned above have highlighted importance of new business models to generate revenue in the electronic age.[104] Adoption of new business policies provided an important argument against enacting an incentive for database producers.[105] Development of business policies reiterates the claim that production of databases to a great extent was market driven. If there was a market, database producers would create new opportunities to recover their investment.[106]

Adoption of new models also represented a situation where old models were no longer sustainable in the electronic age. It became necessary for publishers to change to the new model.[107] If the old business models for database production are not sustainable, then the utility of introducing an incentive for those databases through the enactment of a legislation, which is similar to that of database right is questionable.[108] The transition explained in the Annual Reports of Reed Elsevier would mean similar changes for other database producers.[109]

The presentation of information was considered vital for modern day electronic databases, contrary to the belief that an electronic database would merely represent compilation of factual data.[110] Value added services effectively increased the success rate of a database comprising factual contents. There were two reasons for following the policy of value added service. The first one was market requirement, whereas the second one was in relation to protection. The issue that production was driven by market requirement has already been discussed previously.[111] With regards to protection, publishers may seek copyright protection by adding work, which was original by copyright standard to the already existing factual information.[112] Thus, copyright became a potent tool to protect investment. In the European context, the copyright protection has also been favoured over database right.[113]

While successful transition to new business model temporarily resolved the requirement of database legislation, use of TPM provided an additional layer of security.[114] The effectiveness of TPM in case of electronic databases has already

[104]Bitton (n 56) 132–133.

[105]ibid.

[106]David Fewer, 'A *Sui Generis* Right to Data? A Canadian Position' (1998) 30(2) Can Bus L J 165,180.

[107]Davison (n 67) 261–263.

[108]Bitton (n 56) 169.

[109]Davison (n 67) 261-263.

[110]COM (92) 24 final, para [3.1.9].

[111]*Supra* section 4.3.2.

[112]With reference to the interpretation of the *Feist* case through various decisions, *supra* chapter 3.

[113]Interestingly the stakeholders in response to the suggestion of the *sui generis* database right in the Green Paper of the Commission, did not show any interest for the enactment of a special right and opted for database protection by copyright, George Metaxas, 'Protection of databases: quietly steering in the wrong direction?' (1990) 12(7) EIPR 227-228.

[114]It is apparently temporary because fresh debate concerning database legislation in US started after 1996.

been observed in this chapter and is further consolidated by news of investment in the annual report.[115] There is no substantial notification of free-riding problem, at least not to the extent anticipated in the explanatory memorandum to the proposal.[116]

The above representation gives a broad picture of the market condition. It does not reflect conditions of all publishers who were likely to be affected because of *Feist*. However, these representations clearly underline the strategy and policy of one of the major players in US.[117] The types of databases produced by the publishers coupled with inaction for five years would give us the impression that *Feist* was not an inhibiting force and an obstacle for investment in the electronic age. There was certain unconfirmed evidence to suggest that after *Feist*, the number of databases rose by 35% in the United States. The numbers jumped from 7637 to 10338 within six years. Further, the private sector investment towards database production rose to 78% after *Feist*.[118] These figures, however, are different from what has been expressed in the first evaluation report.[119]

While there was no visible impact immediately after the *Feist* decision, there were comprehensive debates concerning the requirement of database legislation in US.

4.4 US Database Right Debate and *Feist* Decision

There was a prolonged debate in US questioning the need for database right. It started in 1996 and lasted till 2004.[120] It was a debate between publishers and a group comprising of civil liberty organizations, library associations and scholars.[121] This eight-year period saw number of attempts starting with the Collections of Information Antipiracy Act, May H.R. 2652, 105th Congress to the introduction of Database and Collections of Information Misappropriation Act H.R 3261

[115]*Supra* section 4.1.2.

[116]COM (92) 24 final.

[117]Davison (n 67) 261–263.

[118]'H.R. 2281 (used to be H.R. 2652): The Collections of Information Antipiracy Act' available at <https://www.congress.gov/bill/105th-congress/house-bill/2652> (accessed 30 November 2016).

[119]The figures according to the GDD were over 8000 databases in the year 2004, First Evaluation of Directive 96/9/EC, para [4.4].

[120]The American database initiative started in 1996 in form of The Database Investment and Intellectual Property Antipiracy Act of 1996, House Bill 3531.

[121]'H.R. 2281 (used to be H.R. 2652): The Collections of Information Antipiracy Act' available at <https://www.congress.gov/bill/105th-congress/house-bill/2652> (accessed 30 November 2016); Jonathan Band, 'Armageddon on the Potomac The Collections of Information Antipiracy Act' (1999) D-Lib Magazine 5(1) available at <http://www.dlib.org/dlib/january99/01band.html> (accessed November 2010).

(*Rep. Coble, Howard*), 108th Congress (2003–2004) 10th August 2003.[122] The first database bill was introduced in the year 1996, and the entire period of database debate comprises of two stages. While the first stage began in 1996, the second stage commenced in 1998 and further continued for six years. It is noteworthy to understand the reason that led to the initial database debate because there was inaction for a period of five years after *Feist.*[123] Similar to initial stages, it will be noteworthy to see whether *Feist* had a role to play at the later stages.

4.4.1 EU Influence at Initial Stages in the American Database Debate

In the white paper on *Intellectual Property and the National Information Infrastructure*, there was discussion about the possibility of having a world-wide database protection.[124] The potential disparities in relation to database protection at an international stage were pointed out in the white paper.[125] Suggesting harmonization as a solution to the potential problem, the paper proposed a protection at the Berne level and World Intellectual Property Organization (WIPO) through a Berne Protocol or a New Instrument.[126] Two months subsequent to the publication of this paper, Bruce Lehman, under the Clinton administration, wrote a letter to the Director General of WIPO, Dr. Arpad Bogsch on November 29th, 1995.[127] As in the white paper, this letter proposed for an international protection of databases.[128] The communication,

---

[122]Library of Congress: Bills, Resolutions available at <https://www.congress.gov/> (accessed 30 December 2016); Database and Collections of Information Misappropriation Act 2003 available at <https://www.congress.gov/bill/108th-congress/house-bill/3261?q=H.R.+3261+%28108%29> (accessed 23 October 2016).

[123]*Supra* section 4.2.

[124]Working Group on Intellectual Property Rights, Intellectual Property and the National Information Infrastructure (September, 1995) available at <http://www.uspto.gov/web/offices/com/doc/ipnii/> (accessed 10 November 2010).

[125]While referring to the disparities, they were referring to the conflict of laws. "A user in France can access a database in the United States and have a copy downloaded to a computer in Sweden. Whose copyright law would apply to such a transaction? Because copyright laws are territorial, and the standards of protection embodied in the international conventions leave room for national legislative determinations, acts that may constitute infringement in one country may not be an infringement in another country.", 'Intellectual property and the National Information Infrastructure: The Report of the Working Group on Intellectual Property rights' (*United States Patent and Trademark Office*, 8 January 2007) available at <http://www.uspto.gov/web/offices/com/doc/ipnii/> (accessed 10 December 2009).

[126]ibid, The paper, however, never described the Berne Protocol or the New Instrument; Wayman (n 6) 445.

[127]Letter from Bruce Lehman, Assistant Secretary of Commerce and Commissioner of Patents and Trademarks in Wayman (n 6).

[128]ibid.

however, did not provide for any proposal of a new database right, and was "the first submission to WIPO" in relation to an international database treaty.[129]

Meanwhile, Europe made own submission for an international database protection at the WIPO. In December 1994, delegates of the European Commission informed the Committee at WIPO about the ensuing Database Directive in Europe, including the enactment of database right for protecting investments in non-original databases.[130] The representatives of the European Commission in September 1995 presented a paper titled "The *sui generis* right provided for in the Proposal for a Directive on the legal protection of databases".[131] In February 1996, the European Commission provided for a proposal harmonizing database right at an international level. The proposal included substantive provisions of the treaty.[132]

In reply to EU's proposal at WIPO, US submitted a treaty proposal on May 23, 1996.[133] This was the 'second submission' of US at the WIPO. For the first time, US proposed for a database right at an international level.[134] Based on the joint proposal submitted by Europe and the United States, a draft database treaty was formulated and distributed in September 1996. This draft treaty was shared among States, Government and Non-Governmental organizations with intention to discuss the same at the diplomatic conference in December 1996.[135] At the diplomatic conference the issue of enacting database legislation was not discussed, however, a recommendation concerning an international treaty on database legislation was adopted. The recommendation highlighted further preparatory work other than suggesting importance of databases.[136] Starting from 1997 to 2005, the idea of an

[129]Pamela Samuelson, 'The U.S. Digital agenda at the World Intellectual Property Organization' (1998) available at <http://people.ischool.berkeley.edu/~pam/courses/cyberlaw98/docs/wipo.pdf> (accessed 12 January 2011).

[130]World Intellectual Property Organisation, 'Basic Proposal for the Substantive Provisions of the Treaty on Intellectual Property in Respect of Databases to be Considered by the Diplomatic Conference' (WIPO, 30 August 1996) available at <http://www.wipo.int/meetings/en/doc_details.jsp?doc_id=2487> (accessed 10 December, 2010).

[131]ibid.

[132]The substantive clauses proposed were similar to the structure of the European Database Directive, World Intellectual Property Organisation 'Proposal Submitted by the European Community and its Member States' (*WIPO,* February 1996) available at <www.wipo.int/mdocsarchives/BCP_CE_VI_1996/BCP_CE_VI_13_E.pdf> (accessed 10 December, 2010); Wayman (n 6) 450–451.

[133]ibid.

[134]Samuelson (n 129).

[135]Diplomatic Conference on Certain Copyright and Neighboring Rights Questions: Basic Proposal for the Substantive Provisions of the Treaty on Intellectual Property in respect of Databases to be considered by the Diplomatic Conference (Geneva, December 2 to 20, 1996) available at <www.wipo.int/edocs/mdocs/diplconf/en/crnr_dc/crnr_dc_6.doc> (accessed 10 January 2010).

[136]Information Meeting on Intellectual Property in Databases: Existing National and Regional Legislation concerning Intellectual Property in Databases (Geneva, September 17 to 19, 2010) available at <http://www.wipo.int/edocs/mdocs/mdocs/en/db_im/db_im_2.pdf> (accessed 10 January 2010).

international treaty was contemplated at various meetings at WIPO but so far nothing of an international treaty concerning legal protection of databases has been adopted.[137] There was no single reason for the situation with database legislation at WIPO. In the opinion of Davison there was no concentrated effort on one particular form of treaty.[138] Although there was obvious support from the European Union and its member states, there were many developing countries including India and China that opposed any change in the existing legal system without substantial evidence suggesting inclusion of *sui generis* database right.[139] Mark Davison further suggested that concerns of the developing countries and countries that opposed database right should be addressed before the passage of an international treaty.[140] These concerns mostly were related to access to information for educational, scientific and research purposes and information that were produced with public funds.[141] This delayed the process and ultimately there was no consensus on the issue of an international treaty on the protection of non-original databases.[142] Similar arguments were made by Annemarie Beunen.[143]

To understand the reasoning as to why the initiative at the WIPO did not materialize into an international treaty one has to divide the entire period of deliberations into number of stages. At the initial stages when the proposal was presented to the member countries at WIPO, sufficient time was not given to the participants.[144] One can relate this to the subsequent event where the issue of database legislation was not at all discussed at the diplomatic conference in December 1996 for which it was slated.[145] The deliberation on the topic only started once the Committee of Experts at the WIPO commissioned the International Bureau to prepare a document on the existing national laws and legislations

---

[137] For instance, Standing Committee on Copyright and Related Rights: A Study on the Impact of Protection of Unoriginal Databases on Developing Countries: Indian experience (Geneva, may 13-17, 2002) available at <www.wipo.int/edocs/mdocs/copyright/en/sccr_7/sccr_7_5.pdf> (accessed 10 January 2010); Standing Committee on Copyright and Related Rights (Geneva, June 23 to 27, 2003) available at <http://www.wipo.int/edocs/mdocs/copyright/en/sccr_9/sccr_9_11.pdf> (accessed 15 January, 2010); Standing Committee on Copyright and Related Rights (Geneva, Nov 21 to 23, 2005) available at <www.wipo.int/edocs/mdocs/copyright/en/sccr_13/sccr_13_6.doc> (accessed 15 January 2010).

[138] Davison (n 67) 231.

[139] ibid 231–233.

[140] ibid 234.

[141] ibid 233–234.

[142] ibid 233–234.

[143] Annemarie Beunen, *Protection for databases: The European Database Directive and its effects in Netherlands, France and United Kingdom* (Wolf Legal Publishers Leiden 2007), 21–22.

[144] The draft treaty was distributed amongst member countries in September 1996 for the December conference.

[145] Information Meeting on Intellectual Property in Databases: Existing National and Regional Legislation concerning Intellectual Property in Databases (Geneva, September 17 to 19, 1997) available at <http://www.wipo.int/edocs/mdocs/mdocs/en/db_im/db_im_2.pdf> (accessed 15 January 2010).

protecting databases.[146] The deliberation died down in 2005 with the withdrawal of the item of database legislation from the agenda list.[147] It was a gradual process and was an outcome of anxiety and lack of participation involving a large number of countries. Anxiety resulted because there was no clear indication of what might result out of implementing legislation protecting unoriginal databases.[148] For instance, the delegation of Indonesia representing countries in Asia and Pacific said that there was no clear indication of whether database legislation was required at national, regional and international level. In their opinion more information was required in the context of research, education and keeping data in the public domain.[149] Although Europe came out with Database Directive, there was no indicative evidence suggesting the benefit of such legislation. Other than presentations of the European member states suggesting that database legislation was helpful and provided extra incentive to the database producers, there was no empirical evidence corroborating the claims made in those presentations.[150] United States presentations were equally not convincing, since there was nothing concrete in terms of results. US, in fact was still debating on the nature of protection.[151] Therefore, it was difficult for them to suggest the right kind of protection.[152] There was enough deliberation at the initial stages followed by regional studies, covering Asia, pacific and developing countries but all of these did not go beyond the stage of reports.[153] Broadly these reports suggested that the requirement of a database right was unproven.[154] The fact that the issue of database legislation remained so long could possibly give the impression that issue of database was discussed till

---

[146]ibid.

[147]Standing Committee on Copyright and Related Rights (Thirteenth Session, Geneva, November 21 to 23, 2005) available at <http://www.wipo.int/edocs/mdocs/copyright/en/sccr_13/sccr_13_6.pdf> (accessed 15 January 2010) (SCCR 13(6), November 2005).

[148]Standing Committee on Copyright and Related Rights (Third Session, Geneva, November 16 to 20, 1999) available at <http://www.wipo.int/edocs/mdocs/copyright/en/sccr_3/sccr_3_11.pdf> (accessed 15 January, 2010) (SCCR 3(11), November 1999).

[149]ibid.

[150]For instance, ibid; SCCR 3(11), November 1999 (n 148).

[151]*Supra* section 4.4.

[152]Davison (n 67) 232.

[153]Standing Committee on Copyright and Related Rights: The Impact of Protection of Non-original Databases on the Countries of Latin America and the Caribbean (Geneva, November 4 to 8, 2002) available at <http://www.wipo.int/edocs/mdocs/copyright/en/sccr_8/sccr_8_6.pdf> (accessed 20 January 2010); Five studies commissioned by the Secretariat at WIPO by the following experts in India, Egypt, US, China and Denmark, Standing Committee on Copyright and Related Rights (Geneva, May 13 to 17, 2002) available at <http://www.wipo.int/edocs/mdocs/copyright/en/sccr_7/sccr_7_10.pdf> (accessed 20 January 2010) (SCCR 7(10), May 2002).

[154]ibid.

2005.[155] In reality, there was not much discussion after 2002.[156] There was lack of participation and the reading of reports suggests that there was no initiative taken by member countries of WIPO to move the international treaty covering databases. The issue was left in the agenda for member states to share their ideas and experiences with reports covering production of databases in their respective countries.[157]

During the time of the debate at WIPO, Congressman Moorhead proposed for the Database Investment and Intellectual Property Antipiracy Bill in the US.[158] While there was a concentrated effort to execute international database legislation, publishers were heavily investing towards production of databases both in electronic and non-electronic format. For instance, the above sections suggested that Reed Elsevier was investing during the window of 1991–1996.[159] This shows in the period subsequent to *Feist* and first legislative bill in US, that big players like Reed Elsevier had engaged themselves in business development. It is difficult to fathom that Reed Elsevier could have made those acquisitions without being fairly certain about protecting their investments.[160]

It is difficult to suggest that *Feist* could have been the starting point of the debate in US. Logically without enough protection in place, it is difficult to comprehend commercial investments towards databases. If any negative jurisprudence of *Feist* had been a reason to worry for publishers, then investments would not have taken place.[161] There must have been enough incentive for producers, since a substantial period of inactivity with respect to proposing similar *sui generis* right existed after *Feist*.[162]

There was an overall acceptance of *Feist* decision as the law of the land, since there was limited consultation about enacting database legislation similar to the one in Europe.[163] The passage of Database Directive in Europe acted as an example, and provided an opportunity to enact similar database legislation in US. Going by the acceptance of *Feist* decision it is difficult to comprehend after *Feist*, publishers

[155] SCCR 13(6), November 2005 (n 147).

[156] SCCR 7(10), May 2002 (n 153); Standing Committee on Copyright and Related Rights (Geneva, November 4 to 8, 2002) available at <http://www.wipo.int/edocs/mdocs/copyright/en/sccr_8/sccr_8_9.pdf> (accessed 10 January 2010); Standing Committee on Copyright and Related Rights (Geneva, June 23 to 27, 2003) available at <http://www.wipo.int/edocs/mdocs/copyright/en/sccr_9/sccr_9_11.pdf> (accessed 15 January 2010); Standing Committee on Copyright and Related Rights (Geneva, June 7 to 9, 2004) available at <http://www.wipo.int/edocs/mdocs/copyright/en/sccr_11/sccr_11_4.pdf> (accessed 10 January 2010).

[157] ibid.

[158] Database Investment and Intellectual Property Antipiracy Act of 1996, House Bill 3531.

[159] *Supra* section 4.3.

[160] Reed Elsevier Annual Reports, *Supra* section 4.3.

[161] ibid.

[162] *Supra* section 4.2.

[163] Started with first proposal with the enactment of the Database Directive in 1996, COM (92) 24 final and Council Directive 96/9/EC.

came to know about the existing law.[164] In the previous chapter through several arguments we have come to the conclusion that *Feist* was a clarification and reinstatement of known position.[165]

At the initial stages of the American database debate, database right could have been a strong point of influence, since it has been established that *Feist* influence was negligible.[166] The first bill protecting databases was introduced in the US in the month of May, which was after the passage of the Directive in March and the WIPO debates as discussed above did not start until 1997. The argument of influence of the EU database right is also strengthened for a different reason. The database right has a reciprocity provision, which meant that databases originating outside the EU could only be protected under database right, if there was a similar legislation in their country of origin.[167] This implied that unless US thought of bringing about a database right, US databases would not receive protection in the EU.

Without the database right as a direct influence in American database debate, it seems that the prolonged debate could be different without such right in place. Other than influence of EU database legislation, there is a WIPO perspective attached to US database bill of 1996 and one has to observe whether the process of WIPO started the debate in the US.[168]

Through the process of harmonization at WIPO, there was a definite attempt to bring about database legislation.[169] As a WIPO signatory, any WIPO treaty would be incorporated in the US national law. The reason behind starting the WIPO initiative was less likely to be *Feist*, since the process did not start until about five years subsequent to *Feist* decision.[170] Further, in the draft international treaty it was stated that commercial databases would meet the threshold of *Feist*.[171] There was a different reason that triggered the WIPO process. There was no example of database right in the world until it was enacted in EU. In the US, the WIPO process was initiated in May 1996, and this step was subsequent to the enactment of European

---

[164] *Supra* chapter 2.

[165] *Supra* chapter 3.

[166] Dov Greenbaum, 'Are We Legislating Away Our Scientific Future? The Database Debate', (2003) 2 *D*uke *L*aw *& T*echnology *R*eview 1-15, available at <http://scholarship.law.duke.edu/dltr/vol2/iss1/20> (accessed 7 October 2010); Xuqiong Wu, 'E.C. Data Base Directive' (2002) 17 Berkeley Tech LJ 571, 572 available at <http://scholarship.law.berkeley.edu/cgi/viewcontent.cgi?article=1368&context=btlj> (accessed 7 October, 2010).

[167] Article 11, Council Directive 96/9/EC; Ewan J Nettleton and Harjinder S Obhi, 'Can US Companies Protect their Databases in Europe with Database Right' (2002) CW 121.

[168] *Supra* section 4.4.1.

[169] ibid.

[170] *Supra* section 4.2.

[171] Diplomatic Conference on Certain Copyright and Neighboring Rights Questions: Basic Proposal for the Substantive Provisions of the Treaty on Intellectual Property in respect of Databases to be considered by the Diplomatic Conference (Geneva, December 2 to 20, 1996) available at <www.wipo.int/edocs/mdocs/diplconf/en/crnr_dc/crnr_dc_6.doc> (accessed 10 January 2010), para 1.09.

Database Directive in March 1996.[172] Therefore, the developments at WIPO resulted as a reaction to EU database legislation.[173] It is also clear that the chain of events happening at the WIPO around 1996 represents that the American effort was only as a reaction to the steps taken by Europe.[174]

The database legislation in Europe was a major, and perhaps, the only influence that started database debate in US. As a result, the immediate action in the US was to incorporate similar legislation through the WIPO route.[175] Effectively database right in EU took centre stage, instead of *Feist*. The interest for enacting database legislation in the US stemmed from the presence of database right in EU, and from a possible competitive disadvantageous position for US produced databases.[176]

Subsequent to the failure of an international database treaty at WIPO, two cases initiated the second stage of American database debate in 1997–98.[177] These decisions were based on the ruling of *Feist*.

4.4.2 *Effect of* Warren Publishing *and* Matthew Bender

Database producers raised fresh arguments for database legislation in US subsequent to two US 2nd Circuit and 11th Circuit decisions in 1997–1998.[178] The decisions in *Warren Publishing* and *Matthew Bender & Co. v. West Publishing Co* (*Matthew Bender*)[179] followed the principles of *Feist*. These decisions, especially the *Warren Publishing* case initiated the second string of database bill in 1998.[180] The case of *Warren Publishing* has already been discussed in the previous chapter.[181] This section will only consider the effect of *Warren Publishing* case, since the *Matthew Bender* case concerned similar situation.[182]

---

[172]'US Copyright Office: Report on Legal Protection for Databases: August 1997' available at <www.copyright.gov/reports/db4.pdf> (accessed 30 November 2016).

[173]Thakur (n 6) 102.

[174]*Supra* section 4.4.1.

[175]ibid.

[176]Thakur (n 6) 102; Citing the competitive disadvantage, John Tessensohn, 'The Devil's in the Details: The Quest for Legal Protection of Computer Databases and the Collections of Information Act' (1997-98) 38(3) IDEA Intell Prop L Rev 439, 466.

[177]*Supra* section 4.4.

[178]*Warren Publications, Inc v. Microdos Data Corp*, 115 F3d 1509 (11th Cir 1997) (*Warren Publishing*); *Matthew Bender & Co. v. West Publishing Co.*, 158 F.3d 674, (2d Cir.1998).

[179]*Warren Publications* (n 178); *Matthew Bender* (n 178).

[180]'US Copyright Office: Report on Legal Protection for Databases: August 1997' available at <www.copyright.gov/reports/db4.pdf> (accessed 30 November 2016).

[181]*Supra* section 3.3.

[182]In the case of *Matthew Bender* (n 178), *West Publishing* published compilations of case reports. The contentious issue in this case involved judicial opinions, which was claimed copyrightable by West. The 2nd circuit held that alterations undertaken by West in this regard involved the addition and arrangement of facts. In relation to arrangement, the effort on the part of West was merely

Due to the *Warren Publishing* case in 1997, the US Copyright Office, under the advice of Senator Orrin Hatch, published a report concerning the issue of database protection.[183] It has been suggested that in terms of lobbying, publishers had negligible presence in Washington immediately after *Feist*.[184] There was evidence to suggest that under the aegis of the Information Industry Association in US, publishers did initiate the lobbying process in response to the European initiative surrounding the Database Directive.[185] Further, subsequent to the *Feist* decision there was some discussion that happened on the part of the database providers.[186]

The arguments posed immediately after *Warren Publishing Case*, in favour of a new legislation, were not based on sound reasoning. The argument that publishers were unable to proceed with database legislation in US is weak and would essentially mean that only anticipation fuelled investment towards databases, even after six years subsequent to *Feist* decision.[187] After the EU Directive they had a stronger basis for having similar database legislation in the US.[188] It would be difficult to establish a link between continuous investment and future database legislation. The link between the two is unlikely, since it takes considerable length of time to pass legislation in US.[189] Moreover, this argument essentially indicates that publishers would wait for future database legislation to protect their current investments.

A report funded by publishers suggests that even though empirical data after *Feist* decision confirms prosperity of US database market, such situation does not exclude the requirement of statutory protection of databases in the US. According to the report, database market developed in the US because publishers anticipated future legislative measures.[190] Although there was production after *Feist*, market performed at a sub-optimal level due to inadequate protection of comprehensive useful databases.[191] Based on *Warren Publishing* case, the publishers demanded adequate

(Footnote 182 continued)

re-arrangement of data in those judicial opinions. Thus, the only way to assess creativity in the compilation of West depended on selection or arrangement. In this context, such selection or arrangement lacked minimum creativity as it was obvious and typical and hence, there was no copyright infringement.

[183]'US Copyright Office: Report on Legal Protection for Databases: August 1997' available at <www.copyright.gov/reports/db4.pdf> (accessed 30 November 2016).

[184]Stephen M Maurer and others 'Europe's database right experiment (2001) 294 Science (26 October 2001) 769-770.

[185]Steven J Metalitz, 'Response of the Information Industry Association for the Hearing on Databases Chapter 6 of the Green Paper on Copyright and the Challenge of Technology' in Jon A Baumgarten (ed) *'Fact' and Data Protection After Feist* (Prentice Hall Law & Business, New Jersey 1991).

[186]Robert A Simons, 'Industry Impact (Database Providers)' in Jon A Baumgarten (ed) *'Fact' and Data Protection After Feist* (Prentice Hall Law & Business, New Jersey 1991).

[187]*Supra* section 4.2.

[188]Bitton (n 56) 93 and 96.

[189]The database debate continued for a period of more than eight years.

[190]Tyson and Sherry (n 65).

[191]ibid.

database protection.[192] A report in the Financial Times even observed drop in share prices of Reed Elsevier.[193] The newspaper report that focused on share prices of Reed Elsevier must be re-visited. Reed Elsevier confirmed that drop in share price and the case of *Warren Publishing* were two separate incidents.[194] There was no negative effect in case of Reed Elsevier, although Warren Publishing and Reed Elsevier belonged to similar publishing business.[195] The reason behind such difference in impact may be due to the business models adopted by the respective companies. We have noticed that to suit electronic age, Reed Elsevier developed new business models during the transition from print to electronic media. If the Annual Reports of Reed Elsevier for 1997–98 are considered, one clearly observes a shift in business policy in the context of changes required in the electronic age.[196] The adopted business method in *Warren Publishing* case was not similar to the standard adopted by Reed Elsevier. Warren published a directory comprising of information about US cable television network. The directory was non-electronic in nature, something similar to the type of telephone directory that was published by Rural publishing in the *Feist* decision.[197] This was not however the trend adopted by publishing houses at the time of the decision in *Warren Publishing*. Publishing houses, including Reed Elsevier, and Thomson were engaged in manufacturing products that heavily depended on existing technology.[198] Greater emphasis was placed on the presentation of information contrary to just relying on mere collection of information as was done by Warren.[199] It is clear that Warren was relying on outdated business methods. This policy would have eventually decreased their market competitiveness, and was not sustainable for a long time.[200] These decisions do not highlight the problem of data piracy, but only reflects the inability of the business model to compete with market requirement in the information age.[201] This situation indicated that business houses were lagging behind in adopting new business methods that were imperative to sustain themselves in the internet age.[202] It seems correct to contend that outdated business model cannot be a good justification for new legislation.[203] Cases, similar to the one in *Warren Publishing*, were examples of publishers who failed to meet the

---

[192]115F3d 1509 (11th cir 1997).

[193]Raymond Snoddy, 'Reed Elsevier Shares Drop on US Legal Ruling' Financial Times, 23 May 1997.

[194]ibid.

[195]*Supra* section 4.3.

[196]Reed Elsevier annual report 1997 (n 95).

[197]*Feist Publications* (n 86).

[198]'Thomson annual report 1998' available at <https://bib.kuleuven.be/files/ebib/jaarverslagen/Thomson_1998.pdf> (accessed 10 December 2010).

[199]Reed Elsevier annual report 1997 (n 95).

[200]Bitton (n 56) 146.

[201]ibid 169.

[202]ibid.

[203]In agreement with Bitton (n 56) 169.

requirement of the information age. Introduction of new legislation is not desirable to protect publishing industries that are not competent enough to survive market transformation.[204] As to the *Warren Publishing*, opponents argued that the eleventh circuit reached to a wrong conclusion by misapplying copyright law.[205] While *Warren Publishing* started fresh rounds of debate in US, there was no explanation as to why cases like *BellSouth*, which were similar to the decision in *Warren Publishing*, never prompted for database legislation in US.[206] Moreover, there was no pressing need for database legislation after *Feist*.[207] Again, one observes no real position of *Feist* or the new cases in the second stage of American database debate.

Database legislative efforts in US received vociferous opposition. The Collections of Information Antipiracy Act introduced in 1997 largely received

---

[204]In the words of David Fewer, "Legislating windfalls and sheltering markets from the rigours of competition through *sui generis* property rights, especially in the absence of market failure or a pressing social need, cannot be easily squared with traditional notions of democratic governance and responsible policy-making", Fewer (n 106) 165 and 180.

[205]This case was especially considered by the proponents of the database bill in 1998. The opponents did concede that *Warren Publishing* was wrongly decided but argued that one decision does not call for new legislation; *Supra* (n 121).

[206]One has to remember that *Warren Publishing* and the *Bellsouth Advertising & Publishing* reach the same conclusion, although different approach was followed, *Warren Publishing* (n 178); *BellSouth Advertising & Publication Corp v Donnelley Information Publishing Inc*. 999 F2d 1436 (11th Cir 1993). In the case of *Bellsouth Advertising & Publishing* the 11th circuit held that the act of inserting the information in the yellow pages telephone directory in a computer did not constitute any infringement. The claimant said that selection has been made by following certain parameters and the listings were not exhaustive. Nevertheless, the court held that the selection level did not meet the requirement of *Feist*. The decision of this case is questionable, since the 11th circuit court in *Southern Bell Telephone* found copyright infringement in yellow pages directory, *Southern Bell Telephone v. Associated Telephone* 756 F 2d 801 (11th Cir. 1985) 809. In this case, the *Feist* criteria was fulfilled by "... preparing artwork and layout, and in the selection, compilation and arrangement of the information contained therein".

[207]Ian Kyer and Steve Moutsatsos, 'Database Protection: The Old world heads off in a new direction' (1993) 9(1) CLSR 11; Shelly Warwick in her PhD thesis have successfully argued that there was little evidence to support the need to provide greater legal protection for factual works subsequent to the *Feist* decision, especially in the presence of available legal and technological protection. Based on *Feist* enacting database protection law in US would be unnecessary, unconstitutional and poor policy, Shelly Warwick, 'The Judicial Influence and Policy Implications of *Feist* in regard to the protection of Databases and Compilations'(PhD thesis, Graduate School-New Brunswick, Rutgers, The State University of New Jersey 1999); Similar contention has been raised, while using trespass to chattels in solving database protection case (*eBay v Bidders' Edge* 100 FSupp 2d 1058(ND Ca 2000)) and Computer Fraud and Abuse Act as amended in 1996 (*Register.com v Verio* 126 F Supp 2d 238(SNDY Dec 12 2000), Jonathan Band, 'New theories of database protection'(March 2003) Managing Intellectual Property 1; Contrary to the above outlined viewpoints legislation has been regarded as the way after the *Feist* decision, James E Schatz and others, 'What's mine is yours? The dilemma of factual compilations' (1991–92) 17(2) U Dayton L Rev 423, 439–440; In the absence of empirical evidence, the proposition that there is a problem with database protection, is unclear, Jacqueline Lipton, 'Databases as Intellectual Property: New Legal Approaches' (2003) 25(3) EIPR 139, 773 and 825.

criticisms. It was believed that the legislation appeased publishing houses.[208] In particular, opposition was against LexisNexis (owned by Reed Elsevier) and West Publishing (owned by Thomson).[209] Starting from 1998 onwards the representatives of the districts of North Carolina and Virginia planned for different versions of bill in the House Judiciary Committee.[210] Although American organizations eventually joined the database debate, Reed Elsevier and Thomson were observed as the chief proponents in the debate.[211] Interestingly, the Green Paper on Intellectual property developed by United States Government, which analyzed copyright issues in US, never discussed of adopting something similar to the European Database Directive.[212] Further, the US Chamber of Commerce opposed database legislation and was supported by Dun & Bradstreet, Bloomberg and AT&T.[213] Over the eight years period the opposition grew against any form of database legislation in US.[214]

Feist returned to the forefront after a period of seven years.[215] The opponents said that there was no need for legislation[216] and finds support in the ever-growing US database market.[217] On the other hand, proponents argued that database market in US was performing below par in absence of legislation.[218] One has to remember that the claim of market performance at 'sub-optimal' level was contradictory, since

[208]Nelson (n 58) 469.

[209]ibid.

[210]H.R. 354, (Collections of Information Antipiracy Act, H.R. 354, 106th Cong. (1999)) was introduced by Representative Howard Coble (6th District of North Carolina), and H.R. 1858 (The Consumer and Investor Access to Information Act, H.R. 1858, 106th Cong. (1999)) was introduced by Representative Tom Bliley (7th District of Virginia) in Jonathan Band and Makoto Kono, 'The Database Protection Debate in the 106th Congress' (2001) 62(2) Ohio St L J 869.

[211]Davison (n 67) 261-263; see (n 65); For instance, New York Stock Exchange, NASDAQ in Jonathan Band and Makoto Kono (n 210).

[212]Howard Fogt and others 'An American view on the EU Database Directive' (1995) 46 Managing Intellectual Property 33, 33; Lisa Barr, 'Database Protection Bill' (1997–98) 8(2) DePaul-LCA J Art & Ent 371.

[213]Chamber raises concern over database legislation' (*US Chamber of* Commerce, 22 September 2003) available at <https://www.uschamber.com/press-release/chamber-raises-concern-over-database-legislation> (accessed 10 August 2011).

[214]Jonathan Band and Makoto Kono (n 210).

[215]*Supra* section 4.4.

[216]*Supra* (n 213).

[217]*Supra* section 4.3.

[218](Reference to the words use by register of copyrights) Submission of David O Carson and the contemplation of a gap in the database market, which is difficult to fill up with technology, David O Carson, 'General Counsel, United States Copyright Office before the Subcommittee on courts, the internet and Intellectual Property Committee on the Judiciary and Subcommittee on Commerce, Trade and Consumer Protection Committee on Energy and Commerce, 108th Congress' (*United States Copyright Office*, 23 September 2003) available at <http://www.copyright.gov/docs/regstat092303.html> (accessed 15 September 2009); However, Carson statement, representing the US Copyright Office did not take a position on database legislation in US, although the Copyright Office was sympathetic to the efforts made.

the report funded by publishers admitted that the effect of *Feist* towards this alleged sluggish performance was inconclusive.[219] In the background of ever-growing database industry, the claim of sluggish growth is not convincing. Regardless of expected level of production, influence of *Feist* in the possible problem of market performance is inconclusive.[220] Moreover, the value of database legislation is questionable when market is performing without any negative impact from *Feist* decision.[221]

This chapter outlines rather negligible influence of *Feist* in the US more specifically in the area of production of databases. Argument concerning role of 'sweat of the brow' theory in the production of databases is not conclusive.

---

[219]Tyson and Sherry (n 65).

[220]ibid.

[221]It is arguable to have special database legislation in place under these current circumstances even though other existing means may not provide full proof solution. Jane Ginsburg argues that there is the need of carefully carving out a solution measure for database protection and such solution should also consider the problems associated with the *sui generis* database legislation in Europe, Jane C Ginsburg, 'A marriage of convenience? A comment on the *Protection of Databases*' (2007) 82 (3) Chicago-Kent L Rev 1171, 1178.

Chapter 5
Threshold of Author's Own Intellectual Creation

The harmonization of copyright protection for databases was done in the background of uncertainty with the threshold of originality required for protection of compilations in Europe.[1] The Directive left the meaning assigned to AOIC undefined after the harmonization. At the European level, CJEU interpreted the scope of Article 3 in *Football Dataco* decision.[2] According to CJEU there are certain guidelines to be followed by a database maker to merit copyright protection, but the threshold should be decided by the courts in member states.[3] The CJEU held that scope of Article 3 is only limited to storage and processing of existing data.[4] Article 3 does not apply to creation of data but to the creativity towards selection or arrangement of existing data.[5] As to the threshold, the courts in member states have converged to a uniform standard.[6] Examples suggest that modicum of creativity and non-obvious compilations are two important parameters to meet the threshold requirement.[7]

5.1 *Football Dataco* Case in England

Although Article 3 talks about AOIC towards selection or arrangement of contents, the Directive has been silent about the threshold required for a database to merit copyright protection.[8] It was only after CJEU's interpretation in *Football Dataco*

[1]Council Directive of 1996/9/EC of 27 March 1996 on the legal protection of databases [1996] OJ L 77/20 (Council Directive 96/9/EC), art 3.
[2]*Infra* section 5.2.
[3]ibid.
[4]ibid.
[5]ibid.
[6]*Infra* section 5.3.
[7]ibid.
[8]Council Directive 96/9/EC, art 3.

I. Gupta, *Footprints of Feist in European Database Directive*,
DOI 10.1007/978-981-10-3981-2_5

case that the scope of Article 3 became clear.[9] The decision involved ascertaining the copyrightability of a fixture list. The Court of Appeal in England decided to refer this case to the CJEU for further clarification after the preliminary judgement.[10]

As a part of organizing football matches in England and Scotland, *Football Dataco* Limited published annual fixture lists. The publication involved a two-step process including use of computer software in the second step.[11]. The first step was further divided into three stages. It began by drawing fixture schedule or outlining fixture list by the officials of Football Dataco Limited. This schedule simply listed the dates and optional dates, which were available for holding future matches, and did not involve details of clubs. While deciding dates, officials followed three basic parameters, namely: the start and end of season, total number of matches, and international schedule, alongside other national commitments.[12] At the second stage, clubs used questionnaires to convey their requests for "specific date", "non-specific date" and "pairing" in the context of their home and away matches.[13] These requests dealt with particular date, particular time on a non-specific date, and pairing. The completed questionnaires were then reviewed by the leagues.[14] At the final stage, the complex process of 'sequencing and pairing' was carried out. With the objective to perfect home and away sequence, 'Golden rules' were followed for sequencing the fixture.[15] Through sequencing, *Football Dataco* met most specific requests made by clubs at the second stage.[16] In the pairing grid, potential dates clash were retrieved from the sequence and marked with team names. Amendments were carried out to balance 'date clash' and meet specific date request.[17] After the completion of above stages, a computer program was used to produce readable draft of the fixture list from information stated in the pairing grid and sequencing sheet.[18] The preparation of Scottish fixture league was similar to the English fixture.[19]

---

[9]Case C-604/10 *Football Dataco Ltd v Yahoo! UK Ltd* [2012] ECDR 10, 194 (*Football Dataco*).

[10]*Football Dataco Ltd* v *Yahoo! UK Ltd* [2010] EWCA Civ 1380, [2011] ECDR 9; Article 3 of the Database Directive has been incorporated in the UK under section 3A of the Copyright, Design and Patents Act, 1988.

[11]*Football Dataco Ltd v Brittens Pools Ltd* [2010] EWHC 841(Ch) sections 83–90 (*Football Dataco 2*).

[12]ibid, paras [12]–[13].

[13]ibid, para [14].

[14]ibid.

[15]Golden rules: "i) No club shall have 3 consecutive home or away matches (i.e. no HHH or AAA); ii) In any five consecutive matches no club shall have four home matches or four away matches (e.g. AAHAA) is not permissible; iii) As far as possible, each club should have played an equal number of home and away matches at all times during the season; iv) All clubs should have as near as possible an equal number of home or away matches for mid-week matches", *Football Dataco 2* (n 11) para [10]; ibid, paras [15]–[21].

[16]ibid.

[17]*Football Dataco 2* (n 11) paras [15]–[21].

[18]ibid, para [22].

[19]ibid, para [23].

The defendants, representing of a media company, and two other betting companies were involved in exploiting the fixture lists without a valid license from *Football Dataco.* The claimant alleged infringement on three grounds. First, there was infringement of copyright protection of database, which subsisted under section 3A of Copyright, Designs and Patent Act (CDPA).[20] Alternatively, there was infringement of database right under Article 7.[21] Further, the claimants suggested since the fixture list in question was a literary work, there was an additional copyright infringement. Alternatively, fixture lists were tables or compilations other than databases and thus, copyright subsisted in such list irrespective of database protection. Both parties accepted that a fixture list was a database under Article 1 of the Database Directive.[22]

The Court in England was of the opinion that there was no infringement of database right in the fixture list, and no copyright infringement subsisted in an individual fixture list.[23] Further, there was no separate copyright protection for a fixture list under the category of table or compilations. The only available protection was under database copyright which was section 3A.[24] Similarly, there was no copyright protection for individual fixtures.[25] Protection was only available through selecting or arranging them together in a database.[26] At the preliminary level, Court ruled in favour of *Football Dataco*, citing that the defendants had infringed copyright protection for databases, which subsisted under section 3A.[27]

The Court held that the two-step approach followed to complete the entire work of producing the fixture list was not predictable. Makers of fixture list had carved out a unique solution for a unique challenge, i.e. fixture list for a particular year. The method adopted in this fixture list was a solution only applicable to current fixture, and may not be a solution for a different fixture. Therefore, no rigid criterion could have helped in this situation. Production of fixture was not merely an outcome of labour but there was sufficient creativity to merit copyright protection. This is unlike a telephone directory where there is no scope to show judgement and skill. However, the Court in England at the outset suggested that "significant labour and

[20]Council Directive 96/9/EC; In fact, Football Dataco Limited has been trying to invoke licenses on the basis of copyright ever since the BHB decision, Sarah Wright and Priya Vatvani, 'Death of the Database Right' (2005) 153 CW 8.

[21]ibid; Article 7 conferring database right protection to a database maker has been incorporated in the UK under the Copyright and Rights in Databases Regulations 1997/3032 (CRDR).

[22]*Football Dataco 2* (n 11); The ECJ in the case involving Fixture Marketing case [Case C-444/02 *Fixtures Marketing Ltd v Organismos Prognostikon Agnon Podosfairou (OPAP)* [2005] ECDR 3 (Organismos)], said a fixture list comes under the definition of database under Article 1 of the Directive, 42; Article 1 or the definition of database has been incorporated in the UK under CDPA, section 3.

[23]*Football Dataco 2* (n 11).

[24]ibid, paras [67]–[68].

[25]ibid, para [69].

[26]ibid.

[27]ibid, para [101].

skill" would be required to successfully complete the task of preparing a fixture list.[28]

While interpreting Article 3, the Court observed that selection or arrangement of pre-existing data is covered within the ambit of said Article. Selection decisions taken at the time of creating data, "which necessarily involve adopting one alternative and rejecting others, are properly to be regarded as part of the selection or arrangement of the contents of a database."[29] Thus, selection decisions concerning creation of contents should come under overall selection or arrangement in creating the final database. Leaving out initial selection decisions from overall selection or arrangement would be "…arbitrary and conceptually fraught with difficulty".[30]

Further, Floyd J referred to Recital 19 of the Database Directive, and to the jurisprudence that had developed from decisions of European Courts.[31] According to him, it was essential to question "whether the work of selection and arrangement was author's own intellectual creation. In particular, whether it involved author's judgement, taste and discretion"?[32] In addition, "[was] the work quantitatively sufficient to attract copyright protection"?[33] Therefore, Floyd J believed that threshold requirement of AOIC should be based on both qualitative and quantitative criteria. He based his argument on Recital 19 of the Database Directive which reads:

> …as a rule, the compilation of several recordings of musical performances on a CD does not come within the scope of this Directive … because, as a compilation it does not meet the conditions for copyright protection.[34]

Floyd J said that there was a 'quality' requirement in the Recital. This quality would be missing from a CD comprising of several musical recordings. However, the Recital does not say anything explicit about the requirement to meet the threshold of quality. Floyd J also referred to a passage of a book written by Sir Hugh Laddie, Peter Prescott & Mary Vitoria.[35] In this passage, the authors pointed to the possibility that a quantitative factor is attached to the threshold of selection or arrangement. A subjective contribution describing creativity of the author must be

---

[28]ibid, paras [41]–[44].

[29]ibid, para [74]; This view point is also expressed in the seminal article of Robert Denicola where he says that "the effort of authorship can be effectively encouraged and rewarded only by linking the existence and extent of protection to the total labour of production. To focus on the superficial form of the final product to the exclusion of the effort expended in collecting the data presented in the work is to ignore the central contribution of the compiler". Robert C Denicola, 'Copyright in Collections of Facts : A theory for the protection of nonfiction literary works' (1981) 81(3) Colum L Rev 516, 530; The basis, however, is labour and not adoption of creativity in selection or arrangement as expressed in the *Dataco* case.

[30]Floyd J. in *Football Dataco* 2 (n 11) para [82].

[31]ibid, paras [83]–[90].

[32]ibid, para [91].

[33]ibid.

[34]Council Directive 96/9/EC.

[35]Sir Hugh Laddie and others, *The Modern Law of Copyright and Designs* (3rd edn Butterworths 2000) 1068–1071.

accompanied with qualitative requirement. Citing the example of a 1000 favourite poems of an author, Floyd J said that such a database would pass both qualitative and quantitative test to merit copyright protection under Article 3.[36] Such database, both qualitatively and quantitatively would involve a substantial creative contribution.[37] Number of poems holds the key, since the Recital only restricts protection to 'several' recordings.[38] Based on Recital 19, Floyd J. thus introduced a quantitative test to meet the threshold requirement of AOIC.[39]

Other than introducing quantitative test, Floyd J referred to couple of case law to reflect on the threshold requirement. The case of *Infopaq International A/S v. Danske Dagblades Foreing* (*Infopaq*) decided by the ECJ concluded on a note that extraction of 11 consecutive words of a protected work might constitute infringement under Article 2 of Directive 2001/29.[40] Floyd J said that AOIC could have a less stringent threshold "if that extract [ion] contains an element of the work which, as such, expresses the author's own intellectual creation".[41] He then referred to the decision of German Court in *Pharma Intranet Information AG v. IMS Health GmbH & Co. OHG.*[42] In the context of this case, he suggested that there was a difference between pure deterministic work and a work protected under Article 3. To merit protection, there should be an opportunity to manoeuvre the creative mind by showing intellectual ability. There is not much room required to manoeuvre a work to merit protection - *de minimis should be enough.*[43] Before we go through observations made by CJEU, comments made by Floyd J provide some interesting insights about the threshold requirement.

5.1.1 Selection Process Adopted

The judgement identified the type of work, and overall intellectual ability required on the part of author.[44] Floyd J discarded 'sweat of the brow' argument as a basis

---

[36]It must be remembered that the Directive explicitly said: "no criterion other than originality in the sense of the author's intellectual creation should be applied to determine the eligibility of the database for copyright protection, and in particular no aesthetic or qualitative criteria should be applied", Council Directive 96/9/EC, Recital 16.

[37]Laddie and others (n 35) 1070.

[38]The meaning of several is more than two but not many; Oxford Online Dictionary available at <http://oxforddictionaries.com/> (accessed 12 January 2012).

[39]*Football Dataco 2* (n 11) para [91]; "A computer program shall be protected if it is original in the sense that it is the author's own intellectual creation. No other criteria shall be applied to determine its eligibility for protection", Council Directive 1991/250/EEC of 14 May 1991 on the legal protection of computer programs [1991] OJL122/1, art 1 para 3.

[40]Case C-5/08 *Infopaq International A/S v Danske Dagblades Foreing* [2009] ECDR 16, 261.

[41]ibid, para [87].

[42][2005] ECC 12.

[43]*Football Dataco 2* (n 11) para [90].

[44]*Football Dataco 2* (n 11).

for copyright protection of databases.[45] Merely based on 'sweat of the brow' argument an obvious selection or arrangement in a database would not receive copyright protection. There is no scope for including obviousness within the ambit of copyright protection.[46] However, Floyd J did not explicitly state the tool to assess such intellectual ability.[47] If there should be room to manoeuvre at the time of making a database then there must be more than one way to represent the contents of a database. With the expression limited to one way, there is no scope to manoeuvre, thereby resulting in obvious selection or arrangement of the contents.[48]

A second perspective relates to the position of a database maker. The scope of possible maneuvering of the contents of a database is quite important from the point of a second comer who would like to express the contents of a database in a way which is different from the maker of first database.[49] If no such scope exists, then the outcome of such selection or arrangement would be similar to the first database maker. Therefore, the expression would not be a true reflection of the intellectual ability of the second comer. The intellectual ability of the second person should be distinctly identifiable from the first person.[50]

The case also identified role of a non-human tool that plays a vital role in the making of a database. This raises the issue of an acceptable role of a machine at the time of assessing extent of creativity present in a database. The first draft proposal suggested that there would be selection process on the part of author despite using computer technology at some stage of making the database.[51] The role of computers is inevitable and the fact that a computer is used in a database does not altogether exclude a database from protection offered under Article 3.[52] Even while using computer technology, there would be necessary selection or arrangement to suffice the requirement of creativity. The selection or arrangement process in an electronic database may happen at various stages.[53] It is clear that the entire process of database management would involve certain skill sets on the part of a database maker.[54] In the present case, it was contended that in most situations a computer would fail to provide an ideal solution to a given problem and thus, human intervention was

---

[45]ibid, paras [42]–[43] and [82].

[46]ibid.

[47]ibid, para [90].

[48]This is an objective requirement unlike the subjective requirement under author's right system, Ramon Casas Valles, The requirement of originality in Estelle Derclaye (ed), *Research Handbook on the future of EU Copyright* (Edward Elgar 2009); Daniel J Gervais, '*Feist* goes global: A comparative analysis of the notion of originality in copyright law' (2002) 49(4) Journal of Copyright Society of the US 949, 952.

[49]*Football Dataco 2* (n 11) paras [83]–[90].

[50]ibid.

[51]Commission, 'Proposal for a Council Directive on the legal protection of databases' COM (92) 24 final (COM (92) 24 final), para [3.1.8].

[52]Council Directive 96/9/EC.

[53]*Supra* section 2.3.

[54]ibid.

required to resolve such problems.[55] Therefore, the argument of the Court in saying that using computer as a tool does not altogether eliminate the role of discretion or judgement is viable as long as there is enough scope to incorporate discretion and judgement sufficient to merit copyright protection.[56] It is clear that there was enough maneuvering possible in the steps that were followed prior to using computer for the fixture list.[57] With the available scope of maneuvering, the use of computer at a later stage became an irrelevant question. It is also true that a computer can perform all steps that were followed in the preparation of a fixture list if it is programmed accordingly. This would be a departure from the Court's understanding that a computer could not have performed the entire process of creating a fixture list.[58] Therefore, the issue is not whether a computer can perform the steps that are followed by humans, but much rather whether humans used enough discretion and judgement within the given available opportunity.

5.1.2 The Required Threshold of Creativity

There is some case precedence to the idea that selection or arrangement process starts prior to incorporation of contents in a database.[59] In *Football League Limited v. Littlewoods Pools* [1959], a football fixture was held to be copyrightable by virtue of being a literary work under the Copyright Act of 1956.[60] Labour and skill that facilitated in deciding the day and date of the match was relevant in the context of overall labour and skill expended towards the production of the fixture list. Upjohn J. said there was no need to dissect effort; instead any effort leading to final creation of the fixture list was included in overall effort.[61]

Although both Floyd J. and Upjohn J. agreed on the inclusion of prior effort, in the Football *Dataco* case, only prior intellectual effort concerning the creative selection or arrangement of contents was relevant.[62] Unlike the decision in *Football League Ltd* case, Floyd J. did not consider effort as an argument for copyright protection.[63] By designating type of creativity, Floyd J raised a fundamental question about accepting 'sweat of the brow' as an argument for databases to merit copyright protection.

Other than type of creativity, *Football Dataco* decision touched upon the issue of 'timings of creativity'. The recognition of prior creative work should be an accepted

[55]Mr. Glen Thompson representing the claimants and was the person engaged in pairing and sequencing, *Football Dataco 2* (n 11) para [15].

[56]*Football Dataco 2* (n 11) para [44].

[57]ibid, paras [15]–[21].

[58]ibid, para [86].

[59]ibid, para [82].

[60][1959]1 Ch 637.

[61]ibid, 656.

[62]*Football Dataco 2* (n 11) para [82].

[63]ibid.

norm for any work that merits copyright protection.[64] Disregarding prior work would actually ignore creativity that goes into any work at the inception stage. Also it is difficult to segregate one set of creativity that starts a work from the set of creativity that finishes the work. A person making a database comprising of factual contents would start thinking about selecting or arranging before incorporating contents in the database. It involves a lot of planning and an application of intellectual labour.[65] The final structure and functioning of the database is thus dependent on the extent of creativity involved at initial stages. In the context of Article 3 this is an interesting observation which needs to be further analyzed in the background of the CJEU judgement.

The *Football Dataco* decision has followed an interesting approach, while assessing threshold requirement of AOIC. An author needs to fulfill both quantitative and qualitative criteria to satisfy threshold requirement for copyright protection under Article 3.[66] This conclusion was based on the example of a database consisting of 1000 poems subject to the interpretation of Recital 19 of the Directive.[67] Further, the threshold requirement suggested in *Football Dataco* decision to merit AOIC is not stringent.

In the Database Directive, objective surrounding the existence of Recital 19 is not very clear.[68] Recital 19 apparently limits the scope of the broad definition of a database.[69] CD compilations comprising of recorded musical performances is not excluded per se, since the Recital explicitly mentions 'as a rule'.[70] In fact, a CD with musical recordings does come under the purview of a database.[71]

One needs to question appropriateness of using Recital 19 to understand the threshold of AOIC. This Recital does not clearly state the threshold requirement, except saying that there is no protection for a compilation comprising of 'only' several recordings.[72] The number of recordings required to cross the threshold is not clear. Even if there are more than several recordings, such increase in quantity may not be sufficient. For a database maker, protection may not be available only by increasing number of recordings. The first draft proposal and Recitals of the Directive make it very clear that the only criterion for a database to merit copyright protection is the author's intellectual ability.[73] This ability can only be judged in the

[64]ibid.

[65]ibid.

[66]ibid, (n 11) para [98].

[67]ibid, paras [86] and [90].

[68]Council Directive 96/9/EC.

[69]Mark J Davison, *The legal protection of databases* (Cambridge University Press Cambridge 2003), 73; Irini A Stamatoudi, 'The EU Database Directive: reconceptualising copyright and retracting the future of sui generis right' (1997) 50 Hellenic Rev of Int'l L 435; Laddie and others (n 35) 1070.

[70]ibid.

[71]Davison (n 69) 73.

[72]Council Directive 96/9/EC.

[73]COM (92) 24 final, Recitals 14 and 15, para [3.1.8]; Council Directive 96/9/EC, Recitals 15 and 16.

context of selection or arrangement of the contents.[74] There is no explicit quantitative requirement that needs to be fulfilled prior to copyright protection.[75] Going by 1000 poems example[76] and the argument given in this regard, a compiler with 500 poems is less likely to have copyright protection for his database. Let us think of a given situation where a compiler selects 1000, 500 and 250 poems respectively from a total of 1500 poems. The quantitative argument based on the selection of 1000 poems is not tenable because arguably selecting 500 poems or 250 poems for a database from a total number of 1500 poems may involve greater selection process than choosing a total of 1000 poems. A stricter selection process will considerably increase the chance of copyright protection because such selection is likely to be more creative than selecting 1000 poems.[77] Further, there is no threshold attached to quantitative standard, unlike the qualitative standard which has to be measured against the creativity towards selection or arrangement of contents in a database.[78] As such "Copyright laws do not protect disparate facts, data, or information ..., even when arranged in *large quantities...*".[79] Thus, large quantities or quantitative assessment of collection might have lesser effect in relation to copyrightability of a compilation. Looking at the considerable doubt that exists with quantitative requirement under Recital 19, it is preferable to follow only qualitative threshold instead of additional quantitative approach.[80] Floyd J has himself been circumspect about the scope assigned to Recital 19, since he was unsure about the justification behind unavailability of copyright protection for CDs comprising of several musical recordings.[81] However, in the *BHB* decision Laddie J. said, Recital 19 demonstrates "... a quantitative baseline of originality".[82] In spite of the observations made by Laddie J. in *BHB* decision, the requirement of Article 3 according to the Directive is limited to the qualitative analysis of the intellectual ability.[83] Further, reference to the *Infopaq* decision suggests that a mere composition of 11 words may be sufficiently creative and therefore, questions the

[74]Council Directive 96/9/EC, art 3.

[75]ibid.

[76]ibid, paras [86] and [90].

[77]General idea from the *Feist* case, *Feist Publications v Rural Telephone Service*, 499 US 340 (1991).

[78]Council Directive 96/9/EC, Art 3.

[79]Jerome H Reichman and Pamela Samuelson, 'Intellectual Property Rights in data?' (1997) 50(1) V and L Rev 51, 72.

[80]ibid.

[81]*Football Dataco 2* (n 11) para [84].

[82]"...Although there is no requirement to demonstrate aesthetic or qualitative criteria, there must be a quantitative baseline of originality before protection is acquired" [2001] RPC 31 at [28]; this decision is considered in section 7.3.

[83]Council Directive 96/9/EC, Recital 15 and 16.

quantitative baseline argument.[84] The *Infopaq* decision essentially points to the qualitative aspect involved in choosing those 11 words.[85]

Football Dataco's interpretation of the AOIC threshold, with reference to cases in Europe suggests the expected level of creativity. One can understand the reason behind considering *Infopaq* case, since ECJ indicated the threshold that may represent intellectual creation of an author.[86] As per the standard determined by ECJ, a composition of 11 words may be sufficiently original to merit copyright protection.[87] This threshold may serve as an example to decide future copyright cases concerning protection of databases. Going by the reference of *Infopaq* case, Floyd J provided an example of how threshold could be portrayed at the European level. An analogy has been drawn with space to manoeuvre.[88] It represents existing and available opportunity for a producer with reference to creativity in selection or arrangement. While the existing opportunity is for the first producer who comes up with a database, the available opportunity is for the second comer who is interested in producing similar database as the first maker. After using the existing opportunity, if the first database maker produces a database which is purely deterministic in nature, then there is no copyright protection in such database.[89] This reflects that there was not much room to manoeuver for the database maker. Copyright protection is thus linked with existing opportunity. For the second database maker, there may be enough opportunity to show creativity if there is existing opportunity for the first maker. To merit copyright protection, database makers do not require much room, i.e. not much of an opportunity is required to express their creativity.[90] The *Football Dataco* case in England tends to support modicum of creativity required for databases to merit copyright protection.

Further to the preliminary ruling, the Court of Appeal in England referred *Football Dataco* case to the CJEU for further interpretation. The Court of Appeal held that the person responsible for sequencing and pairing had to work within a rigid structure of pre-conceived rules.[91] However, the entire process was far from being purely mechanical.[92] The Court was happy with the reasonable amount of

---

[84]*Infopaq International* (n 40).

[85]ibid.

[86]ibid.

[87]This decision was based on the Copyright Directive (2001/29/EC) where the ECJ said, "storing an extract of a protected work comprising 11 words "may amount to reproduction under copyright, if the elements thus reproduced are the expression of the intellectual creation of their author", Infopaq International (n 40) 272-273.

[88]*Football Dataco 2* (n 11) paras [89]–[90].

[89]ibid, para [90].

[90]ibid.

[91][2010] EWCA Civ 1380, [2011] ECDR 9, para [4].

[92]ibid; Rachel Montagnon and Mark Shillito, 'Requirements for subsistence of database copyright and other national copyright in databases referred to the ECJ: Football Dataco v Yahoo!' (2011) 32 (5) EIPR 324,324.

creativity that was present within the rigid structure.[93] At the hearing, the claimant argued that making of the fixture list, involved selection or arrangement of existing data within the meaning of Article 3. The selection process involved matches played on a particular date, and the work was sufficiently creative and individualistic to merit copyright protection.[94] The defendants contended that the selected data was not 'pre-existing', and suggested that "giving a date to a match (e.g. Arsenal v Chelsea on 26th April) [would amount to] creating data, not selecting or arranging it".[95] Looking at the confusion surrounding interpretation of the section under CDPA, the Court of Appeal in England referred the matter to the CJEU. In the context of Article 3(1), the Court of Appeal asked two questions in particular:

1. "What is meant by "databases which, by reason of the selection or arrangement of their contents, constitute the author's own intellectual creation" and in particular:

(a) Should the intellectual effort and skill of creating data be excluded?
(b) Does "selection or arrangement" include adding important significance to a pre-existing item of data (as in fixing the date of a football match);
(c) Does "author's own intellectual creation" require more than significant labour and skill from the author, if so what?

2. Does the Directive preclude national rights in the nature of copyright in databases other than those provided for by the Directive?"[96]

The first question, 1 (a), relates to created and pre-existing data. Specifically the Court asked whether data created should come under the scope of Article 3.1 (b). It questions whether selection or arrangement involves adding important significance to pre-existing data, while 1 (c) questions the threshold of AOIC. The final question would confirm whether copyright protection is still available to compilations other than protection conferred under Article 3.[97]

5.2 CJEU Observation in *Football Dataco*

According to CJEU, protection under Article 3 is for 'structure' of the database and does not extend towards contents. This is similar to protection offered under Article 10 (2) of the Trade-Related Aspects of Intellectual Property Rights (TRIPS)

---

[93] [2011] ECDR 9, para [4].

[94] ibid, para [16].

[95] [2010] EWCA Civ 1380, [2011] ECDR 9, para [18].

[96] [2010] EWCA Civ 1380, [2011] ECDR 9, Para [22].

[97] One must remember that tables and compilations are still protected as a literary work in the UK and may be protected separately under the 'sweat of the brow' threshold instead of AOIC under section 3A.

agreement.[98] The Court held that selection and arrangement was a process through which "author of the database gives the database its structure".[99]

At the time of deciding the scope of Article 3, CJEU held that it does not extend to creation of data. "Intellectual effort and skill" towards creation of data "[are] not relevant in order to assess the eligibility of the database that contains them for copyright protection".[100] In fact, the objective under the Directive is to stimulate "creation of data storage and processing systems" and "not to protect the creation of materials capable of being collected in a database".[101] The resources used in *Football Dataco* case were for creation of data and hence, were of little relevance to assess copyrightability of the fixture list in question.[102] However, if creativity at the stage of creating the data is supplemented by "elements reflecting originality in the selection or arrangement of the data contained in the database" then such database may be protected by Article 3.[103]

As to the threshold of originality, a database may merit copyright protection where an author by virtue of selection or arrangement expresses "his creative ability in an original manner by making free and creative choices".[104] Further, the threshold of originality is a matter for courts in the member states to determine.[105] The rulings of the national courts are discussed in the following sections.[106] If the creation of a database is "dictated by technical considerations, rules or constraints, [therefore leaving] no room for creative freedom", then such creativity will not satisfy the threshold criterion.[107] Further, any labour or skill will not be counted, which does not express any original selection or arrangement.[108]

Where there is original expression through selection or arrangement, it is irrelevant for the purpose of the Directive, "whether or not that selection or arrangement includes 'adding importance significance' to that data".[109] It is clear that CJEU have

---

[98]'Agreement on Trade-Related Aspects of Intellectual Property Rights: Part II—Standards concerning the availability, scope and use of Intellectual Property Rights' (World Trade Organisation) art 10(2), available at <http://www.wto.org/english/tratop_e/trips_e/t_agm3_e.htm> (accessed 22 November 2008); The Article states, "Compilations of data or other material, whether in machine readable or other form, which by reason of the selection or arrangement of their contents constitute intellectual creations shall be protected as such. Such protection, which shall not extend to the data or material itself, shall be without prejudice to any copyright subsisting in the data or material itself".

[99]*Football Dataco* (n 9) 193.

[100]ibid.

[101]ibid 185.

[102]ibid 194.

[103]ibid.

[104]ibid 185.

[105]ibid 184.

[106]*Infra* section 5.3.

[107]*Football Dataco* (n 9) 193 and 185.

[108]ibid.

[109]ibid 194.

moved away from the decision and argument of the Court of the first instance in England. Their position in *Football Dataco* case needs further analysis.

5.2.1 Creativity in Data Creation

According to CJEU, there is no protection for creation of data under the provisions of Article 3.[110] In the same case, the Court of First Instance in England stated that creativity starts prior to selection or arrangement of the contents in a database.[111] Selection decisions taken while creating data, "which necessarily involve adopting one alternative and rejecting others, are properly to be regarded as part of the selection or arrangement of the contents of a database."[112] CJEU advocated for a separate set of creativity at the time of selecting or arranging data in the database.[113] Going by the interpretation of the Court in England there is a given opportunity for majority of databases to merit copyright protection.[114] This is because the Court held that modicum of creativity requirement covers all intellectual efforts at all stages of the production of a database.[115] By excluding creativity in data creation, CJEU essentially has curtailed the scope of Article 3. One has to understand that with respect to copyright protection, fundamentally, CJEU did not disagree with the proposition that creativity begins prior to selection or arrangement. Such argument, however, does not extend towards the provision of Article 3.[116] This Article is limited to incentivize creation of data storage and processing and not creation of data itself.[117] From the interpretation of CJEU, it seems that the objective behind enacting this Directive is used to encourage collection of data for the end-user.[118] The argument is wholly and squarely based on the interpretation of Recital 12.[119]

---

[110]ibid 194.

[111]*Football Dataco* 2 (n 11) para [82].

[112]ibid para [74]; This view point is also expressed in the seminal article of Robert Denicola where he says that "the effort of authorship can be effectively encouraged and rewarded only by linking the existence and extent of protection to the total labour of production. To focus on the superficial form of the final product to the exclusion of the effort expended in collecting the data presented in the work is to ignore the central contribution of the compiler". Denicola (n 29) 530; The basis, however, is labour and not adoption of creativity in selection or arrangement as expressed in the *Dataco* case.

[113]*Football Dataco* (n 9) 194.

[114]It appears from the explanatory memorandum to the proposal that the Commission expects most databases to fulfil the necessary criteria for copyright protection" Elizabeth Weightman and Jean Hughes, 'EC Database protection: fine tuning the Commission's Proposal' (1992) 14(5) EIPR 147, 148.

[115]*Football Dataco* 2 (n 11) para [90].

[116]*Football Dataco* (n 9) 193.

[117]ibid.

[118]ibid.

[119]ibid.

5.2.2 *Creativity and Single-Sourced Database*

For single-sourced database producers, the requirement of separate creativity under Article 3 is particularly challenging. These producers create data before using them as contents in their database.[120] No amount of initial creativity towards the creation of data will justify protection under Article 3. Single-sourced database producers will have to ensure the application of creativity subsequent to the creation of data, and in the context of selection or arrangement of the created data.[121] Based on the CJEU observation, there may be additional burden on single-sourced database producers before they could claim copyright protection for their databases. The additional burden on database producers is not new in the context of the Directive. There has been similar ruling in the case involving application of Article 7.[122] This ruling may seem to go against the general idea of providing incentive to the producers. However, one observes consistency in both the decisions of the CJEU. The position of single-sourced database producers is further analyzed in the final chapter.[123]

5.3 Overview of AOIC Threshold

There are similarities to what Floyd J said to the observation made by CJEU. In fact, the judgement mostly re-iterated the argument of the Court in England, especially with reference to obviousness and role of computer.[124] The threshold is a matter to be decided by the member courts as long as the general guidelines are followed.

There have been some diverging opinions amongst commentators as to the AOIC. Scholars like Koumantos and Gaudrat have suggested a low threshold requirement for AOIC. According to them a database, which is not copied, will receive copyright protection.[125] In the opinion of Jens Gaster all continental European member states would have to lower their existing requirement for copyright protection.[126] Similarly, Common Law member states must raise the bar of existing copyright protection. This gap is certainly not *de minimis*. Selection or arrangement of contents in a database should provide signs of individuality, although to a modest

[120] Like the database in question involving *Fooball* Dataco.

[121] *Football Dataco* (n 9).

[122] British Horseracing case forms a part of the final chapter, *infra* section 7.3.

[123] *Infra* section 7.3.2.

[124] ibid 185 and 194.

[125] G Koumantos, 'Les bases de donnees dans la directive communautaire', 1997/171 RIDA and Ph Gaudrat, 'Loi de transposition de la directive 96/9 du 11 mars 1996 sur les bases de donnees: dispositions relatives au droit d'auteur' (1 partie), RTDcom 1998 in Annemarie Beunen, *Protection for databases: The European Database Directive and its effects in Netherlands, France and United Kingdom* (Wolf Legal Publishers Leiden 2007) 80.

[126] Jens L Gaster ,'The EU Council of Ministers' common position concerning the legal protection of databases: a first comment' (1995) 6(7) Ent L Rev 258, 260.

degree.[127] The standard of copyright protection in member states and their transition to the AOIC threshold have been considered in the next section. There have been other scholars who thought, "personal creativity is required but of not such a high level as traditionally required in Germany, whereas the thresholds of the United Kingdom and Ireland will need raising".[128] The threshold has been "...decidedly ambiguous" and means that creator must embark upon mental ability instead of the usual "humdrum that anyone else might produce".[129]

One can certainly say that not every database will merit copyright protection based on the reasoning that they are not copied from a different database. Otherwise the argument will be based more on 'sweat of the brow' doctrine than the intellectual labour required for copyright.[130] The protection offered under Article 3 is not 'sweat of the brow' standard, since Article 7 is meant for databases that were previously protected under copyright based on 'sweat of the brow' argument.[131] Going by the first evaluation report there is a clear indication that the enactment of Article 3 suggested moving to a different standard by adopting the standard applied in *Droit d' Auteur* countries.[132] It has to be further observed what 'moving away' means and what was the standard like in *Droit d' Auteur* countries, and countries where 'sweat of the brow' was the argument to merit copyright protection.

5.3.1 Member States' Interpretation of Article 3

Article 3 harmonized the threshold of copyright protection for databases.[133] To observe changes after harmonization, the example of three member states are considered in this section. They are UK, France and Germany.

But before going through the substantive requirement of originality in three member states, it is important to understand the fundamental difference that exists in common and civil law system in relation to 'work'.[134] As a prime example of Common Law system, UK provides copyright protection to a list of eight categories of work.[135] In contrast, France as an example of civil law system provides protection

---

[127]ibid 258 and 260.

[128]Beunen (n 125) 76.

[129]William Cornish and others, *Intellectual Property: Patents, Copyright, Trade Marks and Allied Rights* (7th edn. Sweet & Maxwell London 2010) 449.

[130]*Football Dataco* (n 9) 185.

[131]First Evaluation of Directive 96/9/EC, para [1.1].

[132]ibid; Tanya Aplin, *Copyright Law in the Digital Society: the challenges of multimedia* (Hart Publishing 2005) 55.

[133]Council Directive 96/9/EC.

[134]Tanya Aplin, Subject Matter in Estelle Derclaye (ed), *Research Handbook on the future of EU Copyright* (Edward Elgar 2009) 54.

[135]They are: literary, dramatic, musical and artistic works, sound recordings, films, broadcasting and published editions, Copyright Designs and Patent Act, 1988 section 1(1).

to "all works of mind" that emanates from the author.[136] The resulting protection afforded to a work is categorized under different headings, since these two member states follow different ideological grounds.[137] *Copyright* as a term is used in English speaking countries to describe statutory rights and exceptions granted surrounding the use of a work; whereas in civil law jurisdictions it is *Droit d' Auteur* (author's right).[138] Unlike the Common Law, concept of work in civil law jurisdiction is not an object that results from ability.[139] Instead, the author is present in the created work. As a result, work is the outcome of expressive capacity of human beings.[140] For example, in the French system, only authorial work will receive protection and therefore, entrepreneurial works like sound recording, broadcasting will only receive protection under neighbouring rights instead of copyright.[141] However in the UK, copyright also protects sound recordings and broadcasting.[142]

With the already existing differences in the concept of work, introduction of AOIC meant certain changes in the threshold standard followed in member

---

[136]'Article L112-1 of the Intellectual Property Code' (LexInter) available at <http://www.lexinter.net/ENGLISH/intellectual_property_code.htm> (accessed 10 January 2011); Aplin (n 134) 58.

[137]They are "... derived from different philosophies and the spirit in which protection is acquired is not the same", Michel Vivant, Protection of Raw Data and Data Banks in France in Bernt Hugenholtz & Egbert J Dommering (eds) *Protecting Works of Fact: Copyright, Freedom of Expression and Information Law* (Kluwer law and Taxation publishers, 1991) 74; Kevin Garnett, Gillian Davis, Gwilym Harbottle and others (eds) *Copinger and Skone James on Copyright vol1* (Sweet & Maxwell 2011 16th edn) 6; Stating that copyright and droit d' auteur work share a same ground and the conflict is often exaggerated, Valles (n 48) 109; the concept of work is not harmonized at the European level, Valles (n 48); the term work in Europe is at an unknown level, Christian Handig, 'The copyright term "work" – European harmonisation at an unknown level' (2009) 40(6) IIC 665; At the moment it harmonizes only three categories: computer programs, photographs and databases; It is, however, misleading to suggest that copyright laws were passed in France to promote authorship and in the UK were passed keeping in mind a commercial centric approach. Historically both countries shared same philosophy and purpose in relation to the introduction of copyright and "these laws were of a trade-regulatory nature, employed by the authorities to destroy the monopoly enjoyed by a certain groups" in France and UK, Makeen Fouad Makeen *Copyright in a Global Information Society: The Scope of Copyright Protection Under International, US, UK and French Law* (Studies in Law) (Kluwer Law International 2000) 30.

[138]Copinger and James (n 137) 4; JAL Sterling, Comparison of the copyright and author's right systems (8 June 1998) Institute of Advanced Legal Studies, London, offprint collection, shelf number: X0054.

[139]Valles (n 48); the term work in Europe is at an unknown level, Christian Handig (n 137) 110; Owing to harmonisation at the European level, certain aspects of author's right has been incorporated in the UK. For example the introduction of principal director as one of the authors in a film, along with the producer, Copinger and James (n 137) 6.

[140]As a result the author is granted exclusive rights, including moral rights, ibid; under the author's right, alongside economic rights under copyright system, moral rights are entrenched in it, JAL Sterling (n 138).

[141]'Book II of the Intellectual Property Code' (LexInter) available at <http://lexinter.net/ENGLISH/intellectual_property_code.htm> (accessed January 10 2011); ibid, 57; the moral rights in the UK are provided in the CDPA of 1988.

[142]Copinger and James (n 137) 5.

states.[143] The extent of such changes is best understood by looking at the transition to the AOIC standard. This study of transition will be helpful in two ways. First, it will help us to understand the level of consensus among members states with the threshold of AOIC. Second, the decisions of European Courts concerning the threshold of AOIC will also give an insight of the required standard.

In the UK, only an "original work" is entitled to copyright protection.[144] Section 1(1) (a) of the CDPA, 1988 protects a work under copyright if it is original.[145] Despite the specific provision, there have been varied interpretations of the threshold requirement in UK.

In the case of *University of London Press v. University Tutorial Press*, Mr. Justice Peterson held that for an expression to merit copyright protection there was no requirement of originality in novelty sense.[146] For copyright protection to subsist, the work should have originated from the author, and not a copied expression from a different work.[147] Subsequent cases have upheld that a work is original, if sufficient "skill, judgement and labour" has been expended in the sense that the work in question has not been slavishly copied.[148] Thus, there is a link between the concept of originality and the threshold of skill, judgement or labour.[149] There is, however, little uniformity in the application of the threshold requirement. It is a matter of degree and depends on the facts of a particular case.[150] Originality may be an outcome of either substantial or negligible use of skill, labour or judgement.[151] For example, in the *Football League* case chronological list of matches in four divisions successfully passed the copyright grade.[152] For the purpose of the list, the maker took into account various factors like timings of other matches, clubs willing to play under floodlights and ticket sales. In the opinion of Upjohn J, chronological lists like other "...statistical reference matter such as railway time tables, horse breeding material, catalogues, indices, solar and lunar

---

[143]Council Directive 96/9/EC, Art 3.

[144]Cornish and others (n 129) 9.

[145]CPD of 1988; the requirement that a work needs to be 'original' was only added to the Copyright Act of 1911, Cornish and others (n 129) 447; Keeping an eye on compilation, the originality standard is restricted to literary work.

[146][1916] 2Ch 601, 609; this was said while deciding the copyrightability of mathematics question paper.

[147]ibid.

[148]Lord Atkinson in *Macmillan v Cooper* (1923) 93 LJPC 113; Lord Justice Mummery *Sawkins v Hyperion Records* Ltd [2005] EWCA Civ 565 [2005] 1 WLR 3281 para [31].

[149]Lionel Bently and William R Cornish, United Kingdom in Paul Edward Geller and Melville B Nimmer (eds) *International Copyright Law and Practice* (Lexis Nexis 2009 volume 2) 2[1][b][i].

[150]Lord Atkinson said that the amount of skill, labour or judgement is a matter of degree and depends on the facts of a specific case, *Macmillian v Cooper* (1923) 93 LJPC; Lord Devlin in *Ladbroke v William Hill* [1964] 1 WLR 273 has suggested substantial degree of skill, industry or experience; Upjohn J said some amount of labour, skill, labour or ingenuity in Football League v Littlewoods Pools [1959] Ch. 637, 638-639.

[151]ibid.

[152]ibid.

calendar events, reference directories" possess no literary merit.[153] For these compilations some labour, skill, judgement or ingenuity would be sufficient to merit copyright protection. Moreover, there was considerable attention to detail at the time of making the chronological list.[154] Similar to the *Football League* case, in the *Ladbroke* case, football coupons were sufficiently original to merit copyright protection.[155] Although the way of expressing coupons were common to all bookmakers, the Court said that there was a case of copyright infringement. For copyright protection, labour or expense involved in the compilation of football coupon was sufficient.[156] Similar arguments were followed in the *Blacklock* case where copyright protection existed in an alphabetic list of stations.[157] The defendant publishing company did not expend independent labour to collect the names of stations available in the public domain.[158] Instead, they referred to the list developed by the claimants.

There have been instances where originality was held to be insufficient to merit copyright protection. For example, amount of creativity was not sufficient in selecting different colours with minimal writings at the top. The cards had the words 'name' and 'address' and formed a ready insurance reference for employers to arrange the insurance information of employees.[159] Similarly, there was no copyright protection for the title "The Lawyer's Diary" in the absence of enough effort. The plaintiff claimed copyright infringement, since the defendant had a work titled 'Butterworth's Law Diary'.[160]

In UK, compilations are literary work, and receive copyright protection if they are original.[161] The threshold of originality is not stringent, since "...protection has been given under this head to a wide variety of works and originality has seldom been in issue". [162] At present, tables and compilations receive express protection under the CDPA other than explicit protection for databases.[163] Cases have

---

[153]ibid, 650-651.

[154]ibid.

[155]Ladbroke (n 150) 274.

[156]ibid.

[157]H Blacklock & Co Ltd v C Arthur Pearson Ltd [1915] 2 Ch, 376.

[158]ibid.

[159]*Libraco Ltd v Shaw Walker Ltd* (1913) 58 Sol Jo 48.

[160]*Rose v Information Services Ltd* [1987] FSR 254.

[161]Section 3(1) (a) of the Copyright, Designs and Patent Act, 1988, available at <http://www.legislation.gov.uk/ukpga/1988/48/contents> (accessed 10 November 2010); Moreover in the UK, two different originality standards are maintained for 'compilations' and 'databases'. Compilations are protected as a literary work on the basis of the low standard of sufficient 'labour, skill and judgement (while databases for copyright protection follows the new AOIC criterion (section 3(A) (2)), Aplin (n 132) 52-53; Also see Estelle Derclaye, 'Do sections 3 and 3A of the CDPA violate the Database Directive? A closer look at the definition of a database in the U.K. and its compatibility with European law '(2002) 24(10) EIPR 466.

[162]Copinger and James (n 137) 155.

[163]CDPA s3 (1) (a) & (d).

revealed that hard work and labour is sufficient to merit copyright protection in compilations. As a result, over the years, train timetables, street directories and football fixture lists have received copyright protection.[164]

After the implementation of Article 3 there were certain changes made in the threshold of originality. One of the first cases after the implementation was *Mars v. Teknowledge*.[165] The case involved a semi-conductor programmable chip in Mars coin vending machine and the programmed dimension of coins was stored in an Electronically Erasable Programmable Read-Only Memory (EEPROM) device. This programmed data helped in the working of computer program. It was alleged that Teknowledge decrypted the code contained in the chip, thereby infringing copyright and database right. This case, however, did not explain or consider the threshold requirement of AOIC under Article 3. The defendant conceded infringement of database right in EEPROM.[166] The following year in *Sietech Hearing Limited v. Russell Borland, James Eley, Digital Hearing (UK) Limited* a similar pattern was followed regarding the application of database copyright.[167] This case involved a database containing information about supply of hearing aids. The Court upheld the protection of copyright in such database without giving clear explanation.[168] Other than the *Football Dataco* case discussed earlier, one of the recent decisions explaining the threshold of AOIC is *Football Dataco Ltd* v. *Sportradar GmbH*.[169] The claimant *Football Dataco Ltd* produced "Football Live", (hereinafter the *Live Football* case) a database, which provided live information about football matches in UK. The database included the timings of goals scored, players who scored such goals, players who received yellow and red cards, timings of penalty kicks awarded, and information about player substitution in a particular match. It was claimed, ex-professional footballers compiled Football Live and it involved "considerable skill, effort, discretion and/or intellectual input by experienced personnel to generate, select and/or arrange its contents."[170] The defendants

---

[164]The claimants published compilation of a monthly guide of train timetables of various railways in the United Kingdom. It was comprehensive and was indexed alphabetically with numbers. The Court held copyright infringement in the act of copying such factual index. Blacklock (n 157) 376; There was copyright infringement, since the second comer did not expend the same effort in collecting facts similar to the claimant, *Kelly v Morris* [1959] Ch 637.

[165][2000] ECDR 99.

[166]This decision shows that there is a tension between a computer program and database. The Directive clearly says that it will not apply to computer programs used in the making or operation of databases accessible by electronic means, Database Directive 96/9/EC, art 1(3); Davison (n 69) 71.

[167]'Opinion of Lord Macfadyen in '*Sietech Hearing Limited v. Russell Borland, James Eley, Digital Hearing (UK) Limited*' (Court of Session, 19 February 2003) [2003] E.C.D.R. 26.

[168]In *Royal Mail Group Plc. v. i-CD Publishing (UK) Limited* [2003] EWHC 2038, again the matter of threshold was not discussed.

[169][2011] EWCA Civ 330, [2011] 1 WLR 3044; There has been a recent decision between the same parties where *Sportradar* was not held to be jointly liable for UK users who accessed their database, *Football Dataco Ltd* v *Sportradar GmbH* [2012] EWHC 1185 (Ch), [2012] 26 ECC 273.

[170][2011] EWCA Civ 330, [2011] 1 WLR 3044, para [16].

involving a German and a Swiss company (Sportradar) operated a betting website named bet365.com for the UK audience. It was alleged that, the defendants infringed existing copyright protection in the 'Football Live' database. The defendants said there was no act of copying, as they were generating data independently and the act of data collection in 'Football Live' did not involve any intellectual labour. The alleged infringement related to copying of facts.[171] The Court agreed with the defendants and said that copyright protection was not available for 'Football Live' database. There is no copyright protection for factual data that formed a part of the 'Football Live' database. Further, there is no application of intellectual labour towards the collection of such factual data. Recording of a goal out of goalmouth scramble "...may sometimes involve some skill... but it is not creative skill."[172]

With the incorporation of Article 3, there is a change in the originality requirement for copyright protection in UK. This change is more of an introduction of a new standard in the UK, since there is separate protection for table and compilations under the CDPA.[173] There is an effective distinction between databases and compilations under the UK law.[174] Any compilation that fulfills the requirement of database would, however, be covered under the threshold of Article 3. Therefore, it would be incorrect to say that UK has truly moved away from 'sweat of the brow' theory to originality based on selection or arrangement of the contents.[175] However, there would be a transition from the argument based on 'sweat of the brow' theory given that most compilations in UK would come under the broad definition of database.[176]

This transition is analysed and compared against other two jurisdictions in subsequent sections following the threshold discussions that happened in France and Germany. It is clear that insignificant labour towards writing a few words would not meet the threshold for copyright protection.[177] In the UK, most mundane listings would be protected based on effort expended; and a compilation, which is not a database, will receive copyright protection.[178] There is no indication that such effort would require an independent touch from the author portraying his creativity. The decisions suggest that authors using same information available in the public

---

[171]ibid.

[172]ibid.

[173]Section 3A has been introduced to specifically address the requirement of databases, CDPA, 1988 (1988 c. 48).

[174]ibid, section 3(1) (a) of the CDPA still protects table and compilation other than section 3A which protects databases.

[175]Derclaye (n 161).

[176]After the ECJ decision involving Fixtures Marketing "there are several indications of the intention of the Community legislature to give the term database as defined in the directive, a wide scope, unencumbered by considerations of a formal, technical or material nature", *Organismos* (n 22).

[177]*Libraco* (n 159).

[178]For instance, alphabetic list of stations, *Blacklock* (n 157).

domain must expend independent labour, even if they come to similar results.[179] It has been suggested that copyright in this context compensates for lack of unfair competition law in the UK.[180] These decisions, moreover, were set up in competitive situations where there was the possibility of one individual misappropriating the contents of a compilation.[181] The arguments in the aforementioned cases are similar to US decisions based on the 'sweat of the brow' theory.[182] Although unlike US there is no explicit mention of the term 'sweat of the brow', it is more or less certain that the requirement in UK is similar to 'sweat of the brow' standard.[183]

In France, original "work of mind" receives copyright protection. The copyright statute does not define work of mind, but it is something, which originates from intellectual creation reflecting individual contribution.[184] Originality is the fundamental requirement and a general standard in the French copyright law. However, there is no further statutory guidance on the threshold requirement to fulfil originality.[185] Courts in France tend to find originality in the creative choice exercised by an author. Traditionally, originality is something viewed as an "imprint of the author's personality".[186] There is an inextricable link between creativity and originality where a work must reflect contribution of an author in terms of his intellectual ability. We can observe a marked difference in the understanding of originality in UK where there is no creativity requirement in case of a table and compilation.[187] Originality is measured in terms of independent labour, which is not intellectual labour.[188]

With advancements in technology, the traditional view of originality in France has been questioned.[189] Computer programs have challenged the requirement of 'imprints of author's personality".[190] Article L112-3 of the Code of Intellectual

---

[179]ibid.

[180]The common law countries moved towards "sweat of the brow" copyright in the absence of the law of unfair competition, 'William Rodolph Cornish, 'Protection for and vis-à-vis Databases' in Marcel Dellebeke (ed), *Copyright in Cyberspace: Copyright and the Global Information Infrastructure* (Otto Cramwinckel, Amsterdam, 1997) 436; Daniel Gervais shares the same view but also adds that this originality threshold contravenes the creative originality requirement under the Berne Convention and the TRIPS Agreement, Daniel Gervais, 'The Compatibility of the Skill and Labour Originality Standard with the Berne Convention and the TRIPS Agreement' (2004) 26(2) EIPR 75, 78.

[181]Cornish and others (n 129) 447–448.

[182]*Jeweler's Circular Publishing Co. v. Keystone Publishing Co*, 281 F 83 (CA2 1922).

[183]Davison (n 69) 144; Gervais (n 48) 78.

[184]Andre Lucas, Pascal Kamina & Robert Plaisant, 'France' in Paul Edward Geller and Melville B Nimmer (eds) *International Copyright Law and Practice* (Lexis Nexis 2009 volume 1) s 2[1][b].

[185]ibid, s 2 [1] [b].

[186]s 2[1] [b] [iii] [A]; Vivant (n 137) 74.

[187]*Supra* (n 161) and (n 178).

[188]ibid.

[189]Thomas K Dreier, 'Authorship and New Technologies from the Viewpoint of Civil Law Tradition' (1995) 26(6) IIC 990, 997–999.

[190]In the landmark Pachot decision the cour de cassation, said originality is an "intellectual input" (apport intellectual) and gave the opinion that protection may be refused if an "automated or constraining logic" dictates" and decides the input, Lucas & others (n 184) s 2[2]; The French

Property 1992 provides copyright protection to compilations.[191] It allows for protection of anthologies or collections, if only selection or arrangement of the contents of such anthologies or collections constitutes intellectual creation.[192] French law has protected compilations with contents, which are both informational and works.[193] While dealing with these cases, courts have said that one should identify the originality in selection or arrangement instead of the contents that may not be protectable.[194] A different type of originality is required for compilations in comparison to mere 'sweat of the brow'. The criterion in France is based on originality in selection or arrangement.[195] This criterion is different from the requirement in UK that existed prior to incorporating database copyright provision under Article 3. Although the requirement in France is generally construed differently from 'sweat of the brow', cases have indicated that even prior to incorporating Database Directive, the threshold of such originality was not significantly stringent in terms of requirement of creativity.[196]

(Footnote 190 continued)

approach, which was understandable with regards to writings, paintings and sculptures did not go well with utilitarian work. Thus, the modern test is a subset of the originality requirement that asks "what is it that an author does to show her personality through a work", Elizabeth F Judge & Daniel Gervais, 'Of silos and constellations: comparing notions of originality in copyright law' in Robert F Brauneis, *Intellectual Property Protection of Fact-based Works: Copyright and its Alternatives* (Edward Elgar 2009) 79.

[191]Davison (n 69) 114.

[192]Lucas & others (n 184) s 2[3] [b].

[193]Over the years, protection has been granted to address books, schedule of prices and directory of medical laboratories because of creativity through selection or arrangement, Davison (n 69) 114; On the other hand, protection has been denied for compilations based on 'sweat of the brow' i.e. map of France indicating wine regions, Andre Lucas and Robert Plaisant, 'France' in Melville B Nimmer and Paul Edward Geller (eds) *International Copyright Law and Practice* (Matthew Bender, New York, 1999) in Davison (n 69) 114; CA Douai 7 October 1996 (Sté DDB Needham v. Cie des Courtiers Jurés Piqueurs de Vins de Paris), RIDA 1997/172, 286 in Davison (n 69) 114.

[194]Lucas & others (n 184) s 2[3] [b].

[195]"In theory, the standards of protection are quite high, but in fact, protection is often granted even in cases of weak creativity", Vivant (n 137) 75.

[196]The criterion of originality for collections was revised from the initial standard in France. At the time of implementing TRIPS Agreement in 1996 the cumulative criterion requiring selection and arrangement was changed to selection or arrangement. Hence at the time of incorporating the Database Directive no additional changes were required, Beunen (n 125) 80; In the leading case of *Microfor v Le Monde* [1988] ECC 297, Microfor was involved in publishing an index consisting of titles of French newspaper articles. The compilation of Microfor was further subdivided into two parts. The first part 'analytical' consisted of alphabetic arrangement of articles with 'descriptive' key words, which was followed by a number referring to the chronological section. The second part, the chronological section consisted of the names of the periodicals where the articles were published. This selection or arrangement was considered to be original enough to confer copyright protection. In a different case, a published magazine consisting of a list of car manufacturers in the world was considered creative. The selection or arrangement was considered to be sufficiently creative in an 'organization chart' listing the names of their directors and managers, *SARL v. SA Coprosa Cass.* (1re civ., 2 May 1989) in Beunen (n 125) 81.

After the incorporation of the copyright provision under Article 3, there have been some cases in France, which provide guidelines about the threshold requirement attached to AOIC. In *Editions Législatives v. Le Serveur Administratif, Thierry Ehrmann and others*, (*Editions Législatives*) the claimant published a dictionary of about 400 collective agreements arranged in a thematic method.[197] It was alleged that the defendant had infringed database copyright by reproducing passages. Cour de Cassation held that dictionary of the claimant was not an ordinary compilation of information, which was available in public domain. Instead, the dictionary was a "compilation and summary of a large number of collective agreements in accordance with an original thematic presentation, providing a synthesis of the essential elements of each in accordance with a plan that was unique to the work."[198] Thus, the dictionary was an original work to merit copyright protection and an outcome of personality of the editor. Similarly in *Societe OCP Repartition v Societe Salvea*, the database in question was not a mere compilation consisting of information available in the public domain. On the contrary there was individuality present in the comments, while sources were being integrated in the database.[199]

In *SA Credinfor v. Artprice.com* (*Artprice*), the alleged infringement concerned copyrightability of a database comprising of works of art. Artprice.com maintained a world-wide database, which listed information about paintings from all era including prices paid for such paintings in public auctions.[200] Credinfor was involved with processing of payments and they ran a website of their own. The website of Credinfor provided similar information as Artprice.com. It was alleged that Credinfor infringed copyright in the existing database based on number of hits that Artprice.com received within a short span of time. The Cour D' Appel De Paris held that no evidence was produced by Artprice.com to suggest that any intellectual contribution has resulted such database. Hence, there was no infringement of database copyright.[201] The "intellectual contribution must be assessed [with reference] to the plan, composition, form, structure, language and the expression of the personality of the author".[202] Similar result followed in the case of *Groupe Moniteur et al v. Observatoire des Marchés Publics*. There was no originality

---

[197][2005] ECDR 14; Collective agreements are "written and published agreements between certain parties, who are entitled by law to conclude these agreements, which have general and abstract provisions with binding impacts on the employment relationship", Judge Michel Blatman, Conseiller, 'Chambre sociale de la Cour de cassation, France, "Collective agreements" (International Labour Organisation, 24 September 2006) available at <http://www.ilo.org/wcmsp5/groups/public/—ed_dialogue/—dialogue/documents/meetingdocument/wcms_159942.pdf> (accessed 30 November 2016).

[198]Editions Législatives (n 197) 153.

[199]Tribunal de commerce Paris 19 March 2004 in Beunen (n 125) 106–107.

[200][2006] ECDR 15.

[201]ibid; However, Artprice was entitled for the protection under database right as the producer incurred substantial investment in the production of such database. Accordingly, Artprice has the right to prohibit extraction/re-utilizations of permanent or temporary transfer of the contents of the website to a different medium.

[202]Credinfor (n 200) 203.

present in call for tenders to merit copyright protection. The alleged infringement concerned unauthorized copying and distribution of calls for tender published in a journal. Such compilation was not considered to be a database by the Court and it lacked originality for the purpose of copyright protection.[203]

The cases in France do not bring about a clear indication of the AOIC threshold attached to Article 3. In all of the above cases, there is a uniform distinction between ordinary compilation and compilation where an author incorporates his individual discretion, choice and uniqueness.[204] Ordinary compilations that are likely to be available in the public domain are not protected under AOIC threshold.[205] Databases that pass the grade of copyright have been associated with the traditional requirement of originality which reflects the personality of an author.[206]

With respect to originality requirement, Germany has adopted a different standard.[207] The 1965 Copyright Act is the main legislation in Germany. Article 2 of such Act protects "literary, scientific and artistic works".[208] German copyright law protects a work, which is an outcome of "personal intellectual creation", although

[203]Groupe Moniteur and others v. Observatoire des Marchés Publics, Cour d'appel de Paris 18 June 1999, [2000] 183 RIDA 316 in P. Bernt. Hugenholtz, 'The New Database Right: Early Case Law from Europe', Int'l Intell. Prop. L. & Pol'y 70-1, 70-14 (2002); There were similar cases where copyright protection was refused: *SARL News Invest v. SA PR Line* Court of Appeal (Cour d'appel) Versailles, 11 April 2002–published press releases of the companies enlisted in the stock exchange; La sociéte Sonacotra v. le syndicat Sud Sonacotra District Court (Tribunal de Grande Instance) Paris, 25 April 2003–a database of a company consisting of email addresses of employees.

[204]Editions Législatives (n 197) and Credinfor (n 200).

[205]Societe (n 199).

[206]Credinfor (n 200).

[207]"The work must feature a minimum level of individuality and creativity beyond that of average well-skilled and the trained person in the area (Kleine Munze)", Christian Hertz-Eichenrode, Germany in Dennis Campbell(ed) *World Intellectual property rights and remedies* (Oceana New York 2011) 23 while referring to the Federal Supreme Court's decision at [305] Buromobel programm, and GRUR (1983), 377, Brombeermuster; Article 4 of the German Copyright Act, states that selection or arrangement constitutes a personal intellectual creation, 'Copyright Act (Urheberrechtsgesetz, UrhG)' (Translated by WIPO, 8 May 1998) available at <http://www.iuscomp.org/gla/statutes/UrhG.htm> (accessed 15 March 2011) translated by WIPO, (accessed 15 March 2011); In words of Lewinski selection or arrangement must fulfil the requirement of personal intellectual creation, Silke Von Lewinski, 'Protection of and vis-à-vis Databases: Germany' in Marcel Dellebeke (ed), *Copyright in Cyberspace: Copyright and the Global Information Infrastructure* (Otto Cramwinckel, Amsterdam, 1997) 480; Owing to the harmonization of 'work' constituting of 'author's own intellectual creation' at the EU level, for example in case of computer programs, the standard of originality requires low creativity, Gerhard Schricker, 'Farewell to the "level of creativity" (Schopfungshohe) in German Copyright Law?' (1995) 26(1) IIC 41.

[208]Copyright Act, section 2, paragraph 1, numbers 1-7, 'Copyright Act (Urheberrechtsgesetz, UrhG)' (Translated by WIPO, 8 May 1998) <http://www.iuscomp.org/gla/statutes/UrhG.htm> (accessed 15 March 2011).

nothing definitely has been said about such intellectual creation.[209] In certain cases, instead of stringent standard of originality and individuality, creativity requirement has been interpreted in liberal terms. For example, copyright protection is available for relatively trivial literary work like catalogues, printed forms, etc.[210] There have been three major decisions in Germany prior to incorporating Article 3 of the Database Directive.[211] In the first of these three cases, the Court questioned copyrightability of a compilation of German medieval texts, which were already available in public domain.[212] The Court contended that the act of adding scholarly notes, indexing and arranging individual sections reflected enough creativity to merit copyright protection. In the *WK Documentation* case similar sort of conclusion was reached involving collection of material comprising of the history of German Prisoners of War.[213] The final case involved a degree thesis in biology. It contained examination and description of species that was not protected under copyright except the original contribution towards form and presentation.[214] All three decisions suggested that for material available in public domain, selection or arrangement must be sufficiently creative to justify copyright protection.[215] Moreover, protection is for the form and presentation in a compilation comprising of facts, and not for the information itself. The threshold of originality in Germany requires that compilations by virtue of their selection or arrangement should reflect personal intellectual creations.[216]

In the German case of *R v Unauthorized Reproduction of Telephone Directories in CD-Rom* (*Telephone Directories*), the alleged copyright infringement involved

[209]Adolf Dietz, 'Germany' in Paul Edward Geller and Melville B Nimmer (eds) *International Copyright Law and Practice* (Sweet & Maxwell 2009) sec 2[1][b].

[210]In Germany there is a copyright protection available, which does not need creativity but depends on the time and effort expended. It is called Kleine Munze (a small change), Bernt Hugenholtz, 'Protection of Compilations of facts in Germany and the Netherlands' in Bernt Hugenholtz & Egbert J Dommering (eds) *Protecting Works of Fact: Copyright, Freedom of Expression and Information Law* (Kluwer Tax and Law Publishers 1991) 62.

[211]Monumenta Germaniae Historica BGH-IZR 157/77 – December 7, 1979, BGH- IZR 95/79 June 12, 1981 and BGH-IZR 106/78 November 21, 1980 in Vincent Porter, 'The Copyright protection of compilations and pseudo-literary works in EC member states' (1993) Journal of Business Law 22.

[212]Monumenta Germaniae Historica BGH-IZR 157/77 – December 7, 1979 in Vincent Porter, 'The Copyright protection of compilations and pseudo-literary works in EC member states' (1993) Journal of Business Law 22.

[213]BGH-IZR 95/79 June 12, 1981 in Vincent Porter, 'The Copyright protection of compilations and pseudo-literary works in EC member states' (1993) Journal of Business Law 22.

[214]BGH-IZR 106/78 November 21, 1980, in Vincent Porter, 'The Copyright protection of compilations and pseudo-literary works in EC member states' (1993) Journal of Business Law 22.

[215]Monumenta (n 212); BGH- IZR 95/79 June 12, 1981; BGH-IZR 106/78 November 21, 1980, in Vincent Porter, 'The Copyright protection of compilations and pseudo-literary works in EC member states' (1993) January (22) Journal of Business Law 1.

[216]Copyright Act, 1965, s4 'Copyright Act (Urheberrechtsgesetz, UrhG)' (Translated by WIPO, 8 May 1998) available <http://www.iuscomp.org/gla/statutes/UrhG.htm> (accessed 15 March 2011).

compilation of telephone directories.[217] Deutsche Telekom was involved in publishing telephone directories and customers lists in electronic format. The defendant scanned the contents of all directories, and reproduced subscribers list onto a CD with the option of search for the telephone subscribers. In the context of alleged infringement, the Court held that the directory in question was not an outcome of personal creation.[218] Similar to other telephone directories the claimant gave attention to the general customary needs, and there was no selection process followed at the time of recording data in the telephone directory. There was no creativity present beyond the routine work and hence, the telephone directory in question lacked sufficient creative endeavour to merit copyright protection.[219]

In the *Musical Hits* case, the Court held that there was no case for copyright protection, since the selection or arrangement did not amount to personal intellectual creation.[220] Here, the claimant compiled 'airplay' and music sales chart from musical hits on radio, which was displayed on a weekly basis including current placing, titles, artists, labels, etc. The charts were published in two periodicals. The defendant was engaged in publishing similar charts, although he followed a different selection or arrangement method. Further, in the *Warenzeichenlexika* decision the Federal Supreme Court said that telephone directories need individual decisions at the time of choosing the possibilities of organizing an entry.[221] Even limited opportunities of presentation should be sufficient. This requirement is not significantly stringent.

In Germany there were existing inconsistencies present with the issue of copyrightability of telephone directories.[222] Given that information used in telephone directories is available in the public domain, the only possible creativity in such directory can be attributed to selection, classification or arrangement of the information.[223]

In a different case, a collection of poems was held copyrightable.[224] The published list of poems was a part of the "Classics Vocabulary Project". It comprised of 1100 most important poems in German Literature between 1790 and 1900. There were different stages to the selection process. The first step involved selecting 14 of the 3000 anthologies and they were supplemented by bibliographic compilation of fifty German-language anthologies. This preliminary selection provided a list of 20,000 poems and the final list of 1100 poems was selected based on the number of

[217][2002] ECDR 3.

[218]Dietz (n 209).

[219]ibid.

[220](Bundesgerichtshof (Tele-Info-CD) (I ZR 199/96) (Unreported, May 6, 1999) (Ger), in Mathias Leistner, 'The legal protection of telephone directories relating to the new database maker's right' (2000) 31(7/8) IIC 950.

[221]ibid.

[222]*Supra* (n 220).

[223]ibid.

[224]Case C-304/07 *Directmedia Publishing GmbH v Albert-Ludwigs-Universität Freiburg* [2008] ECR I-7565.

times a particular poem has been mentioned. Poems mentioned at least three times in those anthologies became a part of the published list. The defendant copied 90% of those poems that appeared in the list. The Court held that there was copyright infringement, since the selection or arrangement of poems represents personal creation of the author.[225] Comments suggested that the threshold for this case was somewhat less stringent than the standard expected under AOIC.[226]

The incorporation of Article 3 in the German copyright law may have brought about changes that are different from the traditional requirement.[227] Copyright protection has been favoured in compilations comprising of facts, if such compilations have not been purely expressed in an obvious way.[228] Some amount of creativity is present in all the cases that received copyright protection. This creativity should reflect in the work even if there are limited opportunities to showcase 'author's own personal creation'.[229]

5.3.2 *Convergence to a Uniform AOIC Threshold*

While we observe application of Article 3 to compilations, it is clear that all three jurisdictions have refrained from protecting obvious compilations comprising of materials available in the public domain.[230] These compilations failed to show any creative output either through selection or arrangement of the contents, or author's personal creation or imprints of author's personality.[231]

For instance, in the UK, it was held that a collection of information about goals and description of a live football match may involve labourious work, but that would not satisfy the requirement under Article 3. While providing betting information, there are no two ways of informing a user.[232] The claimant could not have omitted any of the facts, since they were vital for a person interested in placing his bet. The claimant followed an all-inclusive approach. They considered all available information in a live match, since any selection would have rendered the database

---

[225]ibid.

[226]Bundesgerischtshof (German Federal Supreme Court) 24 May 2007 in the case of Directmedia Publishing and Albert- Ludwigs- Universitat-Freiburg in Dietz (n 209) sec 2[1][b]; This case also involved a question of extraction under the database right, which was referred to the ECJ. The ECJ considered that there was a case of database infringement in the context of extraction, Directmedia Publishing GmbH (n 224); Anne Christopher and Kate Freeman, 'Case comment: Directmedia Publishing GmbH v Albert-Ludwigs-Universitat Freiburg (Case C-304/07)' (2009) 31(3) EIPR 151.

[227]Leistner (n 220).

[228]ibid.

[229]ibid.

[230]*Supra* section 5.3.

[231]ibid.

[232][2011] EWCA Civ 330, [2011] 1 WLR 3044.

useless.[233] In cases like the one that we have discussed before, there is little room for any second comer interested in making similar database but to follow same selection or arrangement as the first database maker.[234] This case reveals that with respect to database copyright protection, UK has moved away from 'sweat of the brow' as the basis for granting copyright protection to databases.[235]

In France, the act of compiling information available in public domain would not suffice the requirement of AOIC. There must be some creative aspect beyond deterministic compilation, such as the original arrangement in *Erhmann* case.[236] The courts will not provide protection to compilations, which are obvious.[237] Although obvious compilation will not receive protection, cases do not specify the extent of selection or arrangement to merit copyright protection.[238] At times, as in Artprice.com, not enough evidence has been given to claim copyright protection.[239] In the Artprice.com case in France, there was no opportunity for the Court to provide an elaborate argument on copyright protection.[240] In the context of aforementioned trends, one can comprehend what the Court would have said in the background of the nature of effort expended by Artprice.com. The database consisted of information about paintings from all era, alongside the prices of those paintings at public auctions. There was no primary selection process adopted by the claimant. He opted for an all-inclusive mechanism. There was no unique plan followed, and the French Court in closing remarks suggested possible arrangement in relation to its form, composition, structure and language.[241] For example, claimants could have arranged the database by starting with the price paid for the paintings, the era in which it was painted, and the name of painter. Further, they could have included short descriptions of the paintings similar to descriptions referred at the public auctions, and the names of such auctions.[242] This arrangement

---

[233]This follows the argument taken in the first draft proposal that in useful comprehensive databases there would be less selection, COM (92) 24 final, 17.

[234][2011] EWCA Civ 330, [2011] 1 WLR 3044.

[235]Citing two cases, *Newspaper Licensing Agency, Ltd. v Marks & Spencer, plc,* [2001] UKHL 38, [2013] 1 AC 551and *Designers Guild Ltd. v Russell Williams (Textiles) Ltd.* [2000] 1 WLR 2416 it has been argued that in the UK, ""original skill and labour" cannot have the same meaning as "skill and labour."". It symbolizes creativity-based test. Even the inclusion of originality in the statute has some bearing and logically, it is more than skill and labour; Gervais (n 48) 49.

[236]*Editions Législatives* (n 197).

[237]In *Editions Législatives*, the dictionary was not considered something, which only portrays collection of information available in the public domain.

[238]It has been questioned that "when one selects, does it mean keeping 30%, 60%, 90% or …99% of the source?", Vivant (n 137) 78.

[239]Such criticism has been forwarded by scholars, Beunen (n 125) 83.

[240]Credinfor (n 200).

[241]Credinfor (n 200) 205.

[242]Although the actual requirement is not given, the aforementioned options could provide the required originality going by the previous decisions.

mechanism is likely to merit copyright protection even after the all-inclusive selection.

German cases similar to French decisions show that purely collecting information from public domain would not fetch copyright protection.[243] In the case of *Telephone Directories*, the Court indicated obvious alphabetic arrangement of information available in public domain.[244]

With reference to the issue of obviousness in a compilation, these jurisdictions have struck a uniform note. In the context of the decision in *Football Dataco,* UK interpretation of AOIC also converges with the approach adopted in France and Germany.

5.3.3 *Modicum of Creativity*

Cases that supported copyright protection to factual compilations resorted to the requirement of modicum of creativity. This requirement is adopted if one observes the case involving poems in Germany.[245] The claimant selected a list of poems from a number of anthologies. Poems in the final list only appeared if they had been mentioned three times in the consulted anthologies. Therefore, creativity happens at two stages: first, the author selected some poems from a collection of more than 3000 anthologies, and second, he restricted the collection to the final list of 1100 poems. He did not follow the all-inclusive approach namely, choosing all the anthologies.[246] At the second stage, the list of poems would not represent a comprehensive guide of all poems, but the selection criterion of at least three mentions was adopted. Overall, one would expect some selection in a list featuring selected poems, and not a mere representation of an alphabetic list of all poems for a period of three hundred years.[247] Similar situation is with the Ehrmann decision in France.[248] The arrangement in the dictionary comprising of 400 collective agreements was thematic, and therefore, not a mere alphabetic arrangement of documents that were available in the public domain. With thematic arrangements in place, there was rewriting of the essential elements in the dictionary. Since the adoption of the AOIC threshold in the UK, one observes the requirement of modicum of creativity

[243]This has been somewhat depicted in Telephone Directories (n 217), and in contrast with the Monumenta Germaniae Historica BGH-IZR 157/77 – December 7, 1979 case where the arrangement was found to be sufficient.

[244]*Telephone Directories* (n 217).

[245]Similar to the Feist case, the German courts are inclined to keep scientific knowledge in the public domain, case involving a degree thesis for biology BGH-IZR 106/78 November 21, 1980.

[246]This collection of poems, although useful cannot be referred to as a comprehensive database, COM (92) 24 final, 17.

[247]Following this process would have likely stopped the database from receiving copyright protection, *Supra* section 5.3.

[248]*Editions Législatives* (n 197).

with respect to copyright protection in databases. In the *Live Football* case, the Court did not consider creativity representing the activity of putting down goals scored and information related to a particular live football match as sufficient to merit copyright protection.[249] From the above cases it is clear that creativity that facilitates in crossing the barrier of obvious selection or arrangement would be considered as sufficient creativity. One may want to recall the judgement of the *Football Dataco* case and the interpretation of CJEU.[250] The European Court laid down certain basic guidelines before the national courts could assign the threshold of AOIC.[251] Therefore, it became very important for member states to meet the basic guidelines. The decisions certainly indicate that there is uniformity in this regard. These decisions also indicate that it would not be difficult to meet the threshold requirement and therefore, it would not be farfetched to suggest that most of the databases would actually fulfil the requirement of creativity.[252]

[249][2011] EWCA Civ 330, [2011] 1 WLR 3044.

[250]*Football Dataco* (n 9).

[251]*Supra* (n 184).

[252]Similar suggestions were made in the *Feist* decision, *Feist Publications* (n 77).

Chapter 6
Feist Standard in the Threshold Assigned to AOIC

Harmonization of the threshold of copyright protection (author's own intellectual creation) for databases under Article 3 resembles the standard developed in Feist decision.[1] Following the impact of *Feist*, there have been positive developments such as freeing of factual information available in public domain.[2] Examples suggest that producers are interested in improving the presentation of factual contents in compilations. By virtue of this arrangement, their directories are copyrightable.

6.1 Resemblance of *Feist* Standard

It is interesting to observe that there are some apparent similarities with the guidelines that the US Supreme Court had suggested in the *Feist* decision.[3] This is in relation to the threshold of AOIC suggested by the member courts.[4] One also observes certain similarities with the judgement of CJEU in the *Football Dataco* case.[5]

[1] *Infra* section 6.2.
[2] *Infra* section 6.2.
[3] *Feist Publications v Rural Telephone Service*, 499 US 340 (1991).
[4] *Supra* section 5.3.
[5] Case C-604/10 *Football Dataco Ltd v Yahoo! UK Ltd* [2012] ECDR 10, 194 *(Football Dataco)*.

I. Gupta, *Footprints of Feist in European Database Directive*,
DOI 10.1007/978-981-10-3981-2_6

6.1.1 Minimum Creativity and a Second Comer

In *Feist*, the US Supreme Court suggested that the requirement of creativity in case of compilations need not be novel.[6] Instead, a modicum of creativity was sufficient to hold non-original forms of compilations original.[7]

The cases in Germany, France, UK and US discussed copyrightability of extremely diverse items. These include compilation of poems, a dictionary, football match fixtures and a telephone directory.[8] There could not be one possible standard of creativity set for all these diverse items, since in relative terms, the threshold of creativity required in case of a dictionary is different from the threshold requirement in case of a telephone directory. Therefore, to identify the extent of similarity between threshold of AOIC and the prescribed threshold under *Feist*, we need to identify a common parameter. This parameter should be uniform across any kind of compilations consisting of factual information.

The Court in *Feist* delivered a judgement that not only decided the fate of a telephone directory consisting of factual contents, but also provided a guideline for future cases relating to telephone directories and other similar compilations with factual information.[9] Through *Feist*, the US Supreme Court identified the burgeoning need of freeing up of information, and the role of factual compilations. Although the Court rejected 'sweat of the brow' as an argument for copyright protection with a requirement of minimal threshold of creativity, it provided certain assurance of copyright protection to the makers of factual compilations.[10] With reference to AOIC, cases decided in Europe suggested certain standards of creativity for compilations of diverse nature. In comparison to *Feist, the European Courts* have not explicitly stated that the threshold requirement for any such future compilations is minimal.[11] However, decisions in Europe suggest that requirement for any such similar compilation is likely to be minimal.[12] Jurisprudence surrounding the threshold standard of AOIC is in its formative stage in Europe. It has slowly begun to gain consensus after the passage of the Directive in 1996.[13]

Alongside the minimal requirement of creativity, *Feist* decision provided guidelines for future compilations of similar nature. For any compilation consisting of factual information, selection or arrangement at the stage of compiling such

---

[6]*Feist Publications* (n 3) 358.

[7]ibid.

[8]Case C-304/07 *Directmedia Publishing GmbH v Albert-Ludwigs-Universität Freiburg* [2008] ECR I-7565; *Editions Législatives v. Le Serveur Administratif, Thierry Ehrmann and others* [2005] ECDR 14; [2011] EWCA Civ 330; [2011] 1 WLR 3044; Feist Publications (n 3).

[9]Cases after *Feist* decision in the US followed the guidelines of *Feist*, *supra* section 4.4.

[10]*Feist Publications* (n 3) 362.

[11]*Supra* section 5.3.

[12]ibid.

[13]Council Directive of 1996/9/EC of 27 March 1996 on the legal protection of databases [1996] OJ L 77/20 (Council Directive 96/9/EC).

contents should not be deterministic.[14] It means that in order to make a particular compilation meaningful, the adopted method of selection or arrangement should not be the only way to represent the contents.[15] In case of a compilation, if there are no two ways of representing the contents, then the selection or arrangement in relation to the contents would be obvious.[16] This general criterion in relation to factual compilations can be observed in cases decided so far in Europe. In the case involving the *Live Football* database, there were no two ways of putting across information that were vital for placing bets.[17] For this kind of database, there is little room for a second comer to alter the presentation. The decision indicates agreement with the decision of *Feist.*[18] The case is an example of new-age jurisprudence concerning the future of copyright protection to databases with deterministic or obvious selection or arrangement.[19]

The *Football Dataco* case in UK is one of the many instances wherein the European Courts have implicitly come up with the parameter of obvious and deterministic selection or arrangement.[20] In case of *R v Unauthorized Reproduction of Telephone Directories in CD-Rom (Telephone Directories)*, the German Court indicated that an obvious and deterministic alphabetic arrangement of information available in public domain lacked the creativity threshold required under the AOIC.[21] The French Court in the *Artprice.com* case followed the same argument as the German and the British decisions.[22]

So far, the idea of minimum creativity is present in both continents. These are yet early days to explain whether the existing jurisprudence concerning AOIC threshold exactly matches the threshold of minimum creativity prescribed by *Feist.* It is fair to say that the point of agreement at this stage rests on whether a particular compilation can be compiled in a meaningful manner by a second comer, which will incorporate a different selection or arrangement.[23] Further, it will be different from the first maker, and involves modicum of creativity.[24] This position is somewhat indicated in the UK decision concerning copyrightability of a fixture list wherein Mr. Floyd J suggested that there should be more than one meaningful way

---

[14]*Supra* section 3.3.

[15]*Victor Lalli Enterprises Inc. v. Big Red Apple Inc.,* 936 F 2d 671 (2nd Cir 1991) 673.

[16]ibid.

[17][2011] EWCA Civ 330, [2011] 1 WLR 3044.

[18]If any publisher were to design a similar directory as created by Rural there would be no other way than to strictly follow the procedure followed by Rural in *Feist* decision, *Feist Publications* (n 3).

[19]This is contrary to new line of jurisprudence as proposed in the first draft proposal of the Database Directive, Commission, 'Proposal for a Council Directive on the legal protection of databases' COM (92) 24 final (COM (92) 24 final), para [2.3.3].

[20][2011] EWCA Civ 330, [2011] 1 WLR 3044.

[21][2002] ECDR 3.

[22]*SA Credinfor v. Artprice.com* [2006] ECDR 15 *(Artprice).*

[23]*Feist Publications* (n 3) and *supra* section 5.3.

[24]ibid.

of presenting the contents in a factual compilation.[25] The copyrightability of a factual compilation is thus tested through the lens of creative opportunity available to a second comer. This is an accepted standard that came out of *Feist* decision and is indicative of decisions in Europe.

6.1.2 Pre-existing Work, Use of Computer and Sweat of the Brow

The threshold of AOIC is going through a transition phase where it is noted that manual labour of simply collecting and compiling factual data has been slowly replaced by modern methods of compiling information.[26] One of the important factors in case of factual compilations is the use of technology. Reference to such use is observed in the *Football Dataco* case in UK.[27] Technology in these cases facilitates the collection of data and helps at the stage of data compilation.[28]

The perspective of using a particular technology, and its effect on overall creativity of a compilation was not discussed in the *Feist* case.[29] There was a collection of contact details of customers who subscribed to the telephone service.[30] Even though there were no computers involved in the telephone directory published by Rural, the act of publishing itself was most likely to involve use of certain type of technology. For instance, you would require access to a printing press to publish telephone directories. Similar to a computer used in the football fixture case, the printing press would give final shape to the data collected for the purpose of the telephone directory in question.[31] Therefore, there is broad use of technology in both cases.

The use of technology divides the work into two stages: the first stage is where a person uses his discretion to select and arrange the contents, and the second stage is where the maker of a database uses technology to compile his selection or arrangement.[32] In *Feist*, the US Supreme Court said that the arrangement followed in the white pages was an inevitable outcome for someone interested in producing a

[25] *Football Dataco Ltd v Brittens Pools Ltd* [2010] EWHC 841(Ch) Sections 83–90 (Football Dataco 2); This is an objective requirement unlike the subjective requirement under author's right system, Daniel J Gervais, '*Feist* goes global: A comparative analysis of the notion of originality in copyright law' (2002) 49(4) Journal of Copyright Society of the US 949, 952.

[26] For instance in France, Thomas K Dreier, 'Authorship and New Technologies from the Viewpoint of Civil Law Tradition' (1995) 26(6) IIC 990, 997–999.

[27] *Football Dataco* 2 (n 25) para [22].

[28] ibid.

[29] *Feist Publications* (n 3).

[30] ibid 342.

[31] *Football Dataco* 2 (n 25), para [15].

[32] ibid paras [12] – [21].

telephone directory.[33] Rural issued an application form to the subscribers who were interested in their service. Based on the application form, they alphabetically listed the names of subscribers.[34] In the opinion of Justice O' Connor, "the end product [was] a garden-variety white pages directory, devoid of even the slightest trace of creativity".[35] This statement develops an inextricable link between 'creative work' at the early stages to the final manifestation of the product. The work leading up to the telephone directory has been questioned and usage of words like 'end product' reflects the outcome of creativity depending on prior work. In other words, Rural's approach affected the creative output, and moreover, adoption of a selection mechanism may have resulted in a different outcome. Although there is no reference to the possible use of technology, according to *Feist*, work done at the primary stage will have an overall bearing on the database.[36]

The use of technology would not fundamentally change the extent of creativity in a database if there was little or no creativity at the stage of selecting or arranging data at the initial stages.[37] Therefore, regardless of the use of technology, the preparatory stage is fundamental for a database to merit copyright protection.

Although *Feist* and *Dataco* raised the importance of preparatory work, there is a fundamental difference between these two sets of work. In case of *Feist*, Rural collected pre-existing data; and in the *Football Dataco* decision, Football Dataco created the data for subsequent use.[38] At the time of referral, the CJEU said that the accepted creativity under the AOIC threshold excluded creativity which went into creation of data.[39] Instead, selection or arrangement that went into final database was an accepted threshold under AOIC.[40] The CJEU was silent as to the status of creativity in selecting or arranging factual data, since it considered creativity towards the creation of data and not towards pre-existing factual data.[41]

Though *Feist* and *Football Dataco* are vastly different in their legal approach; nonetheless, there is a fundamental commonality in the two decisions: discarding the 'sweat of the brow argument'.[42] It is on this point that these two cases agreed upon. Both the decisions discussed the nature of work, thereby removing possibility of using 'sweat of the brow' argument to merit copyright protection.[43]

---

[33] *Feist Publications* (n 3) 363.
[34] *Football Dataco* (n 5) 362.
[35] *Feist Publications* (n 3) 363.
[36] ibid 363.
[37] *Football Dataco 2* (n 25), para [44].
[38] *Feist Publications* (n 3); *Football Dataco* 2 (n 25).
[39] *Football Dataco* (n 5) 193–194.
[40] ibid.
[41] ibid.
[42] *Football Dataco 2* (n 25) paras [89]–[90].
[43] *Feist Publications* (n 3); *Football Dataco* (n 5).

6.1.3 Application of Quantitative Factor

Although the quality of selection or arrangement in a compilation merits copyright protection, there is no clear indication about the impact of quantitative factors in a compilation. The *Football Dataco* decision in England suggested that quantity is an important factor to decide copyrightability of a compilation.[44] This is besides the quality of selection or arrangement in a compilation.[45] It is not clear as to what extent quantity plays a role in comparison to quality, and to what proportion the quantity factor should be considered for the purpose of copyright protection. Going back to *Feist*, one observes that *Rural* incorporated large number of subscribers in its compilation.[46] The issue of number of subscribers in *Rural's* telephone directory was not discussed by the US Supreme Court. If quantity had been a criterion, then the US Supreme Court would have possibly agreed with the claim of copyright protection for the directory in question. On the contrary, the US Supreme Court said that the compilation lacked a quality, which was not represented by merely compiling large number of factual data.[47] The US Supreme Court was certainly a lot less interested with total number of subscribers, and was rather concerned with the quality of representation.

From a different perspective, if *Rural's* compilation had a lot less subscribers but satisfied the modicum of creativity requirement, would it have successfully claimed copyright protection? To understand this situation one must understand the significance of less number of subscribers. If the numbers are less, in all likelihood such situation will act for the benefit of the claimant, since it signifies a selection process from a large number of subscribers.[48] On the other hand, the numbers may not be a true representation of any selection process. It depends on total number of subscribers from which selection process was carried out.[49] After all, ending up with a lot less numbers in the final compilation may actually signify all-inclusive selection, if there was small numbers to begin with. Therefore, numbers in a compilation may not be true indicators of creativity. However, numbers are the starting point of assessing creativity, and they are certainly helpful indicators at the time of comparing the selection process. Say for instance, the German case where limited number of poems were selected from a pool of 30,000 anthologies. Here, the final number of 1100 poems did help to fathom the creativity that went through

---

[44]*Football Dataco 2* (n 25), para [86].

[45]ibid.

[46]*Feist Publications* (n 3).

[47]ibid 363.

[48]Selection would entail modicum of creativity as prescribed in the *Feist* case, *Feist Publications* (n 3) 346.

[49]Rural compiled the alphabetical list of all its subscribers as per statutory requirement, *Feist Publications* (n 3) 342.

in selecting the poems.[50] In fact, the Court in England has rightly pointed to the role of the quantitative factor without describing the role.[51] Merely identifying numbers in a compilation would give varied interpretation, and will also mean that database makers would have to ensure that both qualitative and quantitative parameters are satisfied to merit copyright protection.[52] While explaining the threshold for AOIC, there has been an explicit identification of both the parameters.[53] This was a slight departure from *Feist*, although in an implicit way, *Feist* did speak about qualitative and quantitative parameters.[54]

Interpretation of the AOIC threshold broadly talks about the principles that have been put forth by US Supreme Court in *Feist.* Cases concerning AOIC have provided additional clarifications, especially with reference to the impact of technology on compilations.[55] We have not come across situations where two diametrically opposite propositions have been suggested.[56] The interpretation of cases concerning the AOIC threshold shows considerable overall similarity with the broad framework of the *Feist* decision.

6.2 *Feist* Standard in the Formative Stage of Article 3

Following the Green Paper in 1988, the European Commission proposed the first draft of the Database Directive.[57] Harmonization of available copyright protection in European member states led to the development of AOIC threshold.[58]

The Green Paper to the first draft proposal of the Directive reflected upon various challenges that could affect the potential and emerging electronic database market in Europe.[59] Where the contents were not literary or artistic works, there was no

---

[50]Case C-304/07 *Directmedia Publishing GmbH v Albert-Ludwigs-Universität Freiburg* [2008] ECR I-7565.

[51]*Football Dataco* 2 (n 25), para [86].

[52]Stating that " it is not consistent with other areas of copyright law if in fact originality for the purposes of database copyright was to include both a requirement as to [AOIC] and a quantitative requirement but in other areas not", Mark Rodgers, 'Case Comment: Football fixture lists and the Database Directive: Football Dataco Ltd v Brittens Pools Ltd' (2010) 32(11) EIPR 593, 598.

[53]*Football Dataco* 2 (n 25), para [86].

[54]*Feist Publications* (n 3) 363–364.

[55]*Football Dataco* 2 (n 25), para [22].

[56]*Supra* section 6.1.

[57]Commission, 'Copyright and the Challenge of Technology' (Green Paper) COM (88) 172 final (COM (88) 172 final); COM (92) 24 final.

[58]'DG Internal market and services working paper: First Evaluation of Directive 96/9/EC on the legal protection of databases' (*Commission of the European Communities*, 12 December 2005) available at <http://ec.europa.eu/internal_market/copyright/docs/databases/evaluation_report_en.pdf> (accessed 31 October 2016) (First Evaluation of Directive 96/9/EC), para [1.1].

[59]COM (88) 172 final; COM (92) 24 final.

legal certainty in terms of copyright protection to compilations.[60] The Commission perceived that for comprehensive electronic databases comprising of factual contents, it would be difficult to merit copyright protection.[61] There would be little or no selection, and arrangement would be absolutely mundane. This uncertainty and anxiety led to the reference of the issue to the Legal Advisory Board (LAB) and the Senior Advisory Board (SOAG) to unravel the legal challenges that impede the growth of European database market.[62] The Green Paper acted as a prelude to start the process of an emerging idea of creating additional protection for electronic databases comprising of factual contents.[63] At this stage there was no explicit desire to formulate a policy of harmonizing the threshold for copyright protection of databases in Europe. Even though there was no explicit desire, the paper identified difference in copyright protection of databases in the member states.[64] This was owing to the difference in threshold requirement of originality. In response to the Green Paper, the stakeholders overwhelmingly supported the role of copyright in protecting databases.[65] They suggested that there should be harmonization of the existing copyright protection in member states with the criterion being compatible with the Berne threshold.[66] Going by the proposal, the Commission suggested that a Directive proposing harmonization of copyright protection for the legal protection of databases should be adopted.[67]

Similar to the Green Paper, the first draft proposal re-iterated concerns with the protection of databases in Europe. It expressed the desire to create protection measures for electronic databases that contained factual information.[68] In this context, application of Article 2.5 of Berne was questionable, since the scope does not explicitly cover electronic databases.[69] The Proposal for a Directive was only for electronic databases where "contents are arranged, stored and accessed by electronic means".[70] This does not mean that the Directive was in disagreement with the Berne structure or did not conform to the Berne standard. The overall framework for recognizing AOIC by way of selection or arrangement of the contents in a database was followed.[71] However, the proposal in clear terms stated that

[60]COM (88) 172 final, s 6.3.

[61]ibid, para [6.3.2].

[62]ibid, para [6.2.1].

[63]ibid, s 6.1.

[64]COM (88) 172 final, paras [6.2.1] and [6.3.1].

[65]Working programme of the Commission in the field of copyright and neighbouring rights. Follow-up to the Green Paper. COM (90) 584 final, 17 January 1991, 18 (COM (90) 584 final), paras [6.2.1] and [6.2.2].

[66]ibid, para [6.2.2].

[67]ibid, para [6.3.2].

[68]ibid, para [6.2.2].

[69]COM (92) 24 final, para [2.2.4].

[70]ibid, para [3.1.10].

[71]ibid, para [5.3.1].

the scope of the Directive, especially in relation to the copyright protection was not limited to scope determined under Article 2.5 of the Berne Convention.[72] In the background of an ever increasing possibility of the European database market, the Commission was not convinced with non-uniform copyright measures present in the member states.[73] This was in addition to the confusion over the application of Berne standard.[74] Therefore, a basic need was identified to harmonize the level of protection to create a sense of stability among stakeholders. In the course of harmonization, the first draft proposal referred to US Copyright threshold for electronic databases.[75] Although the issue of protecting electronic databases was relatively new in US, the Commission consulted the historic *Feist* decision concerning copyrightability of a telephone directory.[76]

The overall framework relating to selection or arrangement, which was foundational to satisfy the requirement of AOIC was within contemplation even prior to first draft proposal of the Database Directive.[77] At the time of first draft proposal, the Commission was very clear about the scope of the Directive.[78] Although the Directive was proposed to be within the broader framework of the Berne Convention, the purpose behind the Directive was different from the Berne proposal on the collections of literary or artistic works.[79] This shows that the foundation, thought process and threshold standard of the harmonized AOIC in EU was not an exercise to harmonize and reiterate the Berne standard.[80]

6.2.1 *Green Paper to First Draft Proposal: From Berne to* Feist

The biggest challenge at the time of drafting the first proposal was less availability of jurisprudence relating to treatment of electronic databases.[81] Although the Commission believed that electronic databases need further incentive, there was no clear indication through case law about the extent of challenge that electronic

---

[72]ibid, para [2.1].

[73]ibid, para [2.2.3].

[74]ibid, para [2.2.4].

[75]ibid, paras [2.3.1] – [2.3.3].

[76]ibid, para [2.3.3].

[77]COM (88) 172 final.

[78]COM (92) 24 final, s 3.

[79]"Collections of literary or artistic works such as encyclopedias and anthologies which, by reason of the selection and arrangement of their contents, constitute intellectual creations shall be protected as such, without prejudice to the copyright in each of the works forming part of such collections.", Berne Convention for the Protection of Literary and Artistic Work available at <http://www.wipo.int/treaties/en/text.jsp?file_id=283698#P85_10661> (accessed 7 November 2009).

[80]COM (92) 24 final, para [2.2.4].

[81]ibid, paras [2.3.3] and [2.2.9]; *Waterlow Directories v Reed Information Services* [1992] FSR 409.

databases were likely to face in future.[82] The decision in *Waterlow Directories v Reed Information Services* which involved a Solicitor's Diary consisting of names and addresses of firms of solicitors decided copyright protection based on the effort expended towards the collection of the names and addresses.[83] The diary had 12,620 entries and the defendant copied 1600 entries to update its directory named *Butterworths Law Directory.* In this case the defendant had reproduced these entries onto a computer.[84] There was concern about the non-existent basic harmonized structure, and the Commission felt that it needs immediate attention in the wake of electronic database market.[85]

The draft proposal considered most of the arguments and parameters pronounced by the US Supreme Court in *Feist.*[86] The Commission also agreed to the crux of *Feist* judgement, which stated that copyright should not come to the rescue of cases involving an ordinary telephone directory or a mundane bibliographical indexing, where it is not possible to show creativity in terms of selection or arrangement.[87] Role of copyright in case of factual compilations was limited to *Feist* decision and to the standards stated by the US Supreme Court.[88] Further, the Commission was assured that most compilations would come under the prescribed threshold of copyright protection.[89]

The Commission justified enactment of a separate database right, since the theory behind copyright protection does not support mundane collection of information that lack minimum creativity.[90] In the words of the Commission, "it would be an unacceptable extension of copyright and undesirably restrictive measure if simple exhaustive accumulations ..." of information merit copyright protection.[91] This was the argument that led to the separation of copyright protection from the novel database right.[92] Behind this argument, we can see reference to the fundamental axiom that facts do not merit copyright protection.[93] Further, we see reference to the consequence of protecting facts as they may undesirably restrict access, thereby impeding dissemination of information.[94] *Feist* decision referred to these fundamental issues before discarding 'sweat of the brow' argument.[95] Similar to the guidelines of *Feist* the act of harmonizing copyright protection for databases

---

[82]ibid.

[83][1992] FSR 409.

[84]ibid.

[85]COM (92) 24 final, para [2.2.5].

[86]ibid, para [2.3.3].

[87]ibid, paras [3.2.4] – [3.2.6].

[88]ibid.

[89]ibid, para [3.2.5].

[90]ibid, paras [3.2.4] – [3.2.6].

[91]ibid, para [3.2.6].

[92]ibid, paras [3.2.4] – [3.2.6].

[93]*Feist Publications* (n 3) 345.

[94]*Infra* section 7.3.

[95]*Feist Publications* (n 3).

influenced the position of present and future stakeholders involved in producing factual compilations.[96]

The only available option was *Feist* that related to paper-format database in a different jurisdiction.[97] The reference to this decision was again a shift from the Green Paper.[98] In fact, *Feist* case was still at the stage of argument when the report following the Green Paper came out on January 17th, 1991.[99] *Feist* was decided on March 27th, 1991.[100] At the time of the proposal *Feist* decision served as an example to suggest the threshold of originality.[101]

While the first reference to the AOIC threshold can be traced back to the Computer Software Directive, there was no reference point in the Directive to understand the threshold of AOIC.[102]

6.2.2 *Threshold Over the Years*

While *sui generis* has undergone many changes in terms of structure and scope, there has been no change to the AOIC threshold in the period between the first draft and final Directive.[103] One has to remember that the primary objective of the Directive was to design a *sui generis* right for electronic databases that are unlikely to come within the ambit of copyright protection.[104] Logically, the starting point had to be copyright, since it provided a primary basis for protecting compilations in the member states.[105] Moreover, the harmonized threshold of copyright protection for databases could only ensure uniform application of *sui generis* right in the member states.[106]

The harmonized copyright protection had to be stable to maximize the objective of introducing a special right, which would uniformly protect investment made by database makers.[107] On one occasion, the European Parliament said that a substantial change must be borne by a second comer towards the selection or arrangement of the contents if that database were to be considered for copyright

[96] This led to the development of the idea behind the enactment of the database right, *Infra* chapter 7.

[97] ibid, para [2.3.3].

[98] COM (88) 172 final.

[99] COM (90) 584 final.

[100] *Feist Publications* (n 3).

[101] *Supra* section 6.1; COM (92) 24 final, para [2.2.9].

[102] Council Directive 1991/250/EEC of 14 May 1991 on the legal protection of computer programs [1991] OJL122/1.

[103] *Infra* section 7.1.

[104] COM (92) 24 final, para [3.2.8].

[105] ibid, para [2.2.3].

[106] ibid, para [2.2.11].

[107] COM (92) 24 final, para [2.2.11].

protection.[108] Contrary to the position of the European Parliament, different official documents that were drawn at the stage of enacting the Directive made it very clear that there was no such requirement of showing any aesthetic or qualitative criteria while selecting or arranging contents of a database.[109] More importantly, expectation with the threshold requirement as portrayed by the European Parliament was not the threshold either intended by the first draft and subsequent proposals or followed by the courts in Europe.[110] The test of modicum of creativity was held to be sufficient for a database to merit protection under Article 3 of the Directive.[111] There was consistency with the vision of copyright protection for a period of four years until the passage of the Directive in 1996.[112]

6.3 *Feist* Jurisprudence in Factual Contents and Monopoly

The interpretation of US Constitutional requirement of Progress of Science in the context of a factual compilation suggests that a second comer should be able to use factual contents from a database towards his own database.[113] This is subject to the limitation that he is not allowed to follow the exact way of selection or arrangement as in the first database.[114] By virtue of limited protection offered to first database producer, it is ensured that copyright protection in a case of a factual compilation does not create an "undesirably restrictive measure" for database producers who are interested in making similar databases.[115]

This level of protection available for the first database producer provides incentive for the subsequent database producers to follow.[116] The incentive lies in the free availability of factual information.[117] A database maker, by virtue of his creativity can ensure copyright protection for a compilation.[118] Resemblance of the

---

[108]European Parliament Minutes of Proceedings of the sitting of 23 June 1993 on Part II – Texts adopted by the European Parliament [1993] OJC 194/3, para [2a].

[109]Council Common Position 20/95/EC of 10 July 1995 with a view to adopting the Database Directive [1995] OJC 288/02.

[110]COM (92) 24 final, para [3.2.5]; *Supra* section 5.1.

[111]*Supra* chapter 5.

[112]Council Directive 96/9/EC.

[113]*Feist Publications* (n 3).

[114]ibid 349.

[115]ibid.

[116]This argument runs counter to the thought connected to the fundamental argument of providing incentive to first database producer; First Evaluation of Directive 96/9/EC, s 2.

[117]*Feist Publications* (n 3) 347; *Miller v Universal City Studios, Inc* 650 F.2d 1365 (5th Cir 1981) 1369.

[118]*Infra* section 6.4.

Feist jurisprudence can be found in the case involving a live football database.[119] Here the English Court suggested that there was no protection for collection of data, which was devoid of any creativity.[120] Although labour was involved in such collection, it was not the right kind to ensure copyright protection.[121] This decision prevented the use of 'sweat of the brow' argument.[122] Similar observation was also made in the *Football Dataco* case where labour towards making of a database was identified as not the right kind to merit copyright protection.[123] Although there was no explicit mention of the outcome of such decisions, one can identify the possible consequence. By way of refusing copyright protection in the aforementioned cases, the respective courts ensured free availability of factual data for a subsequent database maker.[124] However, one must remember that the change as a result of incorporating the *Feist* standard was mostly felt in UK in the context of databases.[125] The change only related to the shift in argument for copyright protection, meaning from 'sweat of the brow', to originality required through creativity in selection or arrangement of contents.[126] This shift in argument ensured extensive change in the field of copyright law in UK.[127] For instance, long before the enactment of the Directive, the second comer in the *University of London Press case* was asked to expend similar effort in collecting factual information as the first database maker.[128] This decision ensured that even facts available in public domain were monopolized by the first compiler owing to the 'sweat of the brow' argument.[129] Therefore, the second compiler, instead of building on the information available in the first compilation, had to expend similar amount of resources to get hold of the same factual information.[130] Any other database maker subsequent to the first and second database maker would need to follow similar steps.[131] This situation may reduce the incentive for producing similar databases, and implies use of huge amount of resources to collect the same data on more than one occasion.[132]

---

[119][2011] EWCA Civ 330, [2011] 1 WLR 3044.

[120]ibid, para [16].

[121]ibid.

[122]ibid.

[123]*Football Dataco* 2 (n 25) para [82].

[124]*Feist Publications* (n 3) 347; *Miller* (n 117) 1369.

[125]*Supra* section 5.3.

[126]ibid.

[127]ibid.

[128][1916] 2Ch 601, 609.

[129]ibid.

[130]*H Blacklock & Co Ltd v C Arthur Pearson Ltd* [1915] 2 Ch, 376; *Ladbroke v William Hill* [1964] 1 WLR 273, 274.

[131]ibid.

[132]There is the barrier of high cost associated with the production of databases, Jerome H Reichman and Pamela Samuelson, 'Intellectual Property Rights in data?' (1997) 50(1) V and L Rev 51, 81.

The presence of *Feist* jurisprudence in *Live Football* and *Football Dataco* decisions were pivotal in ensuring that factual information remained free for subsequent use.[133]

While *Feist* decision freed up information, there was a belief that production would decrease as a negative effect.[134] Producers would have no incentive as a result of non-availability of copyright protection.[135] Although the above arguments suggest enough incentive for subsequent compilers, there is no guarantee that a compiler would be ready to invest with the knowledge that there is no protection for contents.[136] It would be worthwhile to note the approach of compilers in the midst of the idea that freeing up of information is necessarily detrimental for future production of databases.[137] The Commission was not convinced with the idea that copyright would still continue to protect exhaustive compilations.[138] The consequences of this idea created database right.[139] General observations surrounding this right in the context of *Feist* decision will be discussed in the next chapter.

6.4 *Feist*, Non-electronic Databases and Article 3

While electronic comprehensive databases are likely to possess required creativity, there is doubt as to extending copyright protection to comprehensive databases that are non-electronic in nature.[140] If copyright protection is available for databases in non-electronic format, it propagates the idea to look at databases in a way different from what has been necessarily portrayed at various quarters.[141] This is in relation to citing the fundamental argument that comprehensive databases would lack necessary selection or arrangement to merit copyright protection.[142] The *Feist* decision stated that most databases comprising of factual contents would receive protection.[143] If this observation holds true for databases in non-electronic format then the similar *Feist* jurisprudence that has been followed in Europe does not create a negative impact with reference to copyright protection.[144] The nature of

---

133[2011] EWCA Civ 330, [2011] 1 WLR 3044; *Football Dataco* (n 5).

134COM (92) 24 final, para [2.3.3].

135ibid.

136Previously we have seen how producers in US have invested without a particular protection in place for databases, *Supra* section 4.3.

137ibid.

138COM (92) 24 final para [2.3.3].

139First Evaluation of Directive 96/9/EC, s 2.

140Based on argument of the structure; *Supra* section 2.3.

141Comments on the concern with electronic databases (COM (92) 24 final), para [3.2.5].

142ibid.

143*Football Dataco* (n 5).

144We have observed that there was no appreciable impact of *Feist* decision in Europe, *Supra* chapter 3.

consequence and the issue of absence of creativity are observed through the lens of two comprehensive non-electronic databases.

Two Yellow/White pages directory are considered in this section.[145] White pages telephone directory, and in some cases yellow pages directory are typical examples that are least likely to follow the requisite selection or arrangement standard.[146] A non-electronic yellow pages directory (not colour specific, and may be white in colour) titled 'Thomson Local Directory of Croydon Area' (near London) and the telephone directory of 'British Telecom for South-West London' have been considered.[147]

Thomson Directory is useful for people who have moved to Croydon area for the first time. It provides guidance in finding essential information, having[148] two broad divisions of the directory: 'Business by Type' and 'Business by Name'. Further, they are sub-divided into many categories like 'New To The Area', 'Getting Married', 'Improving Your Home', 'Senior Living', 'Going Out/Having Fun', 'Well Being' etc.[149]

On the other hand, 'the phone book' of British Telecom for South-West London is divided into three parts: classifieds, business telephone numbers and residential telephone numbers.[150] 'Classifieds' consists of information about utilities/services, and companies engaged in delivering such services provide advertisements in this section.[151] Under the classified directory, the phone book listed advertisers by type of business. The business and residential phone numbers are arranged alphabetically from A to Z. Further, the phone book included 'a hair and beauty guide', 'a menu guide for restaurants and takeaways' and 'a leisure, sport and tourism guide'. These two directories need further analysis in the context of copyright protection.[152]

---

[145]Feist said no protection to mundane garden-variety telephone directories, which are arranged alphabetically, *Football Dataco* (n 5) 362.

[146]*Feist Publications* (n 3).

[147]In practical terms it is difficult to scan each and every page of a printed database. On the other hand if someone manages to bypass the TPM, it is easier to copy data from an electronic database. The type of TPM includes both access control mechanisms and copy control mechanisms. User id/Password that comes under the access control mechanism may be breached, although this is not the only kind of access control mechanism that may be used by a database producer. Other forms of access control mechanisms are encryption technologies, digital signatures etc., Aashit Shah, 'UK'S Implementation of the Anti-Circumvention Provisions of the EU Copyright Directive: An analysis' (2004) Duke Law and Technology Review 3.

[148]Thomson Directories Ltd, Thomson local.com: Directory 2011-12 (2011).

[149]There is little issue of frustration on the part of the user if the decision to include such selection or arrangement is market driven; This is again contrary to the proposition that ".the greater variety of classifications, the more frustrated the user of the yellow pages is likely to become" Jane C Ginsburg, 'No "Sweat"? Copyright and the Protection of Works of Information after *Feist v Rural*' (1992) 92(2) Colum L Rev 338, 345.

[150]British Telecom, London South West 2011/2012: The Phone Book (2011).

[151]ibid.

[152]ibid.

6.4.1 Unique Arrangement in Competitive Situation

The Thomson Directory would ideally like to include local information pertaining to Croydon, which may be required by a person living in this area. That does not mean they have been able to include such information successfully, since there are inherent challenges.[153] It is in fact true that not all traders and businesses may choose to include their details recorded in the Thomson Directory.[154] Therefore, the nature of the directory is such, that there is an automatic selection process in place. This selection will entail originality as per requirement and would differentiate from a directory of similar nature.[155] One needs to also contextualize any selection process in the background of the objective behind creation of the directory. While compiling, Thomson included only information, which in their opinion was important for an individual moving to Croydon.[156] Therefore, it is possible that a different company compiling a database of similar nature would consider different information. However, there is an obvious convergence between Thomson Directory and any other similar directory.[157] Both companies involved in publishing would ensure that the information in their respective directories is comprehensive, and they would include all possible information about Croydon. This means that in both directories the selection procedure may be of minimal standard, if one follows the objective of creating a directory consisting of factual information.[158]

Further we have to locate the factor that influences an individual to choose between the available directories. This depends on how effectively a person can find the desired information from either of the directories.[159] Therefore, arrangement of information and the effective design in helping to identify such information is essential for a successful directory.[160] The requirement of making a directory effective for an end-user helps in attaining creativity standards, which is essential to

---

[153]This is contrary to what Rural had compiled in their telephone directory, *Feist Publications* (n 3).

[154]This is an obvious outcome of any business strategy. Previously we have come across business strategy of Reed Elsevier, *Supra* section 4.3.

[155]Going by the given threshold, it is expected that this selection would meet the AOIC threshold, *Supra* section 5.1.

[156]*Supra* (n 154).

[157]This is the similarity between two comprehensive databases of similar kind. As said in the *Feist* decision, "Notwithstanding a valid copyright, a subsequent compiler remains free to use the facts contained in another's publication to aid in preparing a competing work, so long as the competing work does not feature the same selection and arrangement". *Feist Publications* (n 3) 349.

[158]ibid.

[159]'Reed Elsevier annual report 1997' available at <http://www.reed-elsevier.com/investorcentre/reports%202007/Pages/1992-2001.aspx> (accessed 10 December 2010). (Reed Elsevier annual report 1997).

[160]"...Arrangement of the compilation will have a bearing on the speed and ease with which the data can be assessed and hence it's commercial success", COM (88) 172 final, para [6.1.5].

meet originality under copyright.[161] Thomson had arranged the data under various categories. Thus, on the basis of specific arrangement, the directory of Thomson is also copyrightable.[162]

6.4.2 Selected Information and Market Demand

In the *Feist* case, Rural was under statutory obligation to publish the details of the subscribers.[163] One might wonder about the outcome if such publication was not a statutory obligation. That situation would surely have given Rural the opportunity to perceive the situation in a different way. Further, subscribers may have chosen to opt out from their names appearing in such directory. In case of the British Telecom white pages telephone directory, the customers always has the option to opt out from their names appearing in the directory.

British Telecom has carefully selected certain specific information for the phone book. This is a part of the business policy.[164] It is logical that British Telecom telephone book included these selections because they were assured of the consumer demand. The decision on their part is purely market driven. For instance, a similar approach has been indicated in the Annual Reports of Reed Elsevier.[165] There is little doubt that the phone book is beyond a database representing only the collection of numbers.[166] Some creative effort has been expended to increase the utility of this book for prospective users. The selective mechanism and discretion has resulted in the inclusion of above outlined categories.[167] Although there are limited ways of arranging customer or business information in a telephone book, the selected categories in classified section should receive copyright protection.[168]

---

[161]ibid.

[162]Justice O'Conner in Feist citing Nimmer said: "...arrang[ing] the collected data so that they may be used effectively by readers" *Feist Publications* (n 3) 340; Discussing usefulness as a primary concept for the compiler and helps in copyright protection, Alan L Durham, *Speaking of the World: fact, opinion and the originality standard of copyright* (2009) 33(3) Arizona State Law Journal 791, 155.

[163]*Feist Publications* (n 3) 342.

[164]ibid; *Supra* (n 154).

[165]Consulted in chapter 4.

[166]These facts, are contrary to the proposition that "for many post-Feist information compilations, the decision to add this kind of "value" may be driven more by a desire to achieve creative originality than by consumer demand", Ginsburg (n 149) 347.

[167]'A hair and beauty guide', 'a menu guide for restaurants and takeaways' and 'a leisure, sport and tourism guide'.

[168]One could arrange by first name (as done in Iceland), by address, by telephone number as well as by surname; From the comments of the reviewer.

It is a fallacy that only comprehensive,[169] alphabetically arranged telephone directories[170] would be useful for a customer.[171] From the point of utility, they are not useful until efficient search mechanisms[172] are associated with the overall comprehensiveness.[173] In other words, it is difficult to comprehend that business houses would produce directories that are purely loaded with information[174] without essential variance through essential selection and arrangement of contents.[175] Therefore, the directories in question, and other similar comprehensive databases are likely to satisfy the less stringent threshold requirement of AOIC under Article 3.[176]

Despite databases satisfying the threshold requirements of Article 3, protection only extends towards structure.[177] Thus, there may be an additional issue of safeguarding contents in such a database.

6.5 Experiments with Database Right

While there was an idea that *Feist* decision would have negative impact, there was no clear jurisprudence concerning the extent of such impact on electronic database market.[178] Even though there have been claims to suggest negative impact of *Feist* decision on US database producers, there were no cases immediately after the decision to suggest any negative impact on producers.[179]

Therefore, the proposed structure of the Database Directive was an outcome of an unknown apprehension and to some extent to the increasing competitive nature of database market at that time.[180] Under these circumstances it was critical to have a right balance in the proposed database right to ensure stability and create enough incentive for the European producers.[181]

---

[169]This was expressed in the first draft proposal. It was further suggested that there would be less selection or arrangement in a comprehensive database, COM (92) 24 final, para [2.3.3].

[170]Like the one developed by Rural in *Feist Publications* (n 3).

[171]Reed Elsevier annual report 1997 (n 159).

[172]ibid.

[173]ibid.

[174]ibid.

[175]ibid.

[176]*Supra* section 5.1.

[177]*Feist Publications* (n 3) 349.

[178]COM (92) 24 final, para [2.3.3].

[179]US Copyright Office: Report on Legal Protection for Databases (August, 1997) available at <www.copyright.gov/reports/db4.pdf> (accessed 30 November 2016).

[180]COM (92) 24 final, s 2.

[181]The balance was questioned in the First Evaluation of the Directive, First Evaluation of Directive 96/9/EC, para [4.3].

At the stage of introducing database right, the uncertainty with the scope of such right was obvious. In four years, from the proposal to final Directive, structure of the database right has changed on more than one occasion.[182] One of the ways to explain these changes would be the following. Database right was an experiment and therefore, changes were required once the exact and precise way of incentivizing production came to knowledge.[183] This argument may act as a justification in explaining the changes that took place in the first structure of the proposed database right.[184] However, there was no such available information suggesting that changes were required.[185] Therefore, the subsequent changes that took place was again an experiment without precise knowledge about the requirement.[186] All other subsequent changes that happened concerning the structure of database right were similar experiments that went on for four years.[187] There was no explicit reasoning given, while making any of these changes.[188] Taking a cue from the first evaluation report, there is uncertainty in the way changes happened to the structure of database right.[189] Therefore, we must understand reasons for changes to be uncertainty and anxiety, which were present in Europe.[190] Interestingly, while experiments continued in the pre-directive stage, there were no amendments made subsequent to the passage of database right.[191] In terms of number of European databases, the database right has not been effective.[192] Therefore, the present structure that was accepted after so many experiments did not cater to increase in number.[193] It may be argued that number of databases was not the ultimate objective behind the enactment of database right. The idea was to instill confidence among European producers.[194] Even if one goes by this argument, the database right failed to instill

[182]*Infra* section 7.2.

[183]The argument that *Sui generis* database right was an experiment, Robin Elizabeth Herr, *Is the Sui Generis Right a Failed Experiment? A legal and Theoretical Exploration of How to Regulate Unoriginal Database Contents and Possible Suggestions for Reform* (DJØF Publishing Copenhagen, Denmark 2008).

[184]Mark J Davison, *The legal protection of databases* (Cambridge University Press Cambridge 2003) 51–102; Annemarie Beunen, *Protection for databases: The European Database Directive and its effects in Netherlands, France and United Kingdom* (Wolf Legal Publishers Leiden 2007) 3–14; Herr (n 183) 85–101.

[185]ibid.

[186]ibid.

[187]ibid.

[188]ibid; First Evaluation of Directive 96/9/EC, s 2.4.

[189]ibid.

[190]With the emergence of the electronic database market there was enough evidence present in the first draft proposal to show anxiety and apprehension, COM (92) 24 final, s 1–3.

[191]There was such suggestion made in the First Evaluation of Directive 96/9/EC, s 6.

[192]ibid, s 2.4.

[193]ibid, s 5.3.

[194]There was such argument made in the first evaluation report wherein the publishers said that there was increase in investments if not increase in number of electronic databases, ibid, s 4.1.3.

such confidence because the production of databases is directly linked to the extent of confidence that is present amongst producers.[195] The jurisprudence that was reiterated in *Feist* created uncertainty, and this uncertainty featured in Database Directive, especially with the legislation of database right.[196] Even the final outcome was not positive in comparison to what the Commission might have predicted at the time of proposal.[197] With the overall uncertainty, it would have been difficult to comprehend certain specificities in the database right.[198] Such protection may lead to monopolization of information, and may be detrimental for the overall growth of the European market.[199] Europe walked the road that was avoided even after *Feist*.[200] Therefore, merely contemplating possible ill-effect without any definitive impact may be over compensating the producers of electronic databases.[201]

With the resemblance of *Feist* standard in Europe, the impact of *Feist* decision is truly global.[202] *Feist* created this jurisprudence surrounding the protection of databases that was debated for more than two decades.[203] The footprints were present in the context of the threshold of AOIC. It remains to be seen how the balance in the Database Right was maintained.

---

[195]There was no evidence given by the publishers or suggested any alternative way to measure incentive amongst publishers, ibid.

[196]COM (92) 24 final, para [2.3.3].

[197]First Evaluation of Directive, 96/9/EC.

[198]Questioning the balance, Estelle Derclaye, 'Intellectual property rights on information and market power—comparing European and American protection of databases' (2007) 38(3) IIC 275, 297.

[199]*Infra* section 7.3.

[200]Council Directive 96/9/EC.

[201]*Supra* sections 7.2 and 7.3.

[202]Gervais (n 25).

[203]If one considers the time till the First Evaluation report in 2005, First Evaluation of Directive 96/9/EC.

Chapter 7
Uncertainties with *Sui Generis* Database Right: Negative Interpretation of *Feist*

The concern with the apparent negative effect as a result of the *Feist* judgment gave rise to the database right in Europe. This chapter observes such negative effect at the formative stage, stage of enactment and post-enactment stage.[1] All these effects are associated with the structure of the database right.[2] Although concern with the right can only be comprehended at the first two stages, ill-effects are truly visible in the post-enactment stage.[3] The database right has led to considerable monopoly concerns, especially with single-sourced databases.[4]

7.1 Requirement of Database Right in the Draft Proposal

The year 1992 saw the passage of a draft proposal suggesting the enactment of a database right in Europe.[5] This proposal envisaged a commercial right that intended to stop misappropriation of contents from an electronic database.[6] Databases containing works protected under copyright or neighbouring right were not covered under this right.[7] Further, the protection did not extend to databases in non-electronic format, and

[1] *Infra* sections 7.1, 7.2, and 7.3.
[2] *Infra* sections 7.2 and 7.3.
[3] *Infra* section 7.3.
[4] *Infra* section 7.3.
[5] Commission, 'Proposal for a Council Directive on the legal protection of databases' COM (92) 24 final (COM (92) 24 final).
[6] ibid, art 2(5).
[7] ibid; In the final version, there was a shift from the first draft proposal, since the proposal recommended that database right should not apply to databases, if copyright or neighbouring rights subsisted in the contents of such database.

I. Gupta, *Footprints of Feist in European Database Directive*,
DOI 10.1007/978-981-10-3981-2_7

scope of the right excluded private use.[8] Where works or contents were difficult to obtain from other source, there were provisions on compulsory licensing of databases.[9] Other than the compulsory licensing provision, a lawful user enjoyed certain additional exceptions in the context of rights enjoyed by a producer.[10] Subject to acknowledging the source, the first draft proposal allowed a lawful user to extract and re-utilize insubstantial portions of the contents of a database for commercial use.[11] There was no such requirement of acknowledgement, if the insubstantial portions were for private and personal use. In the first proposal, the term of protection for database right was ten years.[12]

We have already observed how *Feist* played a major role in bringing about the concept of a separate database right.[13] Other than the Feist decision in place, there were no further guidelines available to suggest the type and nature of protection measure required for database producers.[14] Under these difficult circumstances, the Commission had two options. The first was to do away with the idea of enacting a special right in the backdrop of the *Feist* decision. The other option was to experiment with a special right without any background knowledge concerning protection of non-original databases.[15] Following the second option, the Commission continued on the path of experimentation.[16] At this formative stage of the proposal, jurisprudence developed as a result of the *Feist* decision played a crucial role.[17] The *Feist* case concretized the idea that a new form of legislation was required to create a perfect atmosphere for investment.[18] Even though *Feist* dealt with a phone directory, the comprehensiveness feature was expected to be present in case of both electronic and non-electronic databases.[19] While the idea of protecting comprehensive databases came from *Feist,* the structure of such protection was merely assumed, and requires further analysis.

---

[8]ibid, art 1(1) & 2(5).

[9]COM (92) 24 final, art 8(1); In the opinion of Jane Ginsburg, the best balance in relation to non-original databases is through the compulsory licensing system whereby access to information is maintained, while there is less chance of appropriating the investment of publishers in such databases, Jane C Ginsburg, 'Creation and Commercial Value: Copyright protection of works of Information' (1990) 90(7) Colum. L. Rev. 1865, 1924–1927.

[10]In the first draft proposal, there was no definite indication about the meaning associated with lawful user, although the explanatory memorandum to the first draft proposal suggests that a lawful user is a "person having acquired the right to use a database." Further discussion on a lawful user will be considered in the next section. COM (92) 24 final, art 5(1).

[11]COM (92) 24 final, art 8(4).

[12]ibid, art 8(5).

[13]*Supra* chapter 6.

[14]ibid.

[15]ibid, section 6.5.

[16]ibid.

[17]COM (92) 24 final, para [2.3.3].

[18]ibid.

[19]*Feist Publications v Rural Telephone Service* 499 US 340 (1991).

7.1.1 Limited Protection to Producers

The first draft proposal limited the situations under which a producer could safeguard contents of his database. He could only rely on database right when substantial portions of the contents of his database have been copied or re-utilized.[20] However, such protection was limited only to electronic databases.[21] This implied the impending problem was in relation to databases that were electronic in nature. Databases in non-electronic format were not considered, although the contents in such databases are prone to a greater degree of copying.[22] There was a clear indication that important commercial databases would be electronic in nature.[23] It is also evident that more importance was given to the term 'comprehensive' instead of databases in paper or electronic format.[24] By not extending protection to non-electronic databases, the Commission made it clear that only limited protection was required for producers.

The concern relating to possible monopoly situation as a result of granting protection to contents of a database was addressed in the first proposal.[25] However, this situation might have arisen in case of single-sourced database producers.[26] Although protection was made available to a database producer involved in the production of single-sourced informational database, use of compulsory licensing provisions removed monopoly concern.[27] Further, exceptions provided in the proposal balanced the issue of accessibility of information. According to the first draft proposal, producer of an electronic database enjoyed limited right over contents without giving away unlimited monopoly over information.[28]

---

[20]COM (92) 24 final, art 1[1].

[21]ibid, art 2[5].

[22]In practical terms it is difficult to scan each and every page of a printed database. On the other hand if someone manages to bypass the TPM, it is easier to copy data from an electronic database. The type of TPM includes both access control mechanisms and copy control mechanisms. User id/Password that comes under the access control mechanism may be breached, although this is not the only kind of access control mechanism that may be used by a database producer. Other forms of access control mechanisms are encryption technologies, digital signatures etc., Aashit Shah, 'UK'S Implementation of the Anti-Circumvention Provisions of the EU Copyright Directive: An analysis' (2004) Duke Law and Technology Review 3.

[23]COM (92) 24 final, s 1.

[24]ibid, para [1.2].

[25]ibid, art 8[1].

[26]*Infra* section 7.3.

[27]ibid.

[28]COM (92) 24 final, art 6 and 7.

7.1.2 Limited Incentive for Electronic Database

The limited protection offered to database producers in the first proposal points to the possible requirement of minimum incentive for production of electronic databases.[29] In previous chapters, we have observed that without special incentive in place, production of electronic databases may continue.[30] Further, there is no guarantee that production would be a natural outcome of any additional incentive.[31] Although the explanatory memorandum to the draft proposal identified the immense potential of the European database industry, they offered limited incentive to database producers. This suggests that Europe would not need greater incentive to realize true potential of the database market.[32] The draft proposal has highlighted competitive relationship with the US database market.[33] Introducing limited incentive for producers in the background of increasing competition was particularly interesting. Therefore with limited incentive, the European database market was expected to compete internationally.[34] With no precedent of database right, the first draft proposal adopted a cautious approach.[35]

The proposal of limited incentive relates to the *Feist* jurisprudence. In the context of threshold of creativity, the US Supreme Court stated that most databases will receive copyright protection.[36] Therefore, even in the period of uncertainty immediately after *Feist* decision, the Commission believed that the amount of incentive required for database producers was less.[37] This signifies that producers with a limited amount of incentive will invest towards production of electronic databases that were essentially comprehensive in nature.[38]

Going back to *Feist* decision, one observes that the available protection is essentially thin to prevent monopoly situation out of copyright protection.[39] The limited protection under the first draft proposal is comparable to the thin protection under *Feist* decision. Overall, although the Commission wanted to mend the

---

[29]ibid.

[30]*Supra* section 4.3.

[31]'DG Internal market and services working paper: First Evaluation of Directive 96/9/EC on the legal protection of databases' (*Commission of the European Communities*, 12 December 2005) available at <http://ec.europa.eu/internal_market/copyright/docs/databases/evaluation_report_en.pdf> (accessed 31 October 2016) (First Evaluation of Directive 96/9/EC), para [5.3].

[32]COM (92) 24 final, s 1 and 2.

[33]ibid.

[34]With protection in place the European database industry could not do much in terms of number of databases, First Evaluation of Directive 96/9/EC, para [5.3].

[35]Mark J Davison, *The legal protection of databases* (Cambridge University Press Cambridge 2003) 60.

[36]*Feist Publications* (n 19) 345.

[37]Similarly, there was a gap in the US immediately after the *Feist* decision, *Supra* section 4.2.

[38]*Supra* section 4.3.

[39]*Feist Publications* (n 19) 349.

apprehended post-*Feist* situation, the proposal was kept mostly within the periphery of the boundary created by *Feist*.[40] On the face of it, the fear of *Feist* decision did not result in a proposal that reflects negative impact of the decision.[41]

Four years subsequent to the first draft proposal, the database right was enacted in 1996. This transition from the first proposal and changes mentioned therein are discussed in the following sections.

7.2 Imbalance and Complexities in the Database Right

The Directive provides protection to databases in both electronic and non-electronic formats.[42] Under the new structure, database right exists independent of any copyright protection that may subsist in the contents of a particular database.[43] Contrary to this provision, the first draft proposal provided no protection for a particular database under database right, if copyright or neighbouring rights subsisted in the contents.[44]

Other than including a commercial right to stop misappropriation of contents from an electronic database, application of database right prevents private users from extracting for a non-commercial purpose.[45] In the first draft, private use was not infringing in relation to the use of a database. The question of infringement was only limited to commercial misappropriation.[46] In the final version certain exceptions have been granted to a lawful user under Article 8. He may extract or re-utilize an insubstantial part of the contents for any purpose. However, such act should not interfere with the normal exploitation of such database, or unreasonably prejudice the legitimate interests of the database maker.[47] Other than the mandatory exception under Article 8, the Directive under Article 9 provides an opportunity to member states to legislate optional exceptions for the lawful user, and for the purpose of teaching and research.[48] Under this provision, a lawful user may extract a non-electronic database for private purpose. For the purpose of illustration in teaching or scientific research, member states may provide an exception in relation to extraction of contents.[49] This extraction, however, should be for non-commercial

---

[40]COM (92) 24 final, para [2.3.3] and section 3.

[41]The fact that limited protection was offered in the background of the possible negative effect, COM (92) 24 final.

[42]Council Directive of 1996/9/EC of 27 March 1996 on the legal protection of databases [1996] OJ L 77/20 (Council Directive 96/9/EC).

[43]ibid, art 7(4).

[44]COM (92) 24 final, art 2[5].

[45]Council Directive 96/9/EC, art 9[a].

[46]COM (92) 24 final, art 8[4] and 8[5].

[47]Council Directive 96/9/EC.

[48]ibid.

[49]ibid.

use, and with due acknowledgement of the source.[50] On the other hand, according to Article 15, a database producer cannot contract out the lawful user from legitimate rights under Article 8.[51] The final version of the Directive removed compulsory licensing provision even if contents can only be obtained from a single database producer.[52]

The term of protection of database right was increased from the proposed ten years in the first draft to a period of 15 years in the Database Directive.[53] This is renewable whenever there is substantial qualitative or quantitative change in the contents because of qualitative or quantitative substantial investment. Substantial change may include "… additions, deletions or alterations".[54] Even a substantial verification may be sufficient to start a fresh term of protection for a particular database.[55] The Directive is silent about the number of new terms introduced in the final version of database right, although CJEU/ECJ has provided some explanations.[56]

In the first draft proposal, database right was limited in many respects.[57] There was a balance between requirement of incentive and accessibility of information.[58] Database producers would have enjoyed limited protection for preventing unfair

---

[50]ibid, art 6[2] [b].

[51]As observed in the first draft proposal not much headway has been made in the final version of the Directive regarding the meaning associated to lawful user. According to the explanatory memorandum a lawful user is a person who has acquired the right to use a database. Varied interpretation has been given to the term, since the meaning has not been decided by the ECJ. There are three possible meanings attached to the term lawful user: user relying on statutory or contractual exceptions, license, or he is the lawful acquirer. Out of these, the option of lawful acquirer is the best choice in the opinion of commentators. It has been argued that the lawful user has got similar meaning as in the case of the Software Directive in EU 2009/24/EC. According to the Software Directive, a lawful user lawfully acquires the use of a database by a contract. For example, online databases obtained through subscription at libraries or research institutions. This interpretation seems to have some support, since Article 15 states that a database producer cannot contract out the lawful user from the rights offered under Article 8. Later in the thesis, the two possible meanings attached to lawful user will be analyzed in the context of access and infringement, Estelle Derclaye, *The Legal Protection of Databases: A Comparative Analysis* (Edward Elgar, Northampton 2008) 122–126.

[52]Council Directive 96/9/EC, art 16[3].

[53]ibid, art [10(1)].

[54]ibid, art [10(3)].

[55]ibid, Recital [55].

[56]ECJ's decision in C-46/2, *Fixtures Marketing Ltd v. Oy Veikkaus Ab*, [2005] ECDR 2, C-444/02 *Fixtures Marketing Ltd v Organismos Prognostikon Agnon Podosfairou (OPAP)* [2005] ECDR 3, C-338/02, *Fixtures Marketing Ltd v. Svenska Spel AB* [2005] ECDR 4, Case C-203/02 *The British Horseracing Board Limited v William Hill Organisation Ltd* [2005] ECDR 1, Case C-545/07 *Apis-Hristovich EOOD v Lakorda AD* [2009] ECDR 13, Case C-304/07 *Directmedia Publishing GmbH v Albert-Ludwigs-Universität Freiburg* [2008] ECR I-7565.

[57]Minimalistic solution offered to tackle the lack of uniformity in the laws protecting databases, and was meant to stop commercial copying of the contents of databases if they were not protected by copyright, Davison (n 35).

[58]*Supra* section 7.1.

extraction of their contents.[59] The provisions on compulsory licensing, and the exceptions provided to a lawful user balanced the control over dissemination of factual information.[60] In the final version, changes made in the database right apparently look to provide more to a database producer.[61] There was a change in the overall requirement of incentive in comparison to what was proposed in the first draft proposal. The first draft proposal started on a cautious note. In the space of four years there were certain changes made in the final structure of database right. There have been no explanations given as to why these changes were vital in the context of incentive for European database producers.[62] The proposed changes without reasonable grounds make us wonder about the arguments and logic that spearheaded the changes. It could be that immediate implication of the *Feist* decision was not fully comprehended.[63] The proposal, therefore, suggested limited protection for producers. It was only at a later stage that the effect of the decision was understood, and thus, changes were naturally brought about in the Directive.[64] This understanding is however not based on any concrete evidence.[65]

7.2.1 Threshold of Substantial Investment Uncertain

If database right was created to incentivize prospective database producers, then the threshold of substantial investment would certainly be less stringent.[66] We have already observed that modicum of creativity is not a difficult threshold to meet, and a non-obvious selection or arrangement in a factual compilation can easily fulfill such requirement.[67] Therefore, the word 'substantial' pre-fixed to investment could be misleading.[68] Substantial investment can take either qualitative or quantitative form, but the Directive has been silent about the actual meaning assigned to 'substantial'.[69] If the objective behind creating this right is to protect databases that fail to meet

---

[59]ibid.

[60]ibid.

[61]*Supra* section 7.2.

[62]This is similar to the substantial changes that occurred at the Common Position in case of computer programs Directive in Europe, Council Directive 91/250EEC. There was a major deviation from the proposed text in the context of Article 6 of the said Directive, dealing with de-compilation, Bridget Czarnota and Robert J Hart, *Legal Protection of Computer Programs in Europe- A guide to the EC Directive* (Butterworths London 1991) 23.

[63]There was inaction in US, *supra* section 4.2.

[64]The producers in US did invest towards database, *supra* section 4.3.

[65]Miriam Bitton, 'Exploring the European Union Copyright Policy through the lens of the Database Directive' (2008) 23(4) Berkeley Tech LJ 1411, 1426.

[66]First Evaluation of Directive 96/9/EC, para [4.1.2].

[67]*Supra* section 3.3.

[68]Davison (n 35) 83.

[69]William Cornish and others, *Intellectual Property: Patents, Copyright, Trade Marks and Allied Rights* (7th edn. Sweet & Maxwell London 2010) 877.

modicum of creativity requirement then it is important to understand the nature of the investment protected under database right. It is not necessary to quantify the investment made towards a particular database.[70] This argument has been validated by ECJ in the case involving British Horseracing Board.[71] ECJ pointed to the investment towards creating of data used in a database. Further, Recital 39 talks about protecting outcomes of financial and professional investment.[72] On a similar note Recital 40, talks about deployment of "financial resources and/or the expending of time, effort and energy".[73] All of the above examples state the type of investment that would qualify for protection under Article 7. Further, as discussed in the previous chapter, Recital 19 points to the type of investment that would not qualify for protection.[74] These explanations also suggest that the scope of substantial investment is essentially broad.[75] Essentially any investment qualifies under Article 7 except those that have been explicitly excluded under Recital 19.[76] Keeping a broad coverage would signify the intention to cover maximum number of databases. The wide coverage of substantial investment, under Article 7 suggests that majority of the databases should be protected. It presumes the idea that incentive is required for their production.[77]

By keeping the scope wide enough for database producers, the Article did not manage to avoid uncertainties. The first evaluation report pointed to such uncertainties surrounding 'substantial', which have led to various interpretations in the member states.[78] For instance, the evaluation report specifically considered four decisions on substantial investment. The first two were Dutch case decisions in *NVM v. De Telegraaf* and *Algemeen Dagblad a.o. v. Eureka* (*Kranten.com*).[79] In *De Telegraaf*, cost of collecting and maintaining up-to-date information concerning several thousands of real estate properties amounted to substantial investment. On the other hand, in *Eureka,* headlines of articles published in a newspaper were held to be a mere 'spin-off' of the newspapers' publishing activities. Hence, the Court ruled that there was no substantial investment in spin-off databases.[80] The remaining two cases

[70]Derclaye (n 51) 73–75.

[71]*British Horseracing Board Limited* (n 56).

[72]Council Directive 96/9/EC.

[73]ibid.

[74]*Supra* section 51.

[75]Derclaye (n 51) 75.

[76]Council Directive 96/9/EC.

[77]*Supra* section 4.3.

[78]First Evaluation of Directive 96/9/EC; The scholars are concerned with the delimitation of substantial investment, since the concept of substantial is vague, Mathias Leistner, 'The legal protection of telephone directories relating to the new database maker's right' (2000) 31(7/8) IIC 950.

[79]LJN: AA8588, Rechtbank's-Gravenhage, KG 00/949 and President District Court of Rotterdam, 22 August 2000, Media forum 2000, p. 344, [2000] AMI 205, note K.J. Koelman in P. Bernt. Hugenholtz, 'The New Database Right: Early Case Law from Europe', Int'l Intell. Prop. L. & Pol'y 70–1, 70–14 (2002).

[80]See the ECJ's judgement in C-203/2 where it was held that spin-off databases may be protected if there is a separate substantial investment.

were *baumarkt.de* and *Hit Bilanz* in Germany.[81] In *baumarkt.de*, while website may be a database, it was held that the investment towards construction, maintenance or display of data in that website was not substantial.[82] In *Bilanz,* the plaintiff made a German "Top 10" hit chart of music titles, which was published weekly. Based on their sales number and radio playing times, the Court acknowledged that the plaintiff's effort of collection and verifying such music requires substantial investment.[83]

There is no definite indication about the meaning associated with substantial investment. The decisions have converged to the conclusion that substantial investment has been given a broad scope. On one end of the spectrum, there is monetary investment and at the other end, time and effort spent in databases are considered sufficient to meet threshold of substantial investment.[84] The broad meaning associated with substantial investment is not only confined to these four decisions, but have emerged in other member states as well.[85] Subsequent to the enactment of database right, commentators thought that substantial investment would not necessarily mean a stringent test to be followed by database producers.[86]

Since the definition of database is broad, a wide coverage of substantial investment has resulted in the protection of databases of various kinds.[87] For a particular database, it is difficult to ascertain the exact requirement to meet the threshold of substantial investment. The overall objective of this Directive is to create a sense of stability among producers.[88] It has failed to provide certainty at the first step itself by leaving the definition of substantial investment open for wide interpretation.[89] Therefore, it is not easily explicable why there was no substantial investment in the construction, maintenance or display of a website.[90] In the same jurisdiction, music titles received protection under Article 7.[91] Arguably, other than the types specified under Recital 19, all other investments should be able to qualify

---

[81]*baumarkt.de*, Oberlandesgericht Düsseldorf 29 June 1999, [1999] Multimedia und Recht 729 in Hugenholtz (n 79); Federal Supreme Court (Bundesgerichtshof), 21 July 2005.

[82]ibid.

[83]ibid.

[84]Derclaye (n 51) 75.

[85]ibid 79.

[86]In all likelihood, substantial investment would possibly carry a broad meaning. In addition to financial resource, which is an obvious example of substantial investment, the question of human investment with regards to spending time, effort and energy have been considered, Recital 40 Council Directive 96/9/EC; Juliet Jenkins, 'Database rights' subsistence: under starter's order' (2006)1(7) Journal of Intellectual Property Law & Practice, 467-477.

[87]For instance, a non-copyrightable list of a list of permanent memory addresses of mobile phones to be used in forensic investigations has been found protectable under *sui generis* database right in *Forensic Telecommunications Services Limited v The Chief Constable of West Yorkshire Police and others* [2011] EWHC 2892 (Ch).

[88]First Evaluation of Directive 96/9/EC, s 2.

[89]ibid, para [4.1.2].

[90]*Supra* (n 81).

[91]ibid.

for the threshold of substantial investment.[92] It shows the existing uncertainty with the threshold of substantial investment and it may reduce incentive for producers to invest towards databases.[93]

7.2.2 Limited Exceptions

Following the intent to cover most databases, the final version of the Directive restricted the use of contents fearing misappropriation.[94] There are no generous exceptions in the Directive, especially in the part concerning database right.[95] In the process of creating enough incentive for producers, there are considerable imbalances.[96] This is in contrast to the *Feist* decision in US. Even after acknowledging a creativity threshold that can easily be fulfilled by database producers, the US Supreme Court ensured that there are enough exceptions to such right.[97] The shift in favour of the database producer meant that a lawful user is given limited rights in the final version of the Directive.[98]

In the midst of many possibilities, a lawful user is someone who has lawfully acquired the database either through a license or through a contract.[99] There is a fundamental difference between a license and a contract. Unlike a contract, in a license there is limited possibility of negotiating the terms. For instance, for an end-user, a software license comes bundled with software, where the terms are not negotiable.[100] Arguably, designating a lawful user as 'any user' is erroneous.[101] Since there is no clear indication about the status of a lawful user, two possibilities must be covered, i.e. any user or a lawful acquirer.[102]

---

[92]Council Directive 96/9/EC.

[93]First Evaluation of Directive 96/9/EC, para [4.1.2].

[94]Council Directive 96/9/EC, art 7.

[95]ibid art 9.

[96]Derclaye (n 51); Davison (n 35).

[97]The thin protection limitation, *Feist Publications* (n 19) 349.

[98]Article 8 in comparison to the rights of a lawful user under the first draft proposal, Council Directive 96/9/EC; *supra* section 7.1.

[99]Derclaye (n 51) 124 –126; Lawful user is the person who has obtained the copy of a database in a lawful way, Vinciane Vanovermeire, 'The concept of the lawful user in the database Directive' (2000) 31(1) IIC 63.

[100]Christopher M. Newman, 'A License Is Not a "Contract Not To Sue": Disentangling Property and Contract in the Law of Copyright Licenses' (2013) 98 Iowa L Rev II01, 1104. The first draft proposal talks about shrink-wrap agreements, which are essentially drafted unilaterally by producers. COM (92) 24 final, para [4.2.9].

[101]ibid; arguing against the proposition that a lawful user, under Article 8 is similar to the lawful user under copyright law. Under copyright law there is no need of contract for a lawful use, Davison (n 35) 77–78; Similarly, Grosheide states that they are similar but not identical, F W Grosheide, 'Database Protection-the European Way' (2002) 8(1) Wash U J L & Poly 39, 67.

[102]ibid. Derclaye (n 51) 120.

There was concern that a lawful user (when lawful user is any user), can extract and re-utilize contents of a database for private purposes prejudicing the normal exploitation of a database.[103] As a result, the final version excluded this exception, although such provision was present in the first draft proposal.[104] However, any user simply would not have access to any particular database. The database producer employs several protection measures before releasing a database to the public.[105] Some of these measures encompass the use of Technological Protection Measures and restrictions through password access.[106] Therefore, it is impossible for any user to access a database in the first place, let alone extract and re-utilize for private purpose. There are instances though, when a person may bypass the restrictions.[107] It would constitute an offense relating to cybercrime, and is not a subject matter to be considered under database right.[108] Mere existence of a right because of instances of illegal downloading is not the correct argument. Illegal downloading would continue even in the presence of database right.[109] This justifies strengthening Technological Protection Measures, and not enactment of a new right, which is not suited to control such downloading.[110]

When a lawful user is a lawful acquirer, there may be a possibility that he extracts and re-utilizes a database beyond private purpose. The argument that a lawful acquirer may act against normal exploitation of a database is assessed through the lens of the size of prospective databases.[111] These databases may be small, medium sized, or they may be as big as Westlaw or LexisNexis.

In case of a small or medium size database, a lawful acquirer may be able to copy contents depending on the resources available to him. However, it is questionable whether he would be able to compete where the original database needs regular updates.[112] Useful databases would require regular updates irrespective of the format. Whether it is a telephone directory in paper-format or an electronic database providing information about case law, they all must be updated for the purpose of

[103]Council Directive 96/9/EC Article 8[3].

[104]COM (92) 24 final, art 8[4] and 8[5].

[105]There are two categories of technological protection measures used. They are access control measures and copy control measures. Access control measures include cryptography, passwords and digital signatures. Copy control mechanisms are used in case of audio and video those are in electronic format, Shah (n 22).

[106]ibid.

[107]Derclaye (n 51) 197.

[108]*Supra* section 4.1.2.

[109]Derclaye (n 51) 197.

[110]*Supra* section 4.2.

[111]There is a general understanding that the cost towards the production of databases would act as a barrier for those who are interested in the manufacturing of similar databases, Jerome H Reichman and Pamela Samuelson, 'Intellectual Property Rights in data?' (1997) 50(1) V and L Rev 51, 81.

[112]There is protection for regular updates under the database directive as long as it is substantial either quantitatively or qualitatively, Council Directive 96/9/EC, art [10(3)].

accuracy and acceptability amongst their users.[113] Where there is no need to update a database on a regular basis, it may be possible that a lawful user extracts the database and competes with the original maker. Again, one has to remember that merely copying contents of a database may not be enough. Presentation is very important and holds the key to a commercially successful database.[114]

When the database is big, there are some practical difficulties in re-building a database of the size of Westlaw or LexisNexis. Primarily, large amount of resources would be required to create a database of this size.[115] It is even more difficult to make such database commercially viable, which would be able to compete with other similar databases.[116] In any case, requirement of substantial amount of resources at the initial stages makes database business monopolistic in nature.[117] Removal of the provision (private purpose) in the final version would less likely to have created any difference. This removal signifies over-protective measure, which will ultimately benefit a database producer.[118]

The above outlined argument suggests that private use of a database is seldom going to dislodge the investment made by a commercial database producer. Even if copied in the process, such use is unlikely to create any substantial uneasiness. Restricting private use is a sign of imbalance enshrined in the database right.[119] It is doubtful that database producers, without limited exceptions would not have sufficient incentives to invest towards the production of electronic databases.[120] There is a danger that with severe restrictions to accessibility, the overall impact is damaging for the society.[121] The lawful users in any of the above forms have less scope with regards to the use of information. While *Feist* talked about freeing up of information, the database right presumably did the exact opposite.[122]

---

[113]That is the reason why investment towards renewal is protected, ibid.

[114]*Supra* section 3.2.2.

[115]There is a barrier due to the cost factor towards the production of electronic factors, Reichman and Samuelson (n 111) 8.

[116]The first draft proposal spoke on the issue of making European databases competitive COM (92) 24 final, s1 and 2.

[117]Reichman and Samuelson (n 111) 81.

[118]Competitive databases rarely emerge because of the barrier of high cost of making the database, Reichman and Samuelson (n 111) 81; The OECD published report concerning computerized database market stated that in the field of Science and Technology, there were only seven major International publishers. This number was sure to come down to four to five publishers in the future, Lydia Arossa, *Economic and Trade Issues in the Computerized Database Market* (*Information Computer Communication Policy Paper* (OECD 1993); This shows that database market is essentially monopolistic in nature and the market was performing even prior to the enactment of the database right.

[119]First Evaluation of Directive 96/9/EC, para [4.3].

[120]Even the exceptions provided in the copyright part of the Directive under Article 5(2(b)) are broad than the *sui generis* part; Matthias Leistner, 'Legal protection for the database maker-initial experience from a German point of view' (2002) 33(4) IIC 439,458.

[121]First Evaluation of Directive 96/9/EC, para [4.3].

[122]*Feist Publications* (n 19) 349.

In the context of database right, member states have the opportunity to frame exceptions for a lawful user, but such opportunity is severely limited in many ways.[123] Under this provision, a lawful user can only extract insubstantial portions of a non-electronic database for private purpose.[124] This restriction is difficult to understand since there is no public dissemination in private use, and such use does not seem to affect the investment of a database producer.[125] Furthermore, the exception is only for non-electronic databases. From the point of utility, restricting extraction to non-electronic databases for private purpose is virtually a meaningless right for a lawful user. This is because important databases were believed to be electronic in nature, and database right was enacted in the background of a potential electronic database market.[126]

7.2.3 *Uncertain Term of Protection*

Even with incentive in place and limited exceptions, the term of protection creates a number of ambiguities with respect to the database right.[127] One can say that the issue of creating incentive with limited exceptions for database producers is an outcome of interpreting *Feist*,[128] but the ambiguities have no direct connection with the decision. The extension of the term from 10 to 15 years is indicative of the intention to protect databases for a long period.[129] Extension without adequate concern also reflects uncertainties.[130]

---

[123]This could be more problematic depending on how the exceptions are incorporated by the member states; A comparison with the copyright Directive of 2001 shows that such Directive has a long list of exceptions for the member states. A compulsory exception is there for temporary non-commercial acts of reproduction with a proposal for similar exception for extraction, Annemarie Beunen, *Protection for databases: The European Database Directive and its effects in Netherlands, France and United Kingdom* (Wolf Legal Publishers Leiden 2007) 228.

[124]Council Directive 96/9/EC, art [9(1)].

[125]Derclaye (n 51) 131.

[126]The first draft thought of protecting only electronic databases, Database Directive proposal, COM (92) 24 final.

[127]The fear is with perpetual protection of the contents of a database on every substantial change. If we go by the threshold of substantial investment, the word substantial may be misleading, Simon Chalton, 'The Amended Database Directive Proposal: A Commentary and Synopsis' (1994) 3 EIPR 94, 97; Mark Schneider, 'The European Union Database Directive' (1998) 13 Berkeley Tech LJ 551, 551 at available at <http://scholarship.law.berkeley.edu/btlj/vol13/iss1/35> (accessed 10 November 2010).

[128]*Supra* section 7.2.

[129]Comparing Article 10[1], Council Directive 96/9/EC with COM (92)24 final), Article 9[3].

[130]Debra B Rosler, 'The European Union's proposed Directive for the legal protection of databases: A new threat to the free flow of information' (1995) 10(1) High Tech L J 105, 118; Schneider (n 127) 556; Davide Mula and Mirko Luca Lobina, 'Legal Protection of the Web Page' in Hideyasu Sasaki (ed) *Information Technology for Intellectual Property Protection: Interdisciplinary Advancements* (Information Science Reference 2012) 214.

It is difficult to understand the basis of extending protection to 15 years owing to the dynamic nature of databases.[131] As rightly suggested by Estelle Derclaye, the term of protection required for a database depends on its type, investment made and frequency of update.[132] For a database that needs regular updates, term of protection stretching for a period of 15 years is questionable.[133] For instance, available protection may not be beneficial in case of a database comprising of information required for a stock market.[134] Providing more protection than required to factual information may result in a monopoly situation.[135] Similarly, databases incurring large investment may require more time to recover their cost. For them, the term may be less, and it may offer less incentive for future database producers.[136] The issue may be grave in case of a database producer who not only controls information, but also creates the same information.[137] Depending on the term, protection for single-sourced databases may result in keeping away information from public domain for a longer period.[138] There are various misgivings when the right is not balanced for either a producer or for public at large.[139] Emerging issues relating to single-sourced database producers have been considered in much greater details in the next section.

Much has been said about how indecision exists with reference to the renewal provision under Article 10.[140] Whether it is an issue of substantial investment coupled with substantial change, or the issue of fresh protection towards existing data, the database right stands at crossroad wherein, it may not be useful to database producers or good from the point of dissemination of information.[141] Further to the

---

[131]It has been suggested that it was extended as a result of the influence of publishers. However, there is no existing proof of such incident happening in EU, W Mathew Wayman, 'International Database Protection: A multilateral Treaty solution to the United States Database Dilemma' (1996–97) 37(2) Santa Clara L Rev 427, 439; Schneider (n 127) 556; Derclaye (n 51) 140.

[132]For substantial discussion on the issue of term of protection, Derclaye (n 51) 137–144.

[133]ibid.

[134]The period may be too long for databases with short life span-stock exchange list, fixture list or job vacancy. On the other hand, it may be too short for low sales databases, NautaDutilh Final Report: The Implementation and Application of Directive 96/9/EC on the legal protection of databases (Study commissioned by European Commission) available at <http://ec.europa.eu/internal_market/copyright/docs/databases/etd2001b53001e72_en.pdf> (2002) (accessed 10 February 2010) 494; Beunen (n 123) 36.

[135]Derclaye (n 51) 138.

[136]ibid.

[137]*Infra* section 7.3.

[138]Derclaye (n 51) 138; Single-sourced database may result in absolute monopoly of downstream information of products and services, P Bernt Hugenholtz, 'Abuse of database right: Sole-source information banks under the EU Database Directive' in F. Lévêque & H. Shelanski (eds.), *Antitrust, patents and copyright: EU and US perspectives* (Edward Elgar Cheltenham 2005) 203 and 217.

[139]*Infra* section 7.3.

[140]Derclaye (n 51) 137 and 144.

[141]These aspects have been explained lucidly by Derclaye (n 51) 139-141 and 147; First evaluation of Directive 96/9/EC.

potential problems that already exist, one needs to identify the challenges in framing a right without much previous knowledge.[142]

Theoretically, database right is heavily inclined in favour of a database maker, and has been under scathing attacks, since its enactment in 1996.[143] The first evaluation report of the Database Directive has talked about the existing complexities.[144] On an overall note, the scope and the exceptions suggest that there is a considerable imbalance present in the database right. Over the period of five years from the first proposal to the final version, database right has failed to pinpoint the exact requirement.[145] The ineffectiveness of database right is clear from observations made in the first evaluation report.[146]

7.3 Single-Sourced Databases Under the Directive

As a measure of dualistic approach under the Database Directive, database right ensured codification of 'sweat of the brow' theory.[147] There were anti-competitive concerns with such codification in place. In other words, database right will protect facts, and may result in monopolization of information. The factor which compounded the fear of monopolization was the removal of compulsory licensing provision for single-sourced databases.[148] Removal of compulsory licensing

---

[142]Bitton (n 65) 1426.

[143]The extension of the term of protection to fifteen years was without consulting any economic evidence, Derclaye (n 51) 147; There are several grey areas in the *sui generis* database right. Mainly, the criticisms have surrounded the scope, exceptions and term of protection with its renewal clause, Mark J Davison, 'Proposed U.S. Database legislation: a comparison with the U.K database Regulations' (1999) 21(6) EIPR 279; Mainly with its exceptions and renewal clause with the possible monopoly situation, Derclaye (n 51) paras [138-144]; It is one of the most complex rights and least balanced right to exist, Reichman and Samuelson (n 111) 81; Strong criticisms have been made against the *sui generis* database right part for being vague and uncertain, since it has left many areas open for interpretation, Irini A Stamatoudi, 'The EU Database Directive: reconceptualising copyright and retracting the future of sui generis right' (1997) 50 Hellenic Rev of Int'l L 435; The *sui generis* right is difficult to understand, First Evaluation of Directive 96/9/EC; On the other hand, despite of the criticisms concerning the database right, Jens Gaster is of the opinion that big problems have not resulted because of the database right, Jens Gaster, 'The EC *sui generis* right revisited after two years: a review of the practice of database protection in the 15 EU Member States' (2000) 5(3) Communications Law 87.

[144]First Evaluation of Directive 96/9/EC.

[145]The challenges with a novel right, Mark Powell, 'The European Union's Database Directive: An International Antidote to the side effects of Feist' (1996-97) 20(4) Fordham Int'l LJ 1215, 1217; First Evaluation of Directive 96/9/EC.

[146]First Evaluation of Directive 96/9/EC.

[147]Jens L Gaster, 'New EU Directive Concerning the Legal Protection of Databases' (1997) 20(4) Fordham Int'l L J 1129, 1142.

[148]Removal of compulsory licence was justified based on the argument that reliance must be placed on competition law, Recital 47. Instead a provision under Article 16 of the Directive was included in

provision may effectively lock up information, and increase the problems associated with accessibility.[149] In the background of such concern, opinion of ECJ (the CJEU) in *BHB* is important.[150] The decision of *BHB* represents the first instance when a matter related to database right was referred to ECJ.

BHB managed horseracing industry in the United Kingdom. BHB maintained a database, which contained large amount of information supplied by horse owners, trainers, horse race organizers and others who were involved in the racing world.[151] Amongst other things, the database contained information about one million horses, their pre-race information, including name, place and date of a particular race. The cost of running such database was nearly 4 million pounds per annum at that time.[152] This database was accessible online, and every week the official journal of BHB published some of the contents. The contents for the use of bookmakers and various other subscribers were in the form of a 'Declaration Feed' and 'Raw Data Feed' (RDF).[153] These two sources provided information like name of the horses,

(Footnote 148 continued)

order to assess any abuse of dominant position in case of single-sourced databases. There is a difference between the economic concept of a dominant position and the legal monopoly granted by intellectual property right. The economic concept of a dominant position is scrutinised under the European competition law and mere ownership of intellectual property may not amount to a dominant position, Beunen (n 123) 236; On the issue of information monopolies, the ECJ in Case C 241–242/91P *Radio Telefis Eireann and Independent Television Publications Limited (Intellectual Property Owners Inc. intervening) v E.C. Commission (Magill TV Guide Limited intervening)* [1995] 4 CMLR 718.

[The Magill case] commented that refusal to grant license on an intellectual property may under exceptional circumstances amount to abuse of dominant position. The main issue in this case was sole source database, and refusal to grant license on basic information. However, there is no clear guideline that refusal of license will always amount to an abuse of a dominant position Beunen (n 123) 241; The Directive, however, explicitly states that competition law is applicable to the databases protected under it, Council Directive 96/9/EC art [13] and [47].

149The fear of monopoly in the absence of compulsory provision is real and competition law, as suggested under Recital 47 of the Directive may not provide adequate remedies, Reichman and Samuelson (n 111), Catherine Colston, 'Sui generis Database right: Ripe for Review?" (2001) available at <http://www2.warwick.ac.uk/fac/soc/law/elj/jilt/2001_3/colston> (accessed 10 December 2009); Stephen M Maurer and others Europe's database right experiment (2001) 294 Science (26 October 2001) 769–770; There are quite a few areas in the *sui generis* database right where the issue of monopoly can be raised. They include the term of protection, which currently is based at 15 years. However, this again can be said in the context of sole source databases and the possibility that data can be monopolised for a period of 15 years, Derclaye (n 51) 145; D Vaver has been a critique of extending term protection without respectable empirical foundation in D Vaver, 'The Copyright Mixture in a Mixed Legal System: Fit for Human Consumption?', (2001) available at <http://www.ejcl.org/52/abs52-3.html> (accessed 15 March 2011).

150*British Horseracing Board* (n 56).

151These are synthetic data in the sense they do not exist in natural form. Synthetic data need certain kind of construction, for example data concerning racing information and stock market quotes, Samuel E Trosow, '*Sui Generis* database legislation' (2005) 7(1) Yale J of L & Tech 535, 541.

152British Horseracing Board (n 56) 7.

153ibid.

name of the jockeys, saddlecloth numbers and the weight of each horse running in a particular race. For the public, the general information about a particular race was available via newspapers, ceefax and teletext services.[154]

William Hill, a leading bookmaker in the United Kingdom was a subscriber of both the Declaration feed and the RDF.[155] William Hill provided betting services through its network of offices and over telephone. For the use of betting information, the company paid licensing fees to BHB. Later, William Hill launched its own betting services on two internet sites, which contained name of the horses running at a particular racecourse, date and time of the race, the name of the racecourses, alongside the odds offered by William Hill. The information provided on the betting websites was already made available to the public through newspaper and teletext services.[156]

There were few observations made by the ECJ about the website of William Hill and the BHB database. In comparison to the database of BHB, information displayed on the website of William Hill represented a small amount of data. William Hill only provided name of the horses in a particular race, date and time of a race, alongside name of the racecourses. Moreover, in comparison to the database of BHB, referencing system of information was different in the websites.[157]

In relation to the websites maintained by William Hill, BHB and others brought an action alleging infringement of the database right.[158] The infringement claim was based under Article 7(1) and 7(5) alleging extraction and re-utilization of the contents, and on systematic repeated extraction and re-utilization of insubstantial part.[159] William Hill argued that there was no infringement, since information provided in the websites was already available in the public domain. Moreover, information displayed on their websites was insubstantial and did not infringe the right of BHB.[160]

At the preliminary stage, the Court in England suggested that for the database right to subsist, substantial investment should be made towards gathering or obtaining existing data, and not towards creating those data.[161] However, when creation and obtaining happens simultaneously, which resulted in inseparable substantial investments towards the obtaining of contents, then such investment was within the scope of database right.[162] In other words, a company has protection for overlapping substantial investment at the time of simultaneously creating and

[154]ibid.

[155]ibid.

[156]ibid.

[157]ibid.

[158]ibid.

[159]ibid (n 56).

[160]*The British Horseracing Board Limited, The Jockey Club and Weatherbys Group Limited v William Hill Organization Limited* [2001] ECDR 20, 270.

[161]ibid.

[162]ibid.

incorporating the same data in their database.[163] The database of BHB provides an example where there was overlapping substantial investment in the process of creating and obtaining contents.[164] In this instance, the Court decided the matter in favour of BHB. Prior to the referral to ECJ, the Advocate General agreed with the above view of the Court in England.[165]

The ECJ considered that the purpose of the Directive was to promote and protect investment in data storage and processing system, which will contribute to the growth of the information market.[166] Against this background, investment made towards obtaining the contents of the database was "the resource used to seek out existing independent materials and collect them in the database and not to resources used for the creation as such of independent materials".[167] This opinion was similar to the view expressed by the English Court, and corroborates with the opinion of the Advocate General.[168] Thus, ECJ approved protection of investments directed towards collection of existing data, but not the investment towards creation of such data.

While speaking on the issue of inseparable substantial investment due to simultaneous action of creating or obtaining, ECJ touched upon the situation when a creator of a database was also the creator of contents.[169] According to ECJ, this situation does not automatically preclude the database maker from protection, if he could show substantial investment independent of investment made at the time of creating the data.[170] Ultimately, the matter was decided against BHB because there was no separate substantial investment, while obtaining data for their database.[171] Therefore, the opinion of ECJ differs from the decision of the Court in England, and opinion expressed by the Advocate General.

According to Jens Gaster, there was no intention on the part of the framers to create a distinction between generation of data and collection of data.[172] He suggested that the translation error led to such artificial distinction, and related the meaning of

[163]ibid.

[164]ibid.

[165]Opinion of Advocate General Stix-Hackl, on *British Horse Racing Board v. William Hill* (8 June, 2004) available at <http://curia.europa.eu/jurisp/cgi-bin/form.pl?lang=en> (accessed 10 November 2008).

[166]*British Horseracing Board* (n 56) 10.

[167]ibid 3.

[168]*Supra* (n 160).

[169]*British Horseracing Board* (n 56) 3.

[170]ibid 3 and 10.

[171]There have been two recent decisions in England suggesting the right type of investment towards obtaining, *British Sky Broadcasting Group Plc v Digital Satellite Warranty Cover Ltd* [2011] EWHC 2662 (Ch), [2012] 14 FSR 407; *Flogas Britain Limited v Calor Gas Limited* [2013] EWHC 3060 (Ch).

[172]Jens Gaster, "Obtinere of Data in the Eyes of the ECJ: How to interpret the Database Directive after *British Horseracing Board Ltd et al. v. William Hill Organisation Ltd*" (2005) 5(6) CLR Int'l 129; Commission's intention was to protect non-original databases in widest possible sense, First Evaluation of Directive 96/9/EC; It was suggested previously that ECJ (prior to its decision) should interpret 'obtaining' to include both creation and collection of data, Tanya Aplin, *The EU Database*

'obtinere' to the word 'obtaining' expressed under database right.[173] Further, '*Obtinere*' is a comprehensive term, and includes obtaining subsequent to creation and generation of data.[174] The original version of the Directive was in French because of the French Presidency, and *obtinere* in French has the same aforementioned meaning. In fact, the meaning may vary depending on the selected language.[175]

7.3.1 Type of Investment Under Article 7

To merit any claim under database right, a database producer should meet the threshold of substantial investment, which is a primary requirement under Article 7.[176] However, ECJ did not question the threshold of investment in this case. It only questioned the type of investment expended towards production of the BHB database.[177]

In the context of type of investment required under database right, ECJ demarcated a difference between investment in creating and investment in obtaining.[178] Thus, protection under Article 7 depends on the type of investment. The CJEU in *Football Dataco* decision came to a similar conclusion, while deciding on copyright protection. In the context of creativity, CJEU said that the objective of Article 3 was not to protect creativity in data creation.[179] Thus, the protection under the said Article depends on the type of creativity.[180]

(Footnote 172 continued)

Directive: Taking Stock in Fiona Macmillan (ed) New directions in Copyright Law: Vol 2 *(Edward Elgar, UK 2006) 126.*

In English, Italian, French, Portuguese, and Spanish, obtaining is derived from the Latin term *obtinere*. It yields the same result to receive. "…if we take the umbrella term creation, in other words the supplying of the database with content, as a basis, both existing and newly created data could be covered"., Opinion of Advocate General Stix-Hackl, on *British Horse Racing Board v. William Hill* (8 June, 2004) available at <http://curia.europa.eu/jurisp/cgi-bin/form.pl?lang=en > (accessed 10 November 2008); It is comprehensive term, Gaster (n 172).

173 ibid.

174 It is a term, which includes generation and collecting of data; Opinion of Advocate General Stix-Hackl, on *British Horse Racing Board v. William Hill* (8 June, 2004).

175 There are existing divergences between various language versions. For example in German language the term 'Beschaffung' used under Article 7(1) "…can only concern existing data, as it can only apply to something, which already exists. In that light *Be*schaffung is the exact opposite of *Er*schaffung (creation)". Similarly there are narrow interpretations if one considers Finnish and Danish version, Opinion of Advocate General Stix-Hackl, on *British Horse Racing Board v. William Hill* (8 June, 2004).

176 Council Directive 96/9/EC.

177 *British Horseracing Board* (n 56) 3.

178 ibid.

179 Case C-604/10 *Football Dataco Ltd v Yahoo! UK Ltd* [2012] ECDR 10, 194 *(Football Dataco)* para [53].

180 ibid; *British Horseracing Board* (n 56) 3.

These two opinions summarily rejected any protection for creation of data, either under the threshold of substantial investment, or under the threshold of AOIC.[181] In other words, Database Directive is primarily meant to provide incentive for database producers actively engaged in storing and processing of existing data.[182] Two decisions in the space of eight years have provided similar scope for database right and for copyright protection for databases. This interpretation is counter-productive to the intent of providing incentive to producers who are investing towards production of non-original databases.[183]

7.3.2 Monopoly Over Factual Content

In a single-sourced database, a database maker must ensure a separate substantial investment, while obtaining contents for his database.[184] According to ECJ, investment directed towards creation of data will not be counted.[185] For example, in the database of BHB, investment was towards the creation of data concerning horse racing. There was no separate investment at the point of incorporating such data. In a practical situation, when creation and obtaining happens simultaneously, it may be difficult to separate and identify two separate investments.[186] However, the requirement of separate investment averted possible monopoly situation in relation to single-sourced databases.[187] In the process, ECJ implicitly pointed that database

[181] *British Horseracing Board* (n 56) and *Football Dataco* (n 179).

[182] Council Directive 96/9/EC, Rectial 12.

[183] COM (92)24 final.

[184] The decision is a sign of an attempt to balance between "the database producers' right and access to information". Further, the decision also restricted the scope of database right, which provides intellectual property protection to one of the controversial subject matter, Estelle Derclaye, "The Court of Justice Interprets the Database Sui Generis Right for the First Time" (2005) 30(3) E L Rev 420, 420.

[185] *British Horseracing Board* (n 56) 3 and 10.

[186] Beunen (n 123) 126; it is difficult to show separate investments in financial databases, "since data are collected and aggregated at the source (stock exchange)", Richard Kemp and others "Database Right and the ECJ Judgment in BHB v. William Hill: Dark Horse or Non-Starter?" (2005) 21(2) CLSR 108,109; This distinction is difficult to endorse in terms of practical circumstances, Andrew McGee and Gary Scanlan, "The Database Directive–Sui Generis and Copyright–A Practicable Distinction" (2005) July Journal of Business Law 413, 422.

[187] First Evaluation of Directive 96/9/EC; ECJ's decision also shows that unfair competition law may not provide complete solution in case of problems with single-sourced database; "the … decisio[n] offer a partial solution to … the absence of a regime of compulsory licensing to cure the anti-competitive effects of "sole-source" information monopolies", Mark J. Davison and P. Bernt Hugenholtz, 'Football Fixtures, Horseraces and Spin Offs: The ECJ Domesticates the Database Right' (2005) 27(3) EIPR 11, 115; GM Hunsucker argues that with a compulsory licensing provision in place for single-sourced databases, the European database right can become an international model, GM Hunsucker, 'The European Database Directive: Regional stepping stone to an International model' (1996–97) 7(2) Fordham Intell. Prop. Media & Ent. L.J. 697, 763.

right is monopolistic in nature.[188] The opinion expressed in the first evaluation report indicates that there was no need to further test abuse of dominant position in case of single-sourced databases, especially after the ECJ decision in *BHB* case.[189] Thus, the scope of *sui generis* database right has been severely curtailed.[190]

It is interesting to note that all of the cases which were referred to ECJ, especially in the context of investment towards creating and obtaining, were single-sourced databases.[191] At around the same time when ECJ came up with the *BHB* decision, almost 50% of law suits have been brought forth by companies who were not engaged in collecting data from the outside world.[192] There is relatively less monopoly concern when there are multiple sources in the same situation.[193]

Providing a difference between investments in creation and obtaining of data may not completely remove monopolistic situation in case of a single-sourced database.[194] As correctly explained by Annemarie Beunen database producer may entrust a subsidiary, or an agent, or a third party to generate or create data because of the requirement of showing separate investment. Later on, the same database producer may obtain data for the purpose of database right. The cost acquired in this transaction will amount to substantial investment.[195] Since the threshold of substantial investment is understandably less stringent, the cost of acquiring should suffice requirement of database right.[196] In the same context the Advocate General in the *Football Dataco* case has said that protection under Article 3 may not be used to bypass the decision of ECJ in *BHB*.[197] Other than the aforementioned suggested

---

[188]The possible monopolistic effect of *sui generis* database right has already been under consideration, since Article 16 of the Database Directive has acknowledged such possibility; Recently ECJ in the context of *BHB* dispelled some fear of over protection, Anna Koo, 'Database Right decoded' [2010] 32(7) EIPR 313.

[189]First Evaluation of Directive 96/9/EC.

[190]ibid.

[191]*Oy Veikkaus (*n 56), *Svenska Spel* (n 56), *Organismos* (n 56), *British Horseracing Board Limited* (n 56).

[192]Jorg Hladjk, 'The protection of databases under EU and US law – the *sui generis* right as an appropriate concept? Part-II' (2004) 20(5) CLSR 377, 380.

[193]Multiple source databases may not be that problematic, Derclaye, (n 51) 148; However, creating a database is an expensive process and already creates a barrier, Reichman and Samuelson (n 111) 83.

[194]Owing to the difference in creating and obtaining, a producer of a single-sourced database may be tempted to deny access to data by using technical means. ECJ's decision is a not a foolproof solution and the producers must have access under non-discriminatory and fair grounds in case of impediments because of the technical measures, Davison and Hugenholtz (n 187); In the opinion of Simon Stokes, persons producing or commissioning databases must document the investment made at the stage of creating and obtaining. There must be documentation, while updating for the purpose of renewal, Simon Stokes, *Digital Copyright: Law and Practice* (3rd edn. Hart Publishing 2009) 69.

[195]Beunen (n 123) 127–128.

[196]*Supra* section 7.1.

[197]Case-604/10 *Football Dataco Ltd v Yahoo! UK Ltd* [2012] ECDR 7, Opinion of AG Mengozzi, para [121].

methods, single-sourced databases may be able to fulfil the requirement of substantial investment by showing investment in verification or presentation of the contents.[198] However, the database producer must be able to show separate substantial investment in either of the cases.[199]

7.3.3 Database Right: Extra Layer of Protection

ECJ prevented formation of a monopoly situation in relation to single-sourced databases.[200] The annual reviews of BHB give interesting insight in the context of granting incentive without knowing the actual requirement.

The scenario with BHB is clear from press releases and annual reviews published over three years.[201] Immediately after the decision, they considered cutting down general expenditure but the process of re-designing and re-fitting a database within the criterion set up by ECJ was a relatively easy task to follow. However, the issue of legal cost incurred by BHB came in the way of proceeding further.[202] This shows that there are ways to bypass the decision of ECJ. Single-sourced database makers in future may still have option to follow the protection offered under database right.[203] The threat of monopolizing information in relation to a single-sourced database continues.[204] Even with the ECJ decision in place, there is no easy way to improve such situation other than reviving the compulsory licensing provision.[205]

---

[198] *British Horseracing Board* (n 56) 10.

[199] ibid.

[200] A single-sourced database has the potential to grant a database maker legal and economic monopoly. The user in case of a single-sourced database must abide by the rules and conditions set up by the database maker. Unlike copyright monopolies given to expression, *sui generis* database right, in case of single-sourced databases gives monopoly on information, Derclaye (n 51) 179.

[201] They will be for the year 2004, 2005 and 2006.

[202] 'Prudent Expenditure Reductions Agreed by BHB' (*British Horseracing* Authority, 9 December 2004) available at <http://www.britishhorseracing.com/press_releases/prudent-expenditure-reductions-agreed-by-bhb/> (accessed 30 November 2016).

[203] Beunen (n 123) 127– 128.

[204] ibid.

[205] Although for some poets creativity has a greater value than monetary incentives, the same is unlikely for "prosaic compositions", Ginsburg (n 9) 1908; It may be the case that database producer will produce databases if there is a market for it. There may not be any additional incentives required to fundamentally initiate production of databases. This is clear from the annual reports and production of databases in US, supra chapter 4, section 4.1; This proposition is contrary to the thought that these works (compilation of facts) may require a prompt to their production, Jane C Ginsburg, 'No "Sweat"? Copyright and the Protection of Works of Information after *Feist v Rural*' (1992) 92(2) Colum L Rev 338.

One has to remember that BHB depended on commercial funding mechanism in the form of licensing fees from the bookmakers, since they proposed to move away from the levy structure.[206] After the decision of ECJ, there was imminent problem with the future of licensing fees, and such concern was clearly visible.[207] All these meant less incentive because there was uncertainty with funding further databases. In a contrasting situation, the Annual Review of 2005 states that there was extraordinary success in the midst of these apparent negative effects.[208] Moreover, BHB went on to publish fixture list in 2006, which also required substantial investment.[209] Surely, BHB would not have invested in future databases if they were not sure to recoup their investment.[210] One may possibly think that merger of BHB with British Horse Racing Authority in 2007 was a result of financial difficulties accruing from the decision of ECJ. However, this decision of merger was prior to ECJ judgment in 2004.[211]

BHB did not stop production of databases, and it is questionable whether they needed the incentive of database right to continue investing.[212] Although it is

---

[206]'BHB Annual Review - Presentation by Chief Executive Greg Nichols' (*British Horseracing*, 9 June 2005) available at <http://www.britishhorseracing.com/press_releases/bhb-annual-review-presentation-by-chief-executive-greg-nichols/> (accessed 30 November 2016); The current levy structure from the bookmaker works out a rate of 10.75%, 'Horseracing levy increased to 10.77%' (*BBC* News, 16th February 2011) available at <http://www.bbc.co.uk/news/business-12486813> (accessed 14 April 2011).

[207]'BHB Annual Review – Presentation by Chairman Martin Broughton' (*British Horseracing*, 9 June 2005) available at <http://www.britishhorseracing.com/press_releases/bhb-annual-review-presentation-by-chairman-martin-broughton/> (accessed 30 November 2016), The funding review was set up to look for alternative means of funding in the event Court of Appeals in England upheld ECJ's decision. In fact, the Court of Appeals following the guideline set up by ECJ did find the matter against BHB's favour. This funding review was set up in accordance with the phasing out of the levy system in 2009. The report considered two principal options - one based on picture rights and the other on having a pre-conditioned betting license. The report concluded by saying that there is no viable alternative to statutory levy system, Martin Broughton, 'Governance Structure for British Racing- Letter to the Racing Industry' (*British Horseracing Board,* 19 May 2006) available at <http://www.britishhorseracing.com/press_releases/governance-structure-for-british-racing/> (accessed 30 November 2016); In fact, the levy system still exists in the present day.

[208]ibid.

[209]ibid.

[210]"The prosperity continued with British Horse Racing in 2005….despite the uncertainty caused by unforeseen legal setbacks', 'Berkshire racing industry backs changes to levy' (*BBC News,* 22 July 2011) available at <http://www.bbc.co.uk/news/uk-england-berkshire-14236144> accessed 1 August 2011.

[211]Broughton (n 207).

[212]There are visible alternatives of funding available for databases comprising of information on racing and pre-race information. The levy system exists and currently it is at the rate of 10.75%. There are discussions in the government to change such system to improve British racing industry. On an overall note, there are incentives available for further publications, Roger Blitz, 'Move to clear horserace funding hurdle' available at <http://www.ft.com/cms/s/0/7967e164-773e-11e0-aed6-00144feabdc0.html#axzz1Unn2vGHA> May 5, 2011 (accessed 10 June 2011); In the recent

understandable that BHB wanted to follow commercial licensing of pre-race data, without economic evidence it is difficult to predict the amount of incentive required to initiate such process.[213] Giving such incentive in vacuum may result in harm instead of providing additional incentives to a producer.[214] Previously, annual reports of publishing companies in US showed that database producers invest based on the knowledge that there is adequate opportunity to recover their investment.[215]

There is certain imbalance in the current structure, which is harmful for disseminating information.[216] Although the argument of a database right after harmonization of copyright protection is logical, such an argument must be seriously re-considered in the background of the current structure.[217] In terms of number of databases, database right has proved to be ineffective in incentivizing database production and further implementation of such right must be questioned in the present circumstances.[218]

(Footnote 212 continued)

years there have been reduction in the racing prize money, but it has nothing to do with incentive. There has been a shift from betting in racing to football and to some extent such fall could be attributed to online betting, 'Berkshire racing industry backs changes to levy' (*BBC News*, 22 July 2011) available at <http://www.bbc.co.uk/news/uk-england-berkshire-14236144> (accessed 1 August 2011).

[213]Bitton (n 65) 1426.

[214]The issues that were considered in the First Evaluation of Directive 96/9/EC.

[215]*Supra* section 4.3.

[216]It has been argued by commentators that in fact database right is nothing but what was sweat of the brow. Critiques have been concerned about the overall balance between the requirement for the producer and the final version of the database right, Davison (n 35); Beunen (n 123); over-protection of certain areas in the database right with the fear of monopolization for single source databases, Derclaye (n 51); question of giving property rights to data, Reichman and Samuelson (n 111); about the problems concerning sole source databases, Hugenholtz (n 138).

[217]First Evaluation Report of Directive 96/9/EC para [1.1].

[218]ibid para [5.3].

Concluding Remarks

Amongst all the confusion and ambiguities with the database directive, especially with the *sui generis* part, one needs to re-visit the three options that the first evaluation report had suggested in the context of possible amendments to the Directive.[1] The first proposal relates to the possibility of repealing database right, the second option is maintaining *status quo* and the third option is amending the current structure of the right.[2] While first two options are not desirable, the third option is much more viable.

The report proposed to repeal database right from the Directive.[3] On a practical note, it will be difficult to execute such proposition. One must refer to the view expressed in the report itself. It considered the amount of resistance such action would face from European publishers.[4] There may be additional legal uncertainty to roll back to the time when there was no database right in Europe. The implications would be felt mostly in Common Law jurisdictions.[5] Based on high number of cases that have already been decided, the proposition of rolling back may increase uncertainty, instead of resolving concerns associated with database right.[6] These observations indicate that it is difficult to reach a consensus to remove a piece of legislation.[7] Therefore, repealing database right from the Directive is not an ideal option.

[1]'DG Internal market and services working paper: First Evaluation of Directive 96/9/EC on the legal protection of databases' (*Commission of the European Communities*, 12 December 2005) available at <http://ec.europa.eu/internal_market/copyright/docs/databases/evaluation_report_en.pdf> (accessed 31 October 2016) (First Evaluation of Directive 96/9/EC), para [6].
[2]ibid.
[3]ibid, para [6.1].
[4]ibid, para [1.5].
[5]ibid, para [6.1].
[6]*Supra* section 7.3.
[7]First Evaluation of Directive 96/9/EC, para [6].

I. Gupta, *Footprints of Feist in European Database Directive*,
DOI 10.1007/978-981-10-3981-2

As to the second option of *status quo*, evaluation report suggested that the Directive might be left untouched. In future, database right is unlikely to create any additional burden in the context of dissemination and access to information.[8] This argument was primarily based on the *BHB* decision. It was believed that ECJ ruling in this case successfully removed possible monopoly situation in relation to single-sourced databases.[9] Despite this contention, monopolization of factual information still remains a concern.[10] Hence, the option of *status quo* is not advisable, since there are legitimate concerns associated with this right.

Although the remaining viable alternative is amending the Directive, one has to answer two questions: what kind of amendments are required; and whether these amendments would be able to resolve problems associated with database right. There have been different suggestions associated with the structure of database right.[11] Mark Davison observed that narrower protection should be given based on weak economic argument, and proposed for an unfair competition model.[12] Estelle Derclaye suggested that database right should be crafted in a way to exclude the over-protective elements.[13] Elizabeth Herr noted that some protection is required but the structure must be decided only based on evidence.[14] In his doctoral dissertation, Victor Bouganin proposed for a narrower right with compulsory licensing provision and more exceptions.[15] Similarly, Annemarie Beunen proposed for a narrower right with the inclusion of compulsory licensing provision.[16] Any such suggestion of improving the structure of the right, however, without evidence

[8]This suggestion primarily considered the decision of the ECJ in *British Horse Racing v William Hill*. According to the evaluation report, the ECJ has successfully curtailed some of the existing problems in the directive, Evaluation Report.

[9]In fact, owing to the removal of compulsory licensing provisions for single-sourced databases, under Article 16 of the Directive, periodical evaluation has been made a requirement to oversee any possible anti-competitive effect enshrined in the database right. Although the report did not refer to any independent study about the anti-competitive effect, there was reference to the decision of the ECJ concerning the protection of single-sourced databases under the database right.

[10]*Supra* section 7.3; Annemarie Beunen, *Protection for databases: The European Database Directive and its effects in Netherlands, France and United Kingdom* (Wolf Legal Publishers Leiden 2007) (n 123) 127–128.

[11]Work particularly concentrated on *sui generis* database right has seen three aspects; Narrower right with the inclusion of compulsory licensing provision for sole source databases, Beunen (n 10).

[12]Mark Davison, *The legal protection of databases* (Cambridge University Press Cambridge 2003) (n 35).

[13]Estelle Derclaye, *The Legal Protection of Databases: A Comparative Analysis* (Edward Elgar, Northampton 2008) (n 51).

[14]Robin Elizabeth Herr, *Is the Sui Generis Right a Failed Experiment? A legal and Theoretical Exploration of How to Regulate Unoriginal Database Contents and Possible Suggestions for Reform* (DJØF Publishing Copenhagen, Denmark 2008).

[15]Victor Bouganin, 'The legal protection of databases, from copyright to dataright' (PhD thesis, University of London 1999).

[16]Beunen (n 10).

would be speculative in nature.[17] The need for empirical evidence already exists in the background of criticism surrounding the database right.[18] It would have been much easier to estimate the right at the beginning based on requirement, rather than adjusting the structure of such right subsequent to the enactment.[19]

One might wonder as to what would have happened without *Feist*. As a first reaction, the explanatory memorandum to the first draft proposal would not have contemplated about the apprehended 'new-line' of jurisprudence that *Feist* had developed, nor would it have questioned the role of 'sweat of the brow' argument as a basis for copyright protection.[20] Further, the argument that more incentive is required in the form of a database right for producers would not have garnered any support.[21] The argument that copyright protection for databases in Europe must be harmonized did not originate from the *Feist* decision.[22] However, without the *Feist* decision, the Commission would only have the Berne standard for compilations to follow to decide the scope of Article 3.[23] It is also clear that while the Commission wanted to remain within the broad structure of the Berne Convention, there was no intention to remain within the scope of the same.[24] Therefore, without *Feist*, there would not have been any standard available, and it would have been difficult to predict the shape and structure of the Database Directive.

[17]"It may be regretted that such a strong exclusive right could be introduced on the mere basis of an assumed need", Beunen (n 10) 279.

[18]The author concludes by saying that theoretical and empirical economic studies on the effects of the database right are highly desirable. Estelle Derclaye, 'Intellectual property rights on information and market power – comparing European and American protection of databases' (2007) 38 (3) IIC 275, 298.

[19]'The preferable way' would have been to improve 'legal and factual analysis' before taking up 'far reaching measures' by way of introducing the database right, Annette Kur and others, 'First evaluation of Directive 96/9/EC on the legal protection of databases- comment by the Max Planck Institute for Intellectual Property, Competition and Tax Law, Munich' (2006) 37(5) IIC 551, 551.

[20]ibid.

[21]Miriam Bitton, 'Exploring the European Union Copyright Policy through the lens of the Database Directive' (2008) 23(4) Berkeley Tech LJ 1411, 1426.

[22]Commission, 'Proposal for a Council Directive on the legal protection of databases' COM (92) 24 final, s 1.

[23]ibid, para [2.2.4].

[24]ibid, paras [5.1.3] and [6.1.3].

Bibliography

Statutes/Directives/Official Opinions

Case-604/10 *Football Dataco Ltd v Yahoo! UK Ltd* [2012] ECDR 7, Opinion of AG Mengozzi

Collections of Information Antipiracy Act HR 2652 105th Cong (1998)

Commission, 'Amended Proposal for a Council Directive on the legal protection of Databases' COM (93) 464 final

Commission, 'Copyright and the Challenge of Technology' (Green Paper)' COM (88) 172 final

Commission, 'Follow-up to the Green Paper: Working Programme of the Commission in the field of Copyright and Neighbouring Rights' (Follow-up Green Paper) COM(90) 584 final

Commission, 'Proposal for a Council Directive on the legal protection of databases' COM (92) 24 final

Commission, 'Proposal for a Council Directive on the legal protection of original topographies of semiconductor products' COM (85) 775 final

Commission, 'Report from the Commission to the Council, The European Parliament and the Economic and Social Committee on the Main Events and Developments in the Information Market 1993–1994' COM (95) 492 final

Computer Misuse Act 1990 (c 18)

Consumer and Investor Access to Information Act H R 1858 106th Cong (1999) Copyright Designs and Patent Act 1988 (c 48)

Council Common Position 20/95/EC of 10 July 1995 with a view to adopting the database directive [1995] OJ C 288

Council Common Position of 30th October 1995 regarding the Proposal for a Council Directive on the legal protection of databases [1995] OJ C288

Council Directive 1991/250/EEC of 14 May 1991 on the legal protection of computer programs [1991] OJ L122

Council Directive 2001/29/EC of 22 May 2001 on harmonization of certain aspects of copyright and relation rights in the information society [2001] OJ L167

Council Directive 2001/29/EC of June 22 2001 on the harmonization of certain aspects of copyright and related rights in the information society [2001] OJ L 167

Council Directive of 1996/9/EC of 27 March 1996 on the legal protection of databases [1996] OJ L 77

Council Directive of 87/54/EC of 16 December 1986 on the legal protection of topographies of semiconductor products [1986] OJ L24

Council Directive of 2009/24/EC of 23 April 2009 on the legal protection of computer programs [2009] OJ L 111

Database Investment and Intellectual Property Antipiracy Act H R 3531 104th Cong (1996)

European Parliament Minutes of Proceedings of the sitting of 23 June 1993 on Part II – Texts adopted by the European Parliament [1993] OJ C 194

I. Gupta, *Footprints of Feist in European Database Directive*,
DOI 10.1007/978-981-10-3981-2

Opinion of Advocate General Stix-Hackl, on *British Horse Racing Board v. William Hill* (8th June, 2004) available at <http://curia.europa.eu/jurisp/cgi-bin/form.pl?lang=en> (accessed 10 November 2008)

Opinion of the Economic and Social Committee of 23 April 1986 on the legal protection of original topographies of semiconductor products [1986] OJ C 189

Opinion of the Economic and Social Committee of the Council of 25 January 1993 on the Proposal for a Council Directive on the Legal Protection of Databases [1993] OJ C19

Opinion of the European Parliament on the Directive on the legal protection of databases A3-0183/93 [1993] OJ C194

Reuters Holdings 1992 Annual Report and Accounts (ICC REPORT NO 09165 December 31 1992)

The Computer Fraud and Abuse Act (CFAA) 18 U S C 1030

The Copyright and Rights in Databases Regulations 1997/3032

U.S. Copyright Act 1870 (16 Stat 198)

Cases

Baker v Seldon 101 US 99 (1879)

BellSouth Advertising & Publication Corp v Donnelley Information Publishing Inc 999 F2d 1436 (11th Cir 1993)

British Horse Racing Board v William Hill Organization [2001] PC Case HC 2000 1335 [2001] ECDR 20

The British Horseracing Board Limited, The Jockey Club and Weatherbys Group Limited v William Hill Organization Limited [2001] ECDR 20, 270

British Sky Broadcasting Group Plc v Digital Satellite Warranty Cover Ltd [2011] EWHC 2662 (Ch) [2012] 14 FSR 407

Burrow-Giles Lithograph Co v Sarony 111 US 53 (1884)

CA Douai 7 October 1996 (Sté DDB Needham v. Cie des Courtiers Jurés Piqueurs de Vins de Paris), RIDA 1997/172.

Case C-203/02 *The British Horseracing Board Limited v William Hill Organisation Ltd* [2005] ECDR 1

Case C-444/02 *Fixtures Marketing Ltd v Organismos Prognostikon Agnon Podosfairou (OPAP)* [2005] ECDR 3

Case C-338/02 *Fixtures Marketing Ltd* v *Svenska Spel AB* [2005] ECDR 4

Case C-46/02 *Fixtures Marketing Ltd v Oy Veikkaus Ab* [2005] ECDR 2

Case C-304/07 *Directmedia Publishing GmbH v Albert-Ludwigs-Universität Freiburg* [2008] ECR I-7565

Case C-545/07 *Apis-Hristovich EOOD v Lakorda AD* [2009] ECDR 13.

Case C-5/08 *Infopaq International A/S v Danske Dagblades Foreing* [2009] ECDR 16

Case C 241–242/91P *Radio Telefis Eireann and Independent Television Publications Limited (Intellectual Property Owners Inc. intervening)* v *E.C. Commission (Magill TV Guide Limited intervening)* [1995] 4 CMLR 718

Case C-30/14 Ryanair Ltd v PR Aviation BV, [2015] ECLI:EU:C:2015:10

Case C-490/14 Freistaat Bayern v Verlag Esterbauer GmbH, [2015] ECLI:EU:C:2015:735

Case C-604/10 *Football Dataco Ltd v Yahoo! UK Ltd* [2012] ECDR 10

CCC Information Services Inc v Maclean Hunter Market Reports Inc 44 F3d 61 (2d Cir 1994)

Charles E Schroeder and Marion S Schroeder v William Morrow and Company and George Banta & Co 566 F2d 3 (7th Cir 1977)

Dennis W Eckes and James Beckett v Card Prices Update and Suffolk Collectables 736 F2d 859 (2d Cir 1984)

Designers Guild Ltd. v Russell Williams (Textiles) Ltd [2000] 1 WLR 2416

Dow Jones & Company Inc v Board of Trade of the City of Chicago 546 F Supp 113 (SDNY 1982)
ebay Inc v Bidder Edge Inc 54 U S P Q 2d (BNA) 1798 (N D Cal 2000)
Editions Législatives v. Le Serveur Administratif, Thierry Ehrmann and others [2005] ECDR 14
Eldred v. Ashcroft 537 US 186 (2003)
Feist Publications Inc. v Rural Telephone Service Co 499 US 340 (1991)
Flogas Britain Limited v Calor Gas Limited [2013] EWHC 3060 (Ch)
Financial Info Inc v Moody's Investors Service 808 F2d 204 (2nd Cir 1986).
Football Dataco Ltd v Brittens Pools Ltd [2010] EWHC 841 (Ch) Sections 83-90
Football Dataco Ltd v Sportradar GmbH [2012] EWHC 1185 (Ch), [2012] 26 ECC 273
Football Dataco Ltd v Sportradar GmbH [2011] EWCA Civ 330, [2011] 1 WLR 3044
Football Dataco Ltd v Yahoo! UK Ltd [2010] EWCA Civ 1380, [2011] ECDR 9
Football League Limited v Littlewoods Pools [1959] (Ch) 637
Forensic Telecommunications Services Limited v The Chief Constable of West Yorkshire Police and others [2011] EWHC 2892 (Ch), [2012] 15 FSR 428
Fred L Worth v Selchow & Righter Company 827 F2d 569 (9th Cir 1987)
Gray v Russell (1839) 10 F Cas 1035 (CCD Mass 1839)
H Blacklock & Co Ltd v C Aurther Pearson Ltd [1915] 2 (Ch) 376
Harper & Row Publishers Inc and the Reader's Digest Association v Nation Enterprises and the Nation Associates Inc 471 US 539 (1985)
Harper House Inc. v Thomas Nelson Inc 889 F2d 197 (9th Cir 1989)
Hodge E Mason v Montgomery Data Inc 967 F2d 135 (5th Cir 1992)
Hutchison Telephone Directory v Fronteer Directory Company 770 F2d 128 (8th Cir 1985)
Illinois Bell v Haines and Company 905 F 2d 1081 (7th Cir 1990)
Jeweler's Circular Publishing Co v Keystone Publishing Co 281 F 83 (CA2 1922)
Kelly v Morris (1865–66) LR 1 Eq 697
Key Publications Inc v Chinatown Today Publishing 945 F2d 509 (2d Cir 1991)
Kregos v Associated Press 937 F2d 700 (2d Cir 1991)
Ladbroke v William Hill [1964] 1All ER 465
Leon et.al v Pacific Telephone & Telegraph Company Co 91 F2d 484 (1937)
Libraco Ltd v Shaw Walker Ltd (1913) 58 Sol Jo 48
Lipton v Nature Co 71 F3D 464(2d Cir 1995)
Macmillian v Cooper (1923) 93 LJPC
Mars v Teknowledge [2000] ECDR 99
Mathew Bender & Co v West Publishing Co 158 F3d 693 (2nd Cir 1997)
Microfor v Le Monde [1988] ECC 297
Miguel Figueroa v United States United States Court of Appeals for the Federal Circuit, 05-5144 (October 2006)
Miller v Universal City Studios Inc 650 F2d 1365 (5th Cir 1981)
Mills Music Inc v Synder 469 US 153 (1985)
National Business Lists v Dun & Bradstreet Inc 552 F Supp 89 (N D Ill 1982)
Nester's Map & Guide Corp v Hagstorm Map Co 796 F Supp 729 (EDNY) 1992
Newspaper Licensing Agency Ltd v Marks & Spencer plc [2001] UKHL 38 [2013] 1 AC 551
Orgel v Clark Boardman Co 301 F2d 119 (1962)
ProCD v Zeidenberg 86 F3d 1447 (7th Cir 1996)
R v Unauthorised Reproduction of Telephone Directories in CD-Rom [2002] ECDR 3
Rand McNally & Company v Fleet Management Systems Inc 591 FSupp 726 at 737 (ND Ill 1983)
Register.com Inc v Verio Inc 126 F Supp 2d 238 (SDNY December 12 2000)
Rose v Information Services Ltd [1987] FSR 254
Royal Mail Group Plc v i-CD Publishing (UK) Limited [2003] EWHC 2038 (Ch)
Rural Telephone Service Co. v. Feist Publications, 737 F. Supp. 610 (D. Kan. 1990)
SA Credinfor v Artprice.com [2006] ECDR 15
SARL News Invest v. SA PR Line Court of Appeal (Cour d'appel) Versailles, 11 April 2002

Sawkins v Hyperion Records Ltd [2005] EWCA Civ 565 [2005] 1 WLR 3281
La sociéte Sonacotra v. le syndicat Sud Sonacotra District Court (Tribunal de Grande Instance) Paris, 25 April 2003
Southern Bell Telephone v Associated Telephone 756 F2d 801 (11th Cir 1985)
Stuart Y Silverstein v Penguin Putnam 368 F3d 77 (2nd Cir 2004)
The Trade Mark Cases 100 US 82 (1879)
United States Payphone Inc v Execs Unlimited Inc 18 USPQ 2d 2049 (4th Cir 1991)
United Telephone Company of Missouri v Johnson publishing 855 F2d 604 (8th Cir 1988)
University of London Press v University Tutorial Press [1916] 2 (Ch) 601
Victor Lalli Enterprises Inc v Big Red Apple Inc 936 F2d 671 (2nd Cir 1991)
Warren Publishing Inc v Microdos Data Corp 115 F3d 1509 (11th Cir 1997)
Waterlow Directories v Reed Information Services [1992] FSR 409.

Books/Book Chapters

Aplin T, *Copyright Law in the Digital Society: the challenges of multimedia* (2005, Hart Publishing).

Aplin T, 'The EU Database Directive: Taking Stock' in F Macmillan (ed) *New directions in Copyright Law: Vol 2* (2006, Edward Elgar) 99.

Aplin T, 'Subject Matter' in E Derclaye (ed), *Research Handbook on the future of EU Copyright* (2009, Edward Elgar) 94.

Arossa L, *Economic and Trade Issues in the Computerised Database Market* (*Information Computer Communication Policy Paper* (1993, OECD).

Bently L and Sherman B, *Intellectual Property Law* (3rd edn, 2008, Oxford University Press).

Bently L and Cornish W R, 'United Kingdom' in P E Geller and M B Nimmer (eds) *International Copyright Law and Practice* (Volume 2, 2009, LexisNexis) 2[1][b][i].

Beunen A, *Protection for databases: The European Database Directive and its effects in Netherlands, France and United Kingdom* (2007, Wolf Legal Publishers Leiden).

Borghi M and Montagnani M L, 'Promises and Pitfalls of the European Copyright Harmonisation' in D Ward (ed) *The European Union and the Cultural Industries* (2007, Ashgate Publishing) 213.

Cornish W, 'Protection of and vis-à-vis Databases' in M Dellebeke (ed), *Copyright in Cyberspace: Copyright and the Global Information Infrastructure* (1997, Otto Cramwinckel) 435.

Cornish W and others, '*Intellectual Property: Patents, Copyright, Trade Marks and Allied Rights*' (7th edn, 2010, Sweet & Maxwell).

Curtis G T, '*A Treatise on the Law of Copyright: Books, Dramatic and musical composition, letters and other manuscripts, engravings and sculptures*' (1847, A Maxwell and Son).

Czarnota B and Hart R J, *Legal Protection of Computer Programs in Europe- A guide to the EC Directive* (1991, Butterworths).

Daintith J and Wright E, *The Facts on File Dictionary of Computer Science* (2004, Infobase Publishing).

Dam K W, 'Self-help in the digital jungle' in R C Dreyfuss and others (eds), *Expanding the boundaries of Intellectual Property: Innovation Policy for the Knowledge Society* (2001, Oxford University Press) 103.

Davison M J, *The legal protection of databases* (2003, Cambridge University Press).

Derclaye E, *The Legal Protection of Databases: A Comparative Analysis* (2008, Edward Elgar).

Dietz A, 'Germany' in P E Geller and M B Nimmer (eds) *International Copyright Law and Practice* (2009, Sweet & Maxwell) 2[1][b].

Drone S E, *A Treatise on the Law of Property in Intellectual Productions in Great Britain and the United States: Embracing Copyright in Works of Literature and Art, and Playright in Dramatic and Musical Compositions* (1879, Little Brown).

Drahos P, *A Philosophy of Intellectual Property* (1996, Dartmouth).

Euchenrode C H, 'Germany' in D Campbell (ed) *World Intellectual property rights and remedies* (2011, Oceana) 23.

Garnett K, Davies G, Harbottle G and others (eds), *Copinger and Skone James on Copyright* (6th edn, 2011, Sweet & Maxwell).

Hamilton M A, 'Database Protection and the Circuitous Route around the United States Constitution' in CEF Rickett and G W Austin (eds) *International Intellectual Property and Common Law World* (2000, Hart Publishing) 9.

Herr R E, Is the Sui Generis Right a Failed Experiment? A legal and Theoretical Exploration of How to Regulate Unoriginal Database Contents and Possible Suggestions for Reform (2008, DJØF Forlag).

Hugenholtz P B, 'Protection of Compilations of facts in Germany and the Netherlands' in P B Hugenholtz and E J Dommering (eds) *Protecting Works of Fact: Copyright, Freedom of Expression and Information Law* (1991, Kluwer Tax and Law Publishers) 59.

Hugenholtz P B, 'Abuse of Database Right: Sole-source information banks under the EU database Directive' in F Lévêque and H Shelanski (eds) *Antitrust, patents and copyright: EU and US perspectives* (2005, Edward Elgar) 203.

Judge F E and Gervais D J, 'Of silos and constellations: comparing notions of originality in copyright law' in R F Brauneis (ed) *Intellectual Property Protection of Fact-based Works: Copyright and its Alternatives* (2009, Edward Elgar) 74.

Klipper M R and Senter M S, 'The facts after Feist: The Supreme Court addresses the Issue of the Copyrightability of factual compilations' in J A Baumgarten (ed) *Fact and Data Protection After Feist* (1991, Prentice Hall Law & Business) 343.

Laddie H and others, *The modern law of copyright and designs* (3rd edn, 2000, Butterworths).

Lehman B 'Intellectual Property and the National and Global Information Infrastructures' in P B Hugenholtz (ed) *The future of Copyright in a Digital environment* (1996, Kluwer Law International) 103.

Lewinski S V, 'Protection of and vis-à-vis Databases: Germany' in M Dellebeke (ed) *Copyright in Cyberspace: Copyright and the Global Information Infrastructure* (1997, Otto Cramwinckel) 480.

Lucas A and others, 'France' in P E Geller (ed) *International Copyright Law and Practice* Lexis Nexis 2009 volume 1.

Makeen M F, *Copyright in a Global Information Society: The Scope of Copyright Protection Under International, US, UK and French Law (Studies in Law)* (2000, Kluwer Law International).

Mackaay E, 'The Economics of Emergent Property Rights on the Internet' in P B Hugenholtz (ed) *The future of Copyright in a Digital Environment* (1996, Kluwer Law International) 13.

Metalitz S J, 'Response of the Information Industry Association for the Hearing on Databases Chapter 6 of the Green Paper on Copyright and the Challenge of Technology' in J A Baumgarten (ed) *Fact and Data Protection After Feist* (1991, Prentice Hall Law & Business) 39.

Mula D and Lobina M L, 'Legal Protection of the Web Page' in Hideyasu Sasaki (ed) *Information Technology for Intellectual Property Protection: Interdisciplinary Advancements* (2012, Information Science Reference) 214.

Nimmer M B and Nimmer D, *Nimmer on Copyright: A Treatise on the Law of Literacy, Musical and Artistic Property and the Protection of Ideas* (2011, Mathew Bender).

Phillips J, 'Databases, the Human Rights Act and EU law' in J Griffiths and U Suthersanen (eds) *Copyright and Free Speech, Comparative and International Analyses* (2005, Oxford University Press) 417.

Romme v Van Dale Lexicografie, B.V., Hoge Raad der Nederlanden [HR] [Supreme Court of The Netherlands], 4 January 1991, *translated in Protecting works of facts: Copyright, Freedom of Expression and Information Law*, E J Dommering and P B Hugenholtz (eds) 1991, Kluwer Law International Appendix I, 93.

Simons R A, 'Industry Impact (Database Providers)' in J A Baumgarten (ed) *Fact and Data Protection After Feist* (1991, Prentice Hall Law & Business) 45.
Sterling JAL, *Comparison of the copyright and author's right systems* (1998, Institute of Advanced Legal Studies, London, Offprint collection, Shelf number: X0054).
Sterling JAL, *World Copyright Law* (2008, Sweet & Maxwell).
Stokes S, *Digital Copyright: Law and Practice* (3rd edn, 2009, Hart Publishing).
Vaidhyanathan S, *Copyrights and Copywrongs: The Rise of Intellectual Property and How it Threatens Creativity* (2003, New York University Press).
Vallés R C, 'The requirement of originality' in E Derclaye (ed) *Research Handbook on the future of EU Copyright* (2009, Edward Elgar) 102.
Vivant M, 'Protection of Raw Data and Data Banks in France' in E J Dommering and P B Hugenholtz (eds) *Protecting Works of Fact: Copyright, Freedom of Expression and Information Law* (1991, Kluwer Law) 73.

Journal Articles

Akester P, 'Survey of Technological Measures for protection of Copyright' (2001) 12(1) Ent L Rev 36
Arden T P, 'The conflicting treatments of compilations of facts under the United States and United Kingdom copyright laws' (1992) 3(2) Ent L Rev 43
Austin W L, 'A Thoughtful and Practical Analysis of Database Protection under Copyright Law, and a Critique of *Sui Generis* Protection' (1997)3(1) Journal of Technology Law & Policy available at <http://jtlp.org/vol3/issue1/austin.html#EN97> (accessed 10 June 2010)
Balaban D, 'The Battle of the Music Industry: the distribution of Audio and Video Works via the internet, Music and more' (2001-02) 12(1) Fordham Intell Prop Media & Ent L J 235
Band J 'New theories of database protection' (2003) March, Managing Intellectual Property 1
Band J and Kono M, 'The Database Protection Debate in the 106th Congress' (2001) 62(2) Ohio State law Journal 869
Baron P,' Back to the future: Learning from the past in the Database Debate' (2001) 62(2) Ohio State Law Journal 879
Barr L, 'Database Protection Bill' (1997-98) 8(2) DePaul-LCA J Art & Ent 371
Bergh R V D, 'The role and social justification of copyright: a "law and economics" approach' (1998) 1 IPQ 17
Besen S M & Raskind L J, 'An Introduction to the Law and Economics of Intellectual Property', (1991) 5 J Econ Persp 3
Bitton M, 'Exploring the European Union Copyright Policy through the lens of the Database Directive' (2008) 23(4) Berkeley Tech LJ 1411
Bitton M, 'A New Outlook on the Economic Dimension of the Database Protection Debate' (2006–07) 47(2) IDEA: The Intell Prop L Rev 93
Bitton M, 'Protection for Informational Works after *Feist Publications, Inc v. Rural Telephone Service Co* (2011) 21(3) Fordham Intell Prop Media & Ent L J 611
Bott C M, 'Protection of Information Products: Balancing Commercial Reality and the Public Domain' (1998-99) 67(1) U Cin L Rev 237
Brill C, 'Legal Protection of Collection of Facts' (1998) 2 Computer L Rev & Tech 1
Brown R S, 'Eligibility for copyright protection: a search for principled standards' (1985) 70(2) Minn L Rev 579
Carson D O, 'Copyright protection for factual compilations after *Feist*: A practioner's view' (1992) 17(3) U Dayton L Rev 969

Celedonia B, 'From copyright to copycat: Open season on data?', Publishers Weekly, Aug 16 1991.
Chalton S, 'The Amended Database Directive Proposal: A Commentary and Synopsis' (1994) 16 (3) EIPR 94
Christopher A and Freeman K, 'Case comment: Directmedia Publishing GmbH v Albert-Ludwigs-Universitat Freiburg (Case C-304/07)' (2009) 31(3) EIPR 151
Colston C, 'Sui generis Database right: Ripe for Review?" 2001(3) available at <http://www2.warwick.ac.uk/fac/soc/law/elj/jilt/2001_3/colston> (accessed 10 December 2009)
Copyright Office and Copyright Royalty Tribunal Report Status to House Panel, (April 18, 1991) 41 Pat Trademark & Copyright J. No. 524
Dahl B A, 'Originality and creativity in reporter pagination: a contradiction in Terms? (1989) 74 (4) Iowa L Rev 713
Davison M J and Hugenholtz P B, 'Football Fixtures, Horseraces and Spin Offs: The ECJ Domesticates the Database Right' (2005) 27(3) EIPR 113
Davison M J, 'Proposed U.S. Database legislation: a comparison with the U.K database Regulations' (1999) 21(6) EIPR 279
Denicola R C, 'Copyright in Collections of Facts: A theory for the protection of nonfiction literary works' (1981) 81(3) Colum L Rev 516
Derclaye E, 'Intellectual property rights on information and market power – comparing European and American protection of databases' [2007] 38(3) IIC 275
Derclaye E, 'Databases Sui Generis Right: Should We Adopt the Spin Off Theory?' (2004) 26(9) EIPR 402
Derclaye E, 'Do sections 3 and 3A of the CPDA violate the Database Directive? A closer look at the definition of a database in the U.K. and its compatibility with European law '(2002) 24(10) EIPR 466
Derclaye E, "The Court of Justice Interprets the Database Sui Generis Right for the First Time" (2005) 30(3) Ent L Rev 420
Deveci H A, 'Databases: Is *sui generis* a stronger bet than copyright?' (2004) 12(2) IJLIT 178
Dowd J R, 'A selection view on history: *Feist Publications, Inc v Rural Telephone Service Co.'* (1992-1993) 34(1) BCL Rev 137
Dreier T K, 'Authorship and New Technologies from the Viewpoint of Civil Law Tradition' (1995) 26(6) IIC 989
Durham A L, 'Speaking of the World: fact, opinion and the originality standard of copyright'(2001) 33(3) Arizona State Law Journal 791
Fernandez-Molina J C, 'The legal protection of databases: current situation of the international harmonisation process' (2004) 56(6) Aslib Proceedings 325
Fewer D, 'A *Sui Generis* Right to Data? A Canadian Position' (1998) 30(2) Can Bus L J 165.
Fogt H and others, 'An American view on the EU Database Directive' (1995) 46 Managing Intellectual Property 33
Gaster J L, '"Obtinere" of Data in the Eyes of the ECJ: How to interpret the Database Directive after *British Horseracing Board Ltd et al. V. William Hill Organisation Ltd*' (2005) 5(6) CLR Int'l 129
Gaster J L, 'The EC *sui generis* right revisited after two years: a review of the practice of database protection in the 15 EU Member States' (2000) 5(3) Communications Law 87
Gaster J L, 'The EU Council of Ministers common position concerning the legal protection of databases: a first comment' (1995) 6(7) Ent LR 258
Gaster J L, 'The New EU Directive Concerning the Legal Protection of Databases, (1997) 20(4) Fordham Int'l L J 1129
Gaudrat Ph, 'Loi de transposition de la directive 96/9 du 11 mars 1996 sur les bases de donnees : dispositions relatives au droit d'auteur' (1 partie)' (1998) 51/3 RTDcom 599
Gerdes M B, 'Getting Beyond Constitutionally Mandated Originality as a Prerequisite for Federal Copyright Protection' (1992) 24(4) Ariz St. L J 1461

Gervais D J, '*Feist* goes global: A comparative analysis of the notion of originality in copyright law' (2002) 49(4) Journal of Copyright Society of the US 949.

Gervais D J, 'The Compatibility of the Skill and Labour Originality Standard with the Berne Convention and the TRIPS Agreement' (2004) 26(2) EIPR 75

Gervais D J, 'The protection of databases' (2007) 82(3) Chicago- Kent Law Review 1109

Ghosh S, 'The Intellectual Property Incentive: Not so natural as to warrant strong exclusivity' (2006) 3(2) Script-ed 96

Ginsburg J C, 'A marriage of convenience? A comment on the *Protection of Databases*' (2007) 82 (3) Chicago-Kent L Rev 1171

Ginsburg J C, 'Copyright, Common Law and *sui generis* protection of databases in the United States and Abroad' (1997-1998) 66(1) U Cin L Rev 151

Ginsburg J C, 'Creation and Commercial Value: Copyright protection of works of Information' (1990) 90(7) Colum L Rev 1865

Ginsburg J C, 'No "Sweat"? Copyright and the Protection of Works of Information after *Feist v Rural* (1992) 92(2) Colum L Rev 338

Goldstein P, 'Copyright' (1990–91) 38(3) Journal of the Copyright Society 109

Gorman R A, 'Copyright protection for the collection and representation of facts' (1963) 76(8) Harv L Rev 1569

Gorman R A, 'Fact or Fancy? The Implications for Copyright-The Twelfth Annual Donald C Brace Memorial Lecture' (1982) 29(6) Journal of the Copyright Society 560

Greenbaum D, 'Are We Legislating Away Our Scientific Future? The Database Debate' (2003) 2 Duke Law & Technology Review 1, available at <http://scholarship.law.duke.edu/dltr/vol2/iss1/20> (accessed 7th October, 2010)

Grosheide F W, 'Database Protection- the European Way' (2002) 8(1) Wash U J L & Pol'y 39

Hamilton M A, 'Justice O'Connor's opinion in *Feist Publications Inc v. Rural Telephone Service Co:* An Uncommon Though Characteristic Approach" (1990-91) 38(2) Journal of the Copyright Society 83

Handig C, '*Infopaq International A/S v Danske Dagblades Foreing* (C-5/08): is the term "work" of the CDPA 1988 in line with the European Directives?' (2011) 32(2) EIPR 53

Handig C, 'The copyright term "work" – European harmonisation at an unknown level' (2009) 40 (6) IIC 665

Haungs M J, 'Copyright of factual compilations: Public policy and the First Amendment' (1990) 23(3) Colum J L & Soc Probs 347

Hicks J B, 'Copyright and computer databases: Is traditional compilation Law adequate?' (1987) 65(5) Tex L Rev 993

Hladjk J, 'The protection of databases under EU and US law – the *sui generis* right as an appropriate concept? Part-II' (2004) 20(5) CLSR 377

Hughes J, 'Created Facts and the flawed ontology of Copyright Law' (2007-2008) 83(1) Notre Dame L Rev 43

Hunsucker G M, 'The European Database Directive: Regional stepping stone to an International model' (1996-97) 7(2) Fordham Intell Prop Media & Ent L J 697

Jenkins J, 'Database rights' subsistence: under starter's order' (2006) 7(6) JIPLP 467

Karjala D S, 'Misappropriation as a third Intellectual Property Paradigm' (1994) 94(8) Colum L Rev 2608

Kemp R and others, "Database Right and the ECJ Judgment in BHB v. William Hill: Dark Horse or Non-Starter?" (2005) 21(2) CLSR 108

Koo A, 'Database right decoded' [2010] 32(7) EIPR 313

Koumantos G, 'Les bases de donnees dans la directive communautaire', (1997) 171 RIDA 79

Ku RSR and others, 'Does Copyright Law promote creativity? An Empirical analysis of Copyright's Bounty (2009) 62(6) V and L Rev 166

Kur A and others, 'First evaluation of Directive 96/9/EC on the legal protection of databases - comment by the Max Planck Institute for Intellectual Property, Competition and Tax Law, Munich' (2006) 37(5) IIC 551

Kyer I and Moutsatsos S, 'Database Protection: The Old world heads off in a new direction' 9(1) (1993) CLSR 11
Lai S, 'Recent Developments in Copyright, Database Protection and (On-line) licensing' (1999) 7 (1) IJLIT 73
Landes W M and Posner R A, 'An Economic analysis of copyright law' (1989) 18(2) J Legal Stud 325
Lea G, 'In defence of originality' (1996) 7(1) Ent L Rev 21
Leistner M, 'Legal protection for the database maker- initial experience from a German point of view' (2002) 33(4) IIC 439
Leistner M, 'The legal protection of telephone directories relating to the new database maker's right' (2000) 31(7/8) IIC 950
Lemley M A, 'Property, Intellectual Property and Free Riding '(2004-2005) 83(4) Tex L Rev 1031
Lipton J, 'Databases as Intellectual Property: New Legal Approaches' (2003) 25(3) EIPR 139(6)
Litman J, 'After *Feist*' (1992)17(2) U Dayton L Rev 607
Maurer S M and others, 'Europe's Database Experiment' (2001) 294 Science 26th October, 769
Maurer S M and Scotchmer S, 'Database protection: Is it Broken and Should we fix it' (1999) 284 Science 14 May, 1129
McGee A and Scanlan G, "The Database Directive–Sui Generis and Copyright–A Practicable Distinction" (2005) July Journal of Business Law 413
McManis C R, 'Database Protection in the Digital Information Age' (2001-2002) 7 (1) Roger Williams U L Review 7
Meade T L, 'Ex-post *Feist* : Applications of a landmark Copyright decision' (1994-1995) 2(1) J Intell Prop L 245
Metalitz S, '*Feist* and the Information Industry' (June/July 1991) 17(5) Bulletin of the American Society for Information Science 11
Metaxas G, 'Protection of databases: quietly steering in the wrong direction?' (1990) 12(7) EIPR 227
Miller P H, "Life after *Feist*: Facts, the First Amendment and the Copyright status of automated databases" (1991-1992) 60(3) Fordham L Rev 507
Mitchell R J, 'If at *Feist* You Don't Succeed, Try, Try Again: An Evaluation of the Proposed Collections of Information Piracy Act' (1999) 78(4) Neb L Review 901
Montagnon R and Shillito M, 'Requirements for subsistence of database copyright and other national copyright in databases referred to the ECJ: Football Dataco v Yahoo!' (2011) 32(5) EIPR 324
Nelson R G, 'Seeking Refuge from a Technology Storm: The Current Status of Database Protection Legislation after the Sinking of the Collections of Information Anti-Piracy Act and the Second Circuit Affirmation of Matthew Bender & (and) Co. v. West Publishing Co. Recent Development' (1998-99) 6(2) J Intell Prop L 453
Newman C M, 'A License Is Not a "Contract Not To Sue": Disentangling Property and Contract in the Law of Copyright Licenses' (2013) 98(3) Iowa Law Review 1101
Nimmer R T and Krauthaus P A, 'Information as Property Databases and Commercial Property' (1993-94) 1(1) Int'l J L & Info. Tech 1
Oman R, 'Reflections on the changing shape of database protection' (1993) 40 Federal Bar News & J 232
Oman R, Copyright Office and Copyright Royalty Tribunal Report Status to House Panel, 41 Pat. Trademark & Copyright J. (BNA) No. 524 (April 18, 1991)
Patry W, 'Copyright in Collection of Facts: A Reply' (1984) 6(5) Comm & Law 11
Patry W, 'Copyright in Compilation of Facts (or Why the "White Pages" Are Not Copyrightable) (1990) 12(4) Comm & Law 37
Patry W, 'The Enumerated Powers Doctrine and Intellectual Property: An Imminent Constitutional Collision' (1999) 67(2) The Geor Wash L R 359
Patterson L R and Joyce C, 'Monopolizing the Law: The Scope of Copyright Protection for Law Reports and Statutory Compilations' (1989) 36(4) UCLA L.Rev 719

Patterson L R, 'Copyright overextended: a preliminary inquiry into the need for a federal statute of unfair competition' (1991-92) 17(2) U Dayton L Rev 385

Perlmutter S, 'The Scope of Copyright in Telephone Directories: Keeping Listing Information in the Public Domain' (1991) 38(1) Journal of the Copyright Society 1.

Polivy D R, '*Feist* applied: Imagination protects, but perspiration persists – the bases of copyright protection for factual compilation' (1997–98) 8(3) Fordham Intell Prop Media & Ent L J 773

Porter V, 'The Copyright protection of compilations and pseudo-literary works in EC member states' (1993) January(22) Journal of Business Law 1

Powell M, 'The European Union's Database Directive: An International Antidote to the side effects of *Feist*' (1996-97) 20(4) Fordham Int'l L J 1215

Raskind L J, 'Assessing the Impact of *Feist*'(1992) 17(2) U Dayton L Rev 331.

Reichman J H and Samuelson P, 'Intellectual Property Rights in data?' (1997) 50(1) Vand L Rev 51

Rodgers M, 'Football fixture lists and the Database Directive: Football Dataco Ltd v Brittens Pools Ltd' (2010) 32(11) EIPR 593

Rossler D B, 'The European Union's proposed Directive for the legal protection of databases: A new threat to the free flow of information' (1995) 10(1) High Tech L J 105

Samuelson P, 'Should economics play a role in copyright law and policy' (2003 04) 1(1–2)Univ of Ottawa L T J 14

Saunders E M, 'Copyright protection for compilations of Fact: Does the originality standard allow protection on the basis of industrious collections'(1987) 62(4) Norte Dame L Rev 763

Schatz J E and others, 'What's mine is yours? The dilemma of factual compilations' (1991-92) 17 (2) U Dayton L Rev 423

Schneider M, 'The European Union Database Directive' (1998) 13 Berkeley Technology Law Journal 551, available at <http://scholarship.law.berkeley.edu/btlj/vol13/iss1/35> (accessed 10 November 2010)

Schricker G, 'Farewell to the "level of creativity"(Schopfungshohe) in German Copyright Law?' (1995) 26(1) IIC 41.

Schwarz M, 'Copyright in compilations of facts: Case Comment' (1991) 17(5) EIPR 178

Shah A, 'UK'S Implementation of the Anti-Circumvention Provisions of the EU Copyright Directive: An analysis' (2004) Duke Law and Technology Review 3

Sheils P T and Penchina R, 'What's all the fuss about *Feist*? The sky is not falling on the intellectual property rights of online database proprietors' (1991-1992) 17(2) U Dayton L Rev 563

Sherwood-Edwards M, 'The Redundancy of Originality' (1995) 6(3) Ent L R 94

Spinello R A, 'Intellectual property rights' (2007) 25(1) Library Hi Tech 12

Stamatoudi I, 'The EU database Directive: reconceptualising copyright and retracting the future of *sui generis* right' (1997) 50 Hellenic Rev of Int'l L 435

Tessensohn J, 'The Devil's in the Details: The Quest for Legal Protection of Computer Databases and the Collections of Information Act' (1997-98) 38(3) IDEA: The Intell Prop L Rev 439

Thakur N, 'Database protection in the European Union and the United States: the European Database Directive as an optimum global model' (2001) 1 IPQ 100

Thorner B B., 'Copyright protection for Computer Databases: the threat of *Feist* and a Proposed Solution' (1997) 5(1) VA J L & TECH 27

Trosow S E, '*Sui Generis* database legislation' (2005) 7(1) Yale J of L & Tech 535

Valente D R, 'Feist Overruled? Database Protection in the Next Century' (2000) 17(7) The Computer Lawyer 20

Vanovermeire V, 'The concept of the lawful user in the database Directive' (2000) 31(1) IIC 63

Vaver D, 'The Copyright Mixture in a Mixed Legal System: Fit for Human Consumption?' (2001) available at <http://www.ejcl.org/52/abs52-3.html> (accessed 15 March 2011)

Versteeg R, 'Sparks in the Tinderbox: *Feist*, "Creativity", and the legislative history of the 1976 Copyright Act' (1994-1995) 56(3) U Pitt L Rev 549

Wayman M W, 'International Database Protection: A multilateral Treaty solution to the United States' Database Dilemma' (1996-97) 37(2) Santa Clara L Rev 427
Weightman E and Hughes J, 'EC Database protection: fine tuning the Commission's Proposal' (1992) 14(5) EIPR 147
Westkamp G, 'Protecting Databases Under US and European Law- Methodical Approached to the Protection of Investments between Unfair Competition and Intellectual Property concepts' (2003) 34(7) IIC 772
Williams M E, 'The state of databases Today: 2004', in M E Williams (ed) *Gale Directory of Databases* (2004, Thomson-Gale) 1
Wood E L, "Copyrighting the Yellow pages: Finding originality in factual compilations" (1993-94) 78(5) Minn L Rev 1319
Wright S and Vatvani P, 'Death of the database right' (2005) 153 CW 8
Wu X, 'EC Data Base Directive' (2002) 17 Berkeley Technology Law Journal 571 available at <http://scholarship.law.berkeley.edu/cgi/viewcontent.cgi?article=1368&context=btlj> (accessed 7 October 2010)
Yen A C, 'The legacy of *Feist:* Consequences of the weak connection between Copyright and the Economics of public goods' (1991) 52(5) Ohio St L J 1343
Zimmerman D L, 'Copyright as Incentives: Did we just imagine that' (2011) 12(1) Theoretical Inquiries in Law 29

PhD Theses

Bouganin V, 'The legal protection of databases, from copyright to dataright' (PhD thesis, University of London 1999)
Warwick S, 'The Judicial Influence and Policy Implications of *Feist* in regard to the protection of Databases and Compilations' (PhD thesis, Graduate School- New Brunswick, Rutgers, The State University of New Jersey 1999)

Magazines

Band J, 'Armageddon on the Potomac The Collections of Information Antipiracy Act' (1999) D-Lib Magazine 5(1) available at <http://www.dlib.org/dlib/january99/01band.html> (accessed 24 November 2010)
Lambert W, 'Yellow pages reuse is found not violate Copyright" (September 24, 1991) The Wall Street Journal (Eastern Edition) New York, B1
Nettleton E J and Obhi H S, 'Can US Companies Protect their Databases in Europe with Database Right' (2002) CW 121.

Directories

British Telecom, London South West 2011/2012: The Phone Book (British Telecom, 2011)
Thomson Directories Ltd, Thomson local.com: Directory 2011-12 (Thomson Directories Ltd, 2011)

Newspapers

Snoddy R, 'Reed Elsevier Shares Drop on US Legal Ruling' Financial Times, 23 May 1997: 24

Blitz R, 'Move to clear horserace funding hurdle' Financial Times, 5 May 2011
Waldmeir P, 'Who should own the raw facts? : Database Legislation: Courts must balance the rights to private property and to public access' Financial Times, 22 May 2002:19

Website/Internet Resources

'Agreement on Trade-Related Aspects of Intellectual Property Rights: Part II — Standards concerning the availability, scope and use of Intellectual Property Rights' available at <http://www.wto.org/english/tratop_e/trips_e/t_agm3_e.htm> (accessed 22 November 2008)
'Annual Report and Financial Statements 2008' available at <http://www.relx.com/annualreport08/business/Pages/elsevier.aspx> (accessed 30 November 2016)
'Article L112-1 of the Intellectual Property Code (LexInter)' available at <http://www.lexinter.net/ENGLISH/intellectual_property_code.htm> (accessed 10 January 2011)
Band J, 'Armageddon on the Potomac The Collections of Information Antipiracy Act' available at <http://www.dlib.org/dlib/january99/01band.html> (accessed 24 November 2010).
'*baumarkt.de*, Oberlandesgericht Düsseldorf 29 June 1999, [1999] Multimedia und Recht 729' English version available at <http://www.ivir.nl/files/database/index.html#germany> (accessed 10 March 2009)
'Berkshire racing industry backs changes to levy' available at <http://www.bbc.co.uk/news/uk-england-berkshire-14236144> (accessed 1 August 2011).
'Berne Convention for the protection of Literary and Artistic Works' available at <http://www.wipo.int/treaties/en/ip/berne/trtdocs_wo001.html> (accessed 21 December 2008)
'BHB Annual Review – Presentation by Chairman Martin Broughton' available at <http://www.britishhorseracing.com/resources/about/press/view.asp?item=002877> (accessed 14 April 2011).
'BHB Annual Review - Presentation by Chief Executive Greg Nichols' available at <http://www.britishhorseracing.com/resources/about/press/view.asp?item=002876> (accessed 14 April 2011)
Blatman J M, 'Collective agreements' available at <http://www.ilo.org/public/english/dialogue/ifpdial/downloads/judges06/france2.pdf> (accessed 14 April 2011)
'Book II of the Intellectual Property Code (LexInter)' available at <http://lexinter.net/ENGLISH/intellectual_property_code.htm> (accessed 10 January 2011)
'British Horseracing authority' available at <http://www.britishhorseracing.com/inside_horseracing/about/whatwedo/handicapping.asp> (accessed 10 January 2011)
Broughton M, 'Governance Structure for British Racing- Letter to the Racing Industry' available at <http://www.britishhorseracing.com/resources/about/press/view.asp?item=002877> (accessed 14 April 2011)
Carson D O, 'Database and Collections of Information Misappropriation Act of 2003' available at <http://www.copyright.gov/docs/regstat092303.html> (accessed 15 September 2009)
Carson D O, 'General Counsel, United States Copyright Office before the Subcommittee on courts, the internet and Intellectual Property Committee on the Judiciary and Subcommittee on Commerce, Trade and Consumer Protection Committee on Energy and Commerce, 108th Congress' (United States Copyright Office, 23 September 2003) available at <http://www.copyright.gov/docs/regstat092303.html> (accessed 15 September 2009)
'Chamber raises concern over database legislation' available at <https://www.uschamber.com/press-release/chamber-raises-concern-over-database-legislation> (accessed 10 August 2011)
'Committee Reports - House Report 108-421- Part 1 (108th Congress (2003-2004)): Database and Collections of Information Misappropriation Act (HR 3261)' available at <https://www.congress.gov/bill/108th-congress/house-bill/3261?q=H.R.+3261+%28108%29> (accessed 23 October 2016)
'Copyright Act (Urheberrechtsgesetz, UrhG)' available at <http://www.iuscomp.org/gla/statutes/UrhG.htm> (accessed 15 March 2011)

'DG Internal market and services working paper: First Evaluation of Directive 96/9/EC on the legal protection of databases' available at <http://ec.europa.eu/internal_market/copyright/docs/databases/evaluation_report_en.pdf> (accessed 31 October 2016)

'Equifax', available at <http://www.equifax.com/home/en_us> (accessed 10 February 2010)

'European Commission Press Release: Winners of 2015 European Border Breakers Awards (EBBA) for pop, rock and dance music unveiled' available at <http://europa.eu/rapid/press-release_IP-14-1135_en.htm?locale=en> (accessed 30 December 2016)

'Federal Supreme Court (Bundesgerichtshof), 21 July 2005; English version' available at <http://www.ivir.nl/files/database/index.html#germany> (accessed 10 March 2009)

'Horseracing levy increased to 10.77 %' available at <http://www.bbc.co.uk/news/business-12486813> (accessed 14 April 2011)

'House Report No. 94-1476(US Copyright Act 1976)' available at <http://www.copyright.gov/history/law/clrev_94-1476.pdf> (accessed 27 November 2016)

'H.R.191: American Consumers Health Care Reform Act of 1993' available at <http://www.thomas.loc.gov> (accessed 10 June 2011)

'H.R. 2281 (used to be H.R. 2652): The Collections of Information Antipiracy Act' available at <https://www.congress.gov/bill/105th-congress/house-bill/2652> (accessed 30 November 2016).

'Intellectual property and the National Information Infrastructure: The Report of the Working Group on Intellectual Property rights' available at <https://www.uspto.gov/web/offices/com/doc/ipnii/ipnii.pdf> (accessed 30 November 2016)

'Information Meeting on Intellectual Property in Databases: Existing National and Regional Legislation concerning Intellectual Property in Databases' available at <http://www.wipo.int/edocs/mdocs/mdocs/en/db_im/db_im_2.pdf> (accessed 10 January 2010)

Institute for Information Law, 'The Recasting of Copyright & Related Rights for the Knowledge Economy' available at <http://ec.europa.eu/internal_market/copyright/docs/studies/etd2005imd195recast_report_2006.pdf> (accessed 10 April 2010)

'Library of Congress: Bills, Resolutions' available at <https://www.congress.gov/> (accessed 30 December 2016)

'LexisNexis', available at <http://www.lexisnexis.com> (accessed 9 October 2008)

'LJN: AA8588, Rechtbank's-Gravenhage, KG 00/949, English version' available at <http://www.ivir.nl/files/database/index.html#thenetherlands-nvm> (accessed 10 March 2009)

Maurer S M, 'Raw Knowledge: Protecting Technical databases for science and industry' available at <http://www2.sims.berkeley.edu/courses/is296a-3/s99/database.pdf> (accessed 25 November 2010)

'NautaDutilh Final Report: The Implementation and Application of Directive 96/9/EC on the legal protection of databases' available at <http://ec.europa.eu/internal_market/copyright/docs/databases/etd2001b53001e72_en.pdf> (accessed 24 October 2010)

'Opinion of Lord Macfadyen in *Sietech Hearing Limited v. Russell Borland, James Eley, Digital Hearing (UK) Limited*' available at <http://www.scotcourts.gov.uk/opinions/CA123_00.html> (accessed 3 December 2010)

'Oxford Online Dictionary' available at <http://oxforddictionaries.com/> (accessed 12 January 2012)

'Prudent Expenditure Reductions Agreed by BHB' available at <http://www.britishhorseracing.com/resources/about/press/view.asp?item=002314> (accessed 14th April 2011)

'Reed Elsevier annual report 1992' available at <http://www.reed-elsevier.com/investorcentre/reports%202007/Pages/1992-2001.aspx> (accessed 10 December 2010)

'Reed Elsevier annual report 1993' available at <http://www.reed-elsevier.com/investorcentre/reports%202007/Pages/1992-2001.aspx> (accessed 10 December 2010)

'Reed Elsevier annual report 1994' available at <http://www.reed-elsevier.com/investorcentre/reports%202007/Pages/1992-2001.aspx> (accessed 10 December 2010)

'Reed Elsevier annual report 1995' available at <http://www.reed-elsevier.com/investorcentre/reports%202007/Pages/1992-2001.aspx> (accessed 10 December 2010)

'Reed Elsevier annual report 1996' available at <http://www.reed-elsevier.com/investorcentre/reports%202007/Pages/1992-2001.aspx> (accessed 10 December 2010)

'Reed Elsevier annual report 1997' available at <http://www.reed-elsevier.com/investorcentre/reports%202007/Pages/1992-2001.aspx> (accessed 10 December 2010)

Samuelson P, 'The U.S. Digital agenda at the World Intellectual Property Organization' available at <http://people.ischool.berkeley.edu/~pam/courses/cyberlaw98/docs/wipo.pdf> (accessed 12 January 2011)

'Standing Committee on Copyright and Related Rights' available at <http://www.wipo.int/edocs/mdocs/copyright/en/sccr_3/sccr_3_11.pdf> (accessed 15 January 2010)

'Standing Committee on Copyright and Related Rights: A Study on the Impact of Protection of Unoriginal Databases on Developing Countries: Indian experience' available at <www.wipo.int/edocs/mdocs/copyright/en/sccr_7/sccr_7_5.pdf> (accessed 10 January 2010)

'Standing Committee on Copyright and Related Rights: Five studies commissioned by the Secretariat at WIPO by the following experts in India, Egypt, US, China and Denmark' available at <http://www.wipo.int/edocs/mdocs/copyright/en/sccr_7/sccr_7_10.pdf> (accessed 20 January 2010)

'Standing Committee on Copyright and Related Rights: The Impact of Protection of Non-original Databases on the Countries of Latin America and the Caribbean' available at <http://www.wipo.int/edocs/mdocs/copyright/en/sccr_8/sccr_8_6.pdf> (accessed 20 January 2010)

'Standing Committee on Copyright and Related Rights' available at <http://www.wipo.int/edocs/mdocs/copyright/en/sccr_8/sccr_8_9.pdf> (accessed 10 January 2010)

'Standing Committee on Copyright and Related Rights' available at <http://www.wipo.int/edocs/mdocs/copyright/en/sccr_9/sccr_9_11.pdf> (accessed 15 January 2010)

'Standing Committee on Copyright and Related Rights' available at <http://www.wipo.int/edocs/mdocs/copyright/en/sccr_11/sccr_11_4.pdf> (accessed 10 January 2010).

'Standing Committee on Copyright and Related Rights' available at <http://www.wipo.int/edocs/mdocs/copyright/en/sccr_13/sccr_13_6.pdf> (accessed 15 January 2010)

Swibel M, 'Defending the Database' available at <http://www.forbes.com/2004/03/31/cz_ms_0331beltway.html> (accessed 3rd January 2010)

'Thomson annual report 1998' available at <https://bib.kuleuven.be/files/ebib/jaarverslagen/Thomson_1998.pdf> (accessed 10 December 2010).

'TRIPS Agreement 1994' available at <http://www.wto.org/english/docs_e/legal_e/legal_e.htm> (accessed 18 December 2010)

Tyson L D and Sherry E F, 'Statutory Protection for Databases: Economic and Public Policy Issues', (unpublished report for the Information Industry Association, 1997)

US Congress Office of Technology Assessment, 'Intellectual Property Rights in an Age of Electronics and Information' available at <http://www.princeton.edu/~ota/disk2/1986/8610/8610.PDF> (accessed 30 November 2016)

'US Constitution' available at <http://www.law.cornell.edu/constitution/> (accessed 15 June 2010)

'US Copyright Act 1909' available at <http://www.copyright.gov/history/1909act.pdf> (accessed 15th June 2010)

'US Copyright Act 1976' available at <http://www.copyright.gov/title17/> (accessed 15 June 2010)

'US Copyright Office: Report on Legal Protection for Databases: August 1997' available at <http://www.copyright.gov/reports/db4.pdf> (accessed 27 November 2016)

'US Copyright Office' available at <http://www.copyright.gov/help/faq/faq-general.html#automatic> (accessed 10 Jan 2011)

'US Copyright Office' available at <http://www.copyright.gov/circs/circ01.pdf> (accessed 27 November 2016)

'Westlaw' available at <http://www.westlaw.com> (accessed 9 October 2008)

World Intellectual Property Organisation, 'Basic Proposal for the Substantive Provisions of the Treaty on Intellectual Property in Respect of Databases to be Considered by the Diplomatic Conference' available at <http://www.wipo.int/meetings/en/doc_details.jsp?doc_id=2487> (accessed 10 December 2010)

World Intellectual Property Organisation, 'Proposal Submitted by the European Community and its Member States' available at <www.wipo.int/mdocsarchives/BCP_CE_VI_1996/BCP_CE_VI_13_E.pdf> (accessed 10 December 2010)

'Working Group on Intellectual Property Rights, Intellectual Property and the National Information Infrastructure' available at <https://www.uspto.gov/web/offices/com/doc/ipnii/ipnii.pdf/> (accessed 30 November 2016)

Kolibri 360 GmbH
Ferdinand-Jühlke-Straße 7
99095 Erfurt, Deutschland
produktsicherheit@kolibri360.de